*THE SOCIAL WELFARE FORUM, 1975*

Melvin A. Glasser

# THE
# SOCIAL WELFARE
# FORUM, 1975

OFFICIAL PROCEEDINGS, 102D ANNUAL FORUM

NATIONAL CONFERENCE ON SOCIAL WELFARE

SAN FRANCISCO, CALIFORNIA, MAY 11 –

MAY 15, 1975

*Published 1976 for the*

NATIONAL CONFERENCE ON SOCIAL WELFARE *by*

COLUMBIA UNIVERSITY PRESS, *New York and London*

ISBN: 0-231-03948-4 clothbound
ISBN: 0-231-03949-2
*Library of Congress Catalog Number: 8-85377*
PRINTED IN THE UNITED STATES OF AMERICA

# Foreword

WITH THE THEME of "Health as a Right: the Human and Political Dimensions," the 1975 Forum focused its attention on one of the urgent but unresolved problems facing our nation—the development and implementation of a coherent national health strategy. This is a fateful period in the politics of health. During 1974, annual expenditures for health reached the $104 billion mark and claimed over 7.4 percent of the gross national product. At a time when the national economy is under enormous pressure because of concurrent stagnation and inflation, the nation is having to assess both the issues associated with lack of access to health care for a significant portion of the population and cost control issues associated with the rising cost of health care. It is neither insignificant nor accidental that the ensuing debate at times seems acrimonious and impassioned.

There were many excellent papers at the Annual Forum, and making a choice for publication was a difficult task for the Editorial Committee. The committee hopes that its choices will give readers a sense of the range and depth of the issues debated as the nation moves toward a rationalized and organized health delivery system. The complex dimensions of the problem were highlighted in all the presentations—from the articulation of national goals by Melvin Glasser and Joe P. Maldonado, through the issues raised by Arnold Miller regarding death and disease in the American work place, to the more specific but similarly urgent considerations regarding patterns of utilization addressed by Henrik L. Blum. The international perspective given by "Goals for Health Care in Other Nations" furnished an additional dimension against which to juxtapose our own situation in the United States, while pre-Forum and post-Forum institutes, described by Patrick McCuan, offered participants

at the Annual Forum an opportunity to explore, in more
depth, specific aspects of professional involvement in the
health care delivery system.

With respect to the selections not directly related to health,
the Editorial Committee chose them because of their timeli-
ness and their indication of the broad range of social issues
which continue to engage the attention of social scientists,
economists, and social work practitioners alike. The papers
on the national economy, income maintenance, and aging,
while at times seeming to demonstrate our continuing inability to resolve problems of equity, also provided some newer
insights into the complexity of the social issues which con-
front us as a nation.

My sincerest appreciation and thanks go to the members of
the Editorial Committee—Salvador Alvarez, Adele Braude,
James Leiby, Marion O. Robinson, and Joan Wallace—for
the dedication and ability with which they approached a difficult and demanding job. Marion Robinson's contribution in
synthesizing the papers on the health systems of other countries deserves special recognition. Our nation needs to serve
noble purposes, and the committee sought to reflect in its
selections the manner and spirit in which that message was
presented in this Annual Forum.

Our sincerest thanks are extended for the consultation and
support of Margaret Berry of the NCSW staff and the guidance of John D. Moore of Columbia University Press as the
Editorial Committee sought to balance its ideal goal of representing the Annual Forum's many facets with the reality of
the limited space within which we could record that history.

MAGDALENA MIRANDA
*Chairman, Editorial Committee*

# National Conference on Social Welfare Distinguished Service Awards

THE NATIONAL CONFERENCE on Social Welfare Distinguished Service Aware for 1975 was awarded to Mitchell I. Ginsberg: For his leadership in the social work profession over more than a quarter of a century—as an educator, as an administrator, and as a developer of public policy; and

For his courage, compassion, and keen insight in his approach to people and their needs, which have helped him become an innovator in public welfare reform, and an exponent of the best in social work itself.

May 12, 1975
102d Annual Forum
San Francisco

MELVIN A. GLASSER
*President*
MARGARET E. BERRY
*Executive Director*

## NATIONAL CONFERENCE ON SOCIAL WELFARE DISTINGUISHED SERVICE AWARDS, 1955–1975

1955  EDITH M. BAKER, Washington, D.C.
FEDELE F. FAURI, Ann Arbor, Mich.
ELIZABETH WICKENDEN, New York
1956  TIAC (Temporary Inter-Association Council) PLANNING COMMITTEE, New York
1957  THE REVEREND MARTIN LUTHER KING, JR., Montgomery, Ala.
WILBUR J. COHEN, Ann Arbor, Mich.
1958  THE HONORABLE JOHN E. FOGARTY, R.I.
LEONARD W. MAYO, New York
1959  ELISABETH SHIRLEY ENOCHS, Washington, D.C.
OLLIE A. RANDALL, New York
1960  LOULA DUNN, Chicago
RALPH BLANCHARD, New York
HELEN HALL, New York
1961  THE HONORABLE AIME J. FORAND, R.I.

# Contents

*THE SOCIAL WELFARE FORUM, 1975*

# Health as a Right—
# The Human and Political
# Dimensions

## MELVIN A. GLASSER

As this 102d annual forum convenes our nation is troubled by the most complex social problems since the Second World War. Our economy is in a shambles, the number of unemployed is high and increasing, and specters of shortages of food and energy increase tensions among men and nations. Social programs built painfully over the years are being eroded by inadequate funding and attacked for the philosophy on which they were built. Cynicism following Watergate is breeding a new climate of political apathy.

These trying times must not become cause for despair and defeat. They can be made into opportunities for hope, for progress. It was in the depths of the depression that Franklin D. Roosevelt called for "government with a soul." We had a soul when we built a good Social Security system with benefits for the elderly and the disabled and income insurance for the unemployed. Think how much worse off we would be today without these programs.

In the early 1930s thousands of ragged Americans stood in the cold and sold apples for a nickel each, and President Herbert Hoover's Bureau of the Census classified them as "employed." This nation had the good sense to reject this

MELVIN A. GLASSER is Director, Social Security Department, International Union, United Automobile, Aerospace, and Agricultural Implement Workers of America, UAW, Detroit, and President, National Conference on Social Welfare shameful philosophy, and adopted a system of public welfare.

The problems we face today call for diverse solutions, many over a lengthy period of time. There is one, however, the pervasive issue of inadequate health care in America, for which the solutions are at hand for a country with a soul. Health as a right has in recent years become a generally accepted national goal. My thesis is that the opportunity is at hand to achieve this goal in the years immediately ahead.

Two decades ago former President Harry S. Truman paid a delightful visit to the Annual Forum in Atlantic City. I remember chatting with him afterward and expressing regret that during his presidency he had not succeeded in his fight, in which I had a very small role, for national health insurance. With characteristic ebullience he urged me to keep at it. "The idea is so right," he said, "it's bound to come."

For three quarters of a century NCSW has dealt with health problems. Frank Bruno reported in 1957 that over the years the subject was a second only to the welfare of children in the number of papers presented at the Forum.[1] In 1881 Dr. James Knight told the Annual Forum that "disease and physical injury are symptoms, but they are as well primary factors in the causation of dependency." [2]

But somehow health never achieved the primary focus it demanded. When in 1956 the National Conference of Social Work changed its name to the National Conference on Social Welfare the base was laid for broadened focus. In every other industrialized nation health care programs are considered an integral part of social welfare. They are of concern not only to doctors and nurses and hospital administrators, but as social programs they are a major concern to social workers and to all the American people.

By focusing the 1975 Annual Forum on a health theme we

[1] Frank J. Bruno, *Trends in Social Work* (New York: Columbia University Press, 1957), p. 241.
[2] *Ibid.,*

affirm our conviction that issues of health care, the largest segment of the human services, are part of the central concerns of the field of social welfare.

## THE PROBLEM

For the past seven years experts and laymen, politicians of the whole spectrum, labor leaders, and civil rights activists have repeatedly expressed their recognition that our country was in the midst of a health care crisis. It has not gone away. It is getting worse. Runaway costs, inability to get care, dissatisfaction with the kind of care offered and given, and 60 million Americans who get practically no health services are but a few of the hallmarks of a system in disarray.

Caspar Weinberger, Secretary of the Department of Health, Education, and Welfare (HEW), and the American Medical Association (AMA) tell us infant mortality rates have gone down in the last decade. But they do not tell us that today the United States is seventeenth among the nations in infant mortality. Twenty-five years ago we were fifth. A dozen nations have been able to do better than we in reducing infant death rates. And they do not tell us that with all our progress the death rate for nonwhite babies is 60 percent higher than for white infants.

We are not receiving health services commensurate with our need and our potential.

Underlying this view are three assumptions:

1. The right to health is a social *goal*. Providing full and equal access to personal health services through national health insurance is a *method* of moving toward that goal.

2. Making personal health services more readily and equally available does not necessarily assure good health. People must learn how to use the system. And there are many other factors, such as pollution in the environment and at the workplace, excessive cigarette smoking, alcoholism, narcotics addiction, malnutrition, the stress of a competitive acquisitive society, which are important obstacles to good

health. But there is good evidence that ready access to comprehensive personal health services is an important contributor to safeguarding health.[3]

3. Our country has made admirable progress in the development of new and advanced medical-scientific knowledge. Our physicians and other health professionals are among the best trained and most competent in the world. Yet the gap continues to widen between what we know about health care and the care people actually receive.

Let us look at the root causes of our health care crisis and at solutions which are available to a nation with a soul, and a field of social welfare with commitment.

1. *Absence of a national health policy.* There is an absence of priorities in our programs. We have some two dozen federal programs for personal health services and dozens more at the state and local levels. We spend large sums to detect single health problems from hypertension to tuberculosis, and leave it to the individual to find the funds and means of access to treatment. And we do almost nothing, with either public or private resources, to support preventive health services.

2. *Runaway health care costs.* We are currently spending at a $104 billion annual rate for health—7.7 percent of our gross national product.[4] The numbers are so staggering they are unreal to most of us. They approach reality as we under-

[3] C. E. Gibbs, M.D., and H. William Diserens, M.D. "Infant Mortality Rates," letter to the editor, *American Medical News,* April 10, 1972, p. 5, reported that neonatal mortality at Robert B. Green Hospital, San Antonio, Texas, declined from 24.5 deaths per thousand in 1969 to 13.1 deaths per thousand in 1971 with an actual saving of 53 lives. Reasons given were: (a) improved quality of prenatal care; (b) increase in availability of family planning; (c) development of an intensive care nursery. *Medical World News,* October 27, 1972, p. 80, reported on a three-year demonstration of improved delivery of health services in Holmes County, Miss., which reduced the infant mortality rate from 39 per thousand in 1969 to 21.3 per thousand in 1972. Through establishing the team approach to delivery and grafting new methods of organizing services as well as making available financing to carry them into existing health resources of the county, this dramatic improvement was achieved.

[4] Nancy L. Worthington, "National Health Expenditures, 1929–74," *Social Security Bulletin,* XXXVIII, No. 2 (1975), 3–20.

stand that costs of health services increased at twice the rate of increases in the cost of living index between 1967 and 1972; and in the first quarter of this year they were escalating at more than twice the Consumer Price Index rate.[5]

This is a growing tragedy for most Americans and a disaster for low-income workers and the poor. It now takes the equivalent of one month's wages to pay the annual family premium for health insurance for a Michigan auto worker. By 1980 it will take two months' wages to pay for the same benefits, unless there is major intercession in the system.

The elderly who rely on Medicare are paying out of pocket $179 more per year today for health services than they did before we had a Medicare program.[6] The medically needy who must turn to state Medicaid programs find their benefits reduced in the face of escalating costs. And blacks are particularly disadvantaged by health care inflation. The median income of black families amounts to about 60 percent of white family income.

3. *Lack of access.* Significant portions of our population, particularly low-income workers, the poor, the ethnic minorities, and those who live in the urban ghettos and rural areas, have great difficulty in getting decent health care when they need it. Twice as many nonwhites as whites, and half again as many people with incomes below $3,000 annually, receive what few medical services they seek in the often demeaning settings of hospital clinics and emergency rooms.[7]

Nonwhite Americans constitute less than one percent of all our physicians, and almost all of both groups are moving to the suburbs. In the inner city of Detroit 15 physicians serve more than 200,000 people; in Harlem, New York City, 100 doctors serve a population in excess of 400,000. In twenty

---

[5] Bureau of Labor Statistics *Bulletin, The Consumer Price Index—March 1975,* April 23, 1975, Table 2.
[6] Social Security Administration, "Age Differences in Health Care Spending, Fiscal Year 1974," *Research and Statistics Note,* Note No. 6–1975, May 13, 1975, p. 3.
[7] Department of Health, Education, and Welfare, *The Forward Plan for Health for FY 1976–1980,* Executive Summary, February, 1975, p. 4.

years the city of Chicago lost 35 percent of its physicians while the suburbs had a 130 percent increase in doctors.[8]

Is it any wonder than when Meharry Medical College recently conducted a study of over 1,200 households in the inner city of Nashville, Tennessee, they determined that only 13 percent of those requiring medical care were receiving the care they needed?[9]

Tens of millions of dollars are wasted annually by providing for the care of acute needs more and more hospital beds which are used inappropriately while we require new facilities and approaches to dealing with the problems of long-term illness. This is where the major need is today.

Hundreds of thousands of chronically ill, most of them elderly, without access to decent extended health care or home health services end up in the 22,000 nursing homes in our country.[10] Ninety percent of the beds are operated first for profit and then for patients. It is not surprising that two Congressional investigations and any number of state probes have revealed the scandal of nursing home operators who frequently neglect and often mistreat patients.[11] But more important, should we be asking where is our sense of outrage that these charnel houses have not been closed?

And having money in pocket to buy medical care does not necessarily mean it is available, or that what is available is appropriate to need. Not if you live in an inner city or a rural area—not even if you live in a suburb and need health care at night or on a weekend. And if you have a medical emergency you may well find yourself in a city where five times as many open-heart surgeries are performed as are needed, but which has half the required number of adequately staffed emergency services.

[8] Report of the Committee on Labor and Public Welfare accompanying S. 3585, *The Health Professions Educational Assistance Act of 1974,* p. 59.

[9] Samuel Wolfe, *et al., The Meharry College Study of Unmet Needs for Health and Welfare Services. Phase I: The 1972–73 Study* (Nashville, Tenn: Center for Health Care Research, Meharry Medical College, 1974), p. 40.

[10] Department of Health, Education and Welfare, *op. cit.,* p. 2.

[11] Report of U.S. Senate Subcommittee on Long Term Care, Special Committee on Aging, Frank Church, chairman, Investigations. 1974–75. See also report of Rep.

4. *Fragmented organization of services.* While 60 percent of all out-of-hospital visits are handled by general practitioners, their number has been declining. Only a third of practicing physicians are in so-called "primary care." [12] It is hard to get to see a doctor, regardless of one's income, and little wonder. The trend toward specialization continues, and we have too many of the wrong kinds of doctors concentrated in the wrong places.

The solo-practice, fee-for-service system, essentially similar in organization to the cottage industries before the industrial revolution, is a major factor in fragmentation. The health sciences are today so complex and specialized that they require the team approach to the delivery of care. But such an approach is the exception rather than the prevailing practice.

Since most doctors are in solo practice the patient must fend for himself as he is shunted from specialist to specialist and radiology lab to special treatment center. Not only is this wasteful and costly, but the patient often gets lost in a system that specializes in diseases and organs rather than people.

The waste is exemplified by the solo-practice physician himself. A task force of the American Medical Association (AMA) estimated in 1974 that such a physician—usually well-trained at a cost of almost $100,000, 90 percent of this with public monies—spends only half his working time doing what he was trained to do—seeing patients. The other half of his time is spent on business matters, insurance problems, social, psychological, and related situations—for which he was not trained.

And with more than three million allied health professionals essentially limited in their capacity to function by a solo-practice physician system, there is evidence of tremen-

---

David Pryor, U.S. House of Representatives, *Congressional Record,* 1970, 1971, as well as reports to New York State Legislature by Rep. Andrew Stein, chairman, Special Committee on Nursing Homes reported to New York *Times,* January, February, and March, 1975.

[12] Department of Health, Education and Welfare, *op. cit.,* p. 2.

dous underutilization of their potential contributions. Effective access does not necessarily require training more people. It requires better use of properly trained, properly supervised nurse clinicians, physicians' assistants, social workers, therapists, and other health professionals.

Special health care programs for the disadvantaged have been, under public auspices, underfunded, disorganized, and segregated from the health care mainstream. Poor clients remain ignorant of available services and confused in finding their way through the medical maze. Understandably, the poor and the programs have both failed, and the political realists are busy terminating grants and closing the doors.

This approach was doomed from the start; for the disadvantaged cannot be made physically and mentally whole through special clinics, cash grants, or charity, but only through a reorganized health care system, to which they have a right, and which treats them as equals with correspondent access to our splendid medical competence. We have in the United States today largely separate and less equal health care for the disadvantaged.

5. *Inadequate quality of care.* The quality of health care in this country ranges from superb to horrid. Patients are usually not able to judge the quality of care they are receiving, and we do not have a means of providing them needed protection.

The evidence is alarming. A distinguished anesthesiologist who studied medical care in the United States and in England expressed the belief that as many as half the surgeries performed each year may be unnecessary.[13] Comparative

[13] John P. Bunker, "Surgical Manpower," *New England Journal of Medicine,* CCLXXXII (1970), 135–144. Bunker further indicates that some procedures, particularly those for which surgical intervention is often in doubt (tonsillectomies), were found to be three or four times as prevalent in the United States as in England. Victor R. Fuchs, *Who Shall Live?* (New York: Basic Books, Inc., 1974), p. 73, cites data indicating that substantially too many surgeons are being trained: "Between 1950 and 1970 the number of surgical residencies offered in the U.S. increased by 100%." He indicates that many surgeons perform approximately one-third the number of surgeries their time and skills would permit.

studies between prepaid group practice plans and solo-practice services support this view.[14] A recent study of a union group in New York City reports that 28 percent of the recommended surgeries were unnecessary.[15]

A nationwide federal government study based on a random sample reported less than a month ago that over half the hospitals in the country may be delivering substandard care because they had "significant health and safety deficiencies." [16]

There are some 100,000 hospital admissions annually due to grand negative septicemia caused by adverse reactions to prescribed antibiotics.[17]

Thirty percent of all X rays must be repeated because they were improperly taken.[18]

One hundred and ninety thousand Americans, reported an HEW official, die annually of treatable cancer.[19]

Yet this is only part of the picture. The important role of psychological factors in health and illness is widely recognized. Hence for years health practitioners have pointed out that the function of "caring" is related to "curing." But solo-practice providers, paid a fee for each service, have less and less time for patients, and the "caring" part of health delivery is disappearing.

And so on and on in a country where the AMA spokesmen repeatedly assure us we have "the best medical care in the world."

6. *The failure of the private insurance industry.* Private health insurance played a valuable role in making possible insur-

[14] George S. Perrott, *The Federal Employees Health Benefits Program: Enrollment and Utilization of Health Services, 1961–1968* (Washington, D.C.: Department of Health, Education and Welfare, 1971).

[15] "Program Here Finds 28% of Surgery Unnecessary," report of results of a study and demonstration conducted by Dr. Eugene McCarthy, Cornell Medical College, New York *Times,* Dec. 15, 1974.

[16] New York Times Service, Detroit *Free Press,* "Report of Survey Conducted by Stanley Rosenfeld," Section Chief for Hospitals (Washington, D.C.: Bureau of Health Insurance, Department of Health, Education, and Welfare, 1975).

[17] Henry Simmons, M.D., address to Institute of Medicine, National Academy of Sciences, Washington, D.C., November 7, 1974.

[18] *Ibid.*     [19] *Ibid.*

ance coverage for health needs. But it is now as completely inadequate to meet our problems in health care as private insurance proved to be when it was necessary to replace it with Social Security income benefits for the elderly and the disabled.

At a current annual cost of over $23 billion it still meets only one fourth of our total national expenditures for personal health care.[20] Forty-one million Americans under age sixty-five have no private health insurance at all [21]—and only half as many nonwhite persons as whites have coverage for hospitalization and surgery.

Most health insurance policies provide Swiss cheese coverage, with gaps, loopholes, co-insurance, deductibles, and partial payments which provide more illusion than reality of coverage. Of equal importance is the compelling fact that the private insurance industry does not have the capacity, nor does it claim to have, to control costs or quality of care. Instead, billions of health care dollars are siphoned off annually for competing sales forces, duplicating administrations, retention funds arrived at through a myriad of formulas, profits, and on and on.

We have here ineffectiveness and a waste of health care dollars that even a country as wealthy as the United States can no longer afford.

7. *The interrelationship of the above factors.* For thirty years efforts have been made to deal with all these problems, one by one. The efforts have failed, primarily because the problems are interrelated. They are system problems. They cannot be separated. This brings many of us to the conclusion that we must and we can bring about fundamental system reform. If the system could, through national health insurance, gain access to the better than $90 billion now being spent annually on personal health services and redirect these

---

[20] Worthington, *op. cit.*

[21] Marjorie Smith Mueller, "Private Health Insurance in 1973: a Review of Coverage, Enrollment, and Financial Experience," *Social Security Bulletin*, XXXVIII, No. 2 (1975), 21–40.

expenditures in accordance with thought-through health policies, needed institutional change would be achievable in the immediate future.

Winston Churchill once characterized social insurance as "the miracle of large numbers." That miracle is achievable for health care now.

### PRINCIPLES IN THE SOLUTION

That the American people are aware of the problems in the health care system is evidenced by repeated public opinion polls which show that a majority favor a national health insurance program. I am confident one will be adopted in the near future. The greatest danger we face at this time is that the wrong kind of program will be adopted—one which will not address itself to the problems, or one which will protect the self-interests of the providers or the insurance industry, not those at hazard, the American people.

1. A sound program should provide a single universal national health insurance program covering the entire population regardless of age, race, income, employment or unemployment status. Had such a program been in effect today we would not be faced with the grim specter of more than 30 million people in the families of almost 9 million unemployed workers losing their health care coverage because it is employment-related.

Had the previous Administration's national health insurance proposal passed, or that proposed by the AMA, the health insurance industry, or the American Hospital Association, we would still be in the same dilemma in which we find ourselves. When national health insurance is employer-related and not universal it does not meet the needs.

2. Fully paid health benefits should be available to cover the entire range of personal health services, including the prevention and early detection of disease, the treatment of illness, and physical and mental rehabilitation. Good health care to be effective must consist of much more than the treatment of episodic sickness.

Such coverage could prove to be an important means of bridging the gap between the "haves" and the "have nots" in America. In health care, at least, they would be brought into the mainstream as equals.

3. Financing should be simple and equitable. It should use the tested mechanism of Social Security financing combined with federal general revenues. Such a plan would help relieve states and localities of most of the burden of financing health care programs, permitting them to allocate their scarce funds to other urgently needed services.

4. Incentives should be built in to make possible the delivery of more efficient, high-quality services. There is substantial evidence to demonstrate that nonprofit health maintenance organizations (HMO's) providing complete health care services are able to cut in-hospital use by one-half and reduce surgery rates by one-half or more. A national health insurance program should use the leverage of its funds to encourage health professionals, physicians, nurses, social workers, therapists, and others to practice teamwork health delivery through HMO's, hospital-based organizations, outpatient primary care centers, and other innovative organizational forms. These groups can and should be reimbursed on a capitation basis for enrolled groups, thus encouraging them to maintain health rather than treat illness.[22]

The monopoly of solo-practice medicine should be replaced by competition of alternative delivery systems. While doctors should be given the option of remaining in solo practice, the incentives should be geared to encourage those who wish to innovate.

Social workers have essential roles to play in a reorganized health system. To date, however, they have demonstrated

[22] Sidney Garfield, "The Delivery of Medical Care," *Scientific American*, CCXXII, No. 4 (1970), 15–23. He recognizes that a prepaid group practice or HMO is but one of many alternatives to solo-practice, fee-for-service delivery. For example, he recommends a quadripartite prepaid delivery system consisting of: (*a*) a screening center for the worried well; (*b*) a health maintenance center for immunization and other care of the worried well; (*c*) a center for the chronically ill; (*d*) an acute care center where the bulk of patient contact with physicians would take place.

limited competence and interest. This accounts for the fact that some 30,000 social workers identified with health care serve primarily in treatment roles.[23] Except possibly in mental health, they are noteworthy by their absence from administration, planning, and organization. And that is where the action is.

5. Scrutiny of quality of care must be mandated as an integral part of the program. Once and for all we must eliminate "gang visits," 90-second diagnoses, and 30-second treatment visits which our present arrangements permit, and which occur with depressing frequency.

6. A federal and national plan with decentralized regional administration should replace the present chaos of federal, state, and local programs and 1,800 private insurance companies selling different policies and administering them with thousands of different and often conflicting policies and procedures. Such a federal program would for the first time make possible the planning, budget procedures, and cost controls so desperately required in this sprawling costly industry.

7. Consumers need to be assured a role at every administrative and decision-making level of the program. The time has passed when the patient can or will accept meekly what he is told is good for him. Health care becomes meaningful and relevant when those who pay for and use services play a role in determining the policies.

8. Incentives must be included to overcome the shortages and maldistribution of health personnel. Funds should be available to train and upgrade personnel in those human services professions who are in short supply. Schools of social work and our professional association have an opportunity to define new roles in health for our profession and to lay plans to seek funds to provide training and placement.

The success of a national health insurance program which will bring about substantial institutional change will, I am

[23] Neil F. Bracht, "Health Care: the Largest Human Service System," *Social Work,* XIX, No. 5 (1974), 539 and n. 6.

confident, over time, be dependent on the extent to which it incorporates the eight guiding principles I have enumerated.

Such a national health insurance program, called Health Security, has been fashioned by a group of academicians, health practitioners, and medical economists. Sponsored by Senator Edward Kennedy and Congressman James Corman and over a hundred members from both branches of the Congress, it is at the center of the current national debate on health care.[24] A national coalition of organizations from every field and committees in some thirty-five states has joined in the effort to get national health insurance *and* system reform.[25]

"Give me a lever and we shall move the world," said Thomas Paine at the founding of the Republic. The Health Security program proposes to use the lever of large funds, the more than $90 billion we are spending annually on personal health care, to provide universal comprehensive protection, and evolutionary change in the system.

A number of critics in and out of Congress say we cannot afford such a program. But Health Security would not cost more than we now spend for personal health services. The money would be raised differently and more equitably; it would be spent in quite a different manner—but the totals would be about the same.

And social welfare can bear witness only too well that we can afford even less the present situation where millions are locked into poverty because they are too ill or too handicapped to maintain themselves; where large numbers of the mentally ill are still maintained in warehouses often called mental institutions or, worse still, discharged into communities unwilling or unable to care for them; and where thousands of babies die needlessly each year or suffer lifelong defects because their mothers did not receive decent prenatal care.[26]

[24] The Health Security Program, S.3, H.R. 21, 94th Congress.
[25] This coalition organized under the Health Security Action Council, Washington, D.C.
[26] David M. Kessner *et al., Infant Death: an Analysis by Maternal Risk and Health Care* (Washington, D.C.: Institute of Medicine, National Academy of Sciences, 1973), pp.

Social welfare in the last decade increasingly has seen a major role in advocacy to produce social change. Our field is uniquely qualified for these roles in a democratic society, for we have understanding and a commitment to protecting human values.

I have indicated my conviction that these issues of human services are integral to the field of social welfare, and it is possible to begin to solve them in the present scene. Social welfare has not had nor is it likely ever to have sufficient power on its own to produce major social change. The present scene, however, lends itself to the possibility of an effective power base of social welfare, the ethnic groups to whom we are close, the labor movement, committed to reform of health care, and the rising new force in our country, organized consumers.

I suggest that in time of trouble we have an opportunity for our finest hour—an organized effort to make the goal of the right to health a reality in this generation. Let us not spend our energies cursing the darkness. We can light a candle for the future.

## RESPONSES

### I. JAMES R. DUMPSON

As I READ President Glasser's presidential address, two reactions crowded out almost all others. The first was that in this bicentennial year of the nation's beginning we

JAMES R. DUMPSON is Administrator/Commissioner, New York City Human Resources Administration, Department of Social Services.

1–2. "Generally, adequacy of care . . . is strongly and consistently associated with infant birth weight and survival, an association that is pronounced throughout the first year of life. The findings indicate that if all women had the pregnancy outcare of those receiving adequate health services, the overall 1968 New York City infant mortality rate of 21.9 per 1,000 live births could have been reduced as much as 33 percent to 14.7 per 1,000. . . . (The) death rate was more than two-and-one .half times higher for infants of mothers with inadequate care than it was for infants of mothers with adequate care."

have yet to develop and accept an integrated human resource policy, a national social policy that places individuals
and families, irrespective of their race or age or sex or income, at the center of all of our national activities—social,
political, and economic. And so, as I approached the subject
of health as a right as outlined by Mr. Glasser, I had a need
to start with an understanding of the imperative for change
in our total social, economic, and political system. Until that
premise is accepted and action developed to bring it about,
the concept of health as a right as a goal, and the several
variations on the theme of methods of provision in the several bills in Congress, fails to propel me into immediate action.

My second immediate response was a corollary to the
first—that we may be detoured in achieving implementation
of the concept of health as a right as outlined by Mr. Glasser
until we agree on the urgent need for mechanisms by which
we can achieve an equitable redistribution of wealth in this
country.

Poverty, with all its implications, is the single most influential factor affecting health status; for it is those in the lowest
socioeconomic group who pay the highest price for being
poor in America. And the poorest, for the most part, are
those ethnic groups that we respondents have been called
upon to represent.

Mr. Glasser has given some statistical insight concerning
the service and manpower gaps in the black community. I
wish space permitted me to share even more startling and
shocking data that need to be repeated for the record.

When attempting to find remedies for the health problem,
one is struck by the scarcity of minority health professionals—a situation attributed in no small measure in the past
to policies and procedures that screened out blacks interested
in, and prepared for, a health service career. Blacks, for example, make up approximately 10 percent of the population;
they constitute only 2 percent of the nation's doctors and
dentists. As things stand today, only one in every 3,800

blacks will become a physician in the next decade, compared with one in 560 for whites.

The devastating effect of such a situation becomes clearer when one examines the geographic location of health professionals. Areas with the greatest need are areas with the fewest resources. Southern rural areas, for example, where a large population of blacks lives, and the inner cities, where blacks are becoming the major inhabitants, both cry out for professional health assistance. In 1976 it is estimated that between 35,000 and 40,000 physicians are needed in rural and inner-city areas. The predicament is magnified by statistical estimates showing that 21 percent of the black population have not even seen a doctor in two years or more; while 3 percent have never even been to a doctor. Further, over 25 percent of the black population of this country has never seen a dentist for any kind of care.

Of course, there is need for greater federal support for such problems as sickle-cell anemia and hypertension. But we cannot permit the "cop-out" of the government and society: "Look, we are doing all of this research on sickle-cell anemia to deal with the black health problem." Sickle-cell anemia may kill only blacks; hypertension, to be sure, is the prime killer among blacks. But the struggle for mere existence, in dignity and economic security while attempting to accommodate racism wherever it exists in our society, may be a major contributor to hypertension rates among blacks. If that is so, we may need to reorganize the very foundations of a brutalizing society whose social and economic practices may need to be attacked before health as a right has any meaning to masses of our black population.

What do Mr. Glasser's paper and the theme of the 1975 Forum mean to me from a black perspective?

We need a new federal income-security system that is incapable of depriving, denying, and destroying people—a system that plays a meaningful role in the redistribution of the nation's wealth and assures free access to *all* of the opportunities for achieving wealth. Then health as a right as a goal will have tremendous meaning to the blacks crowded in the ghettoes of our cities.

We need a change in the socioeconomic political system of the country that places human rights for all above any other consideration, foreign or domestic. We need not so much *détente* with foreign powers as a *détente* with the survival problems of the towns and cities throughout the land, where the social and economic deprivations, including the absence of even second-rate health care, may be more threatening to our national survival than what happens across the seas. We need to uproot and destroy eviscerating American poverty, for all times, just as penicillin conquers a host of bacteria laying siege to a human organism.

We need a comprehensive national health care system that makes quality health care available and accessible to all as a matter of right. When we achieve this, there will be no need for a panel to speak for special ethnic group needs. Universal availability of comprehensive, integrated, quality health care will remove all special pleaders for health as a right from most platforms.

We need to get the best possible incentives for entrenching providers, as Mr. Glasser advocated, in areas where they are most needed. Those agencies in government which support health services providers need to look more carefully at what they are purchasing in health care, for whom and for where.

We need to correct the geographic maldistribution of health manpower. One way that would help blacks would be to have government allocate its financial support in such a way as to compensate for past neglect by medical education of blacks and other minorities, and through government policy and fiscal practice give incentives for service to areas that are defined as high-priority health areas.

The road toward making the right to health care a *functioning* reality for *all* Americans will be difficult at times, it will be perilous, and its success will be uncertain. But one thing is clear: it will not come about unless social workers are willing and prepared to lead or join in providing the leader-

ship of a new social, economic, and political order. Black
social workers, all ethnic minority social workers, I believe,
are prepared to accept the challenge for real, basic, change.
A united profession must be the response to the call for the
leadership required for hammering out a national human
resource policy for the protection and care of all our
people—in which health care as a right would take its proper
place. The question is: will the profession respond to the
challenge?

## *II. JOE P. MALDONADO*

I HAVE BEEN ASKED to discuss the most urgent achievable health goals from the standpoint of the Spanish-speaking people.

Obviously, I cannot be the spokesman for all of the
Spanish-speaking people of this country, state or city. However, in order to present a more knowledgeable view I have
consulted with a number of friends and colleagues who are
well-informed about the health needs, resources, and priorities that affect Spanish-speaking people.

First, it should be clear to all of us that regardless of ethnicity we are all in the same human and political boat. All of
us must work together to keep the boat from sinking and to
keep it moving in the direction of good health for all of the
people in this country.

I believe that there are some very important cross-cutting
activities that we must all be a part of, and yet I think there
are some areas of special concern to Spanish-speaking people
that need to be understood. Mr. Glasser has covered the
cross-cutting issues very well. Spanish-speaking individuals
and groups, as well as everyone else, need the following:

1. A national health policy
2. Reasonable health care costs

JOE P. MALDONADO is Regional Director, Department of Health, Education, and Welfare, Region IX.

3. Access to medical care
4. Integration of services
5. Quality care

To achieve these five goals we need to band as allies, then translate this ill-defined tie into easily understood political action that will bring about definable results in the real world.

In the areas of special concern to Spanish-speaking people we need:

1. *Availability of accurate data.* This is essential so that the health status of the Spanish-speaking may be determined. For statistical purposes, Spanish-speaking persons are grouped as "white" by most local, state, and national agencies including the National Center for Health Statistics and the Census Bureau. A method for extracting information regarding this group of approximately twelve million people needs to be developed.

2. *Concentrated efforts to reduce disease rates.* Immediate and special steps must be taken, especially where disease rates are known to be significantly higher than in the white Anglo areas.

3. *Employment.* More Spanish-speaking people are needed in administrative and management positions in health delivery and health-planning structures to provide sensitivity and knowledge in dealing with specific needs, such as the language problem and understanding the culture. This means upward mobility opportunities as well as scholarships and other programs designed to increase the number of Spanish-speaking workers in the health field.

4. *Planning.* More involvement by Spanish-speaking professionals and consumers in the planning of health delivery systems is needed so that consideration will be given to language problems, transportation concerns, and other factors which stand in the way of both utilization of available medical care and the institution of new programs.

5. *Urban areas.* More emphasis should be placed on the health needs and care of the Spanish-speaking population in the urban areas where the majority live as well as on continuing concern for the rural farm worker.

6. *Preventive medicine.* New preventive medicine techniques should be developed for implementation in the home, or at least in the neighborhoods, to take advantage of the strengths and assets of close family ties and the tendency of Spanish-speaking families to care for their own health needs. More health materials need to be printed in the Spanish language.

7. *Policy formation.* There are Spanish-speaking professionals at every level—physicians, social workers, statisticians, and researchers—and more Spanish-speaking students are going into various areas of health care study. Opportunities should be made for them to fill key positions and to assist in the development of policy and program so that the needs of the Spanish-speaking community may be considered and met.

Improving the health care of the Spanish-speaking community revolves around a balanced diet, availability of physicians, greater awareness of *when* one should seek health care, aggressive preventive health maintenance, improved quality of services, health education outreach programs, and increased training and educational opportunities for aspiring medical professionals.

All this suggests, in my opinion, that achievable goals in the health field are obtainable for the Spanish-speaking community, as well as for all of the people, but in order to fulfill a number of the critical basic needs we must work together— the majority as well as the minorities.

## III. EVELYN L. BLANCHARD

THE ISSUE of health care, its human and political dimensions, is a very difficult area for a Native American to discuss. The difficulty arises out of the catastrophically damaging and tragic situation that exists. With few exceptions, the Native American is the most vulnerable human being

EVELYN L. BLANCHARD is Assistant Area Social Worker, Bureau of Indian Affairs, Albuquerque, N. Mex.

who resides in these United States. Health care is not only a right to which we are entitled as human beings, it is also a right which results from the treaty relationship which exists between the federal government and many Indian tribes throughout the country. The federal government in exchange for lands which were taken from the Indians agreed to provide certain services, health care among them. If these treaty arrangements had been heavily weighted in terms of the Indians, one might say that the federal government had long ago met its debt. But the federal government was paid well, in advance. The quest for land and resources continues, and even today Indians are being pressured and coerced to rid themselves of the last holdings they have. It is in this climate that the relationship between the federal government and the Indians exists today.

Let us look at some of the health characteristics of Indians over several decades. Live births per 1,000 persons have been stabilized around 40 percent from 1940 to 1970 with a decrease in infant mortality of 40 percent since 1950. Yet, only 5.7 percent of our population live beyond sixty-five years of age.

What are the causes of our deaths? Diseases of the circulatory system, accidents, poisonings, violence, and digestive disorders are the main causes. Suicides are a prevalent characteristic with incidence beginning to climb at age fifteen with the peak occurring between the ages of twenty-five and thirty-four. There is a gradual decline through the next several years, but at age sixty-five again the incidence rises. The incidence rates for leading notifiable diseases for Indians are astronomical in all categories with amoebic and bacillary dysentery, gonorrhea, hepatitis, measles, mumps, syphilis, and tuberculosis heading the list. These diseases are those for which there are available cures. If this is so, why is it that Indians still suffer and die from these diseases?

There are many miracle drugs, but these must be administered by medical service personnel. The number of doctors available throughout Indian country is small. In addition to this, few of the physicians who serve in our communities have a real commitment to the health of the Indian people. In the main, these have been people who work on reservations as an alternate to military service. One would think that an individual who chooses not to involve himself in a situation where thousands of people are being maimed and killed would have a strong commitment to the preservation of life itself. However, the statistics paint a different picture. In 1966 only 10.2 percent of the U.S. hospital population was Indian. In 1969 this had climbed to 12.1 percent. The 1970 census revealed that there were no Indian chiropractors or podiatrists. Pharmacists, physicians, including medical and osteopathic, and veterinarians numbered only one tenth of one percent. There is one Indian dentist.

Many of our people hesitate to request medical services because of factors of language, customs, and indignity. Yet, no great push has been initiated to educate Indian physicians and other health care personnel to meet the needs of their own people. The quality of preparatory education required to gain entrance to these professions is almost nonexistent for Indians. Yet we frequently hear the cry that Indians need to become self-reliant rather than dependent on the federal government.

The mental health services are even more startling. In spite of the volumes that have been written about the Indian family and its relational, supportive network, most services are delivered on an individual basis. Many of the diseases may afflict the Indian body, but many more afflict his mind and soul. The numbers of our children in non-Indian foster care and adoptive homes can only be described as genocidal. The premise is that Indian families and communities cannot care for themselves and therefore, over and again, they are not given the opportunity. Little wonder that many Indians live in a world of hopelessness and frustration.

This is a sad and inhuman world for many Indian people. It is not realistic to think that this results from happenstance. Meaningful and quality health care is not available to Indian people because it is not planned for them. How can it be that the preservation of the life of a people is either overlooked or left out of the budget? Who makes the decision to continue this arrangement? Is it you? Is it I? How is that decision really made?

## IV. TSUGUO IKEDA

Acknowledgment is critical that Asians have health and related needs like any other citizen in this country who is affected by factors of racism, neglect, and just plain ignorance by the general public.

[The] planners of the 1971 White House Conference on Aging . . . . failed to include a Special Concerns Session for Asian American elderly as part of its original agenda. While the planning for other Special Concerns Sessions had been in process for many months, the decision to hold a Special Concerns Session for Asian Americans was made only . . . because a special request was made by concerned Asian Americans.[1]

This omission of Asians as being in need continues to be a major problem. In 1974, the Social Security Administration published a position paper on Asian Americans. The following are a few of the significant findings:

Because of the dearth of Asian American clinical psychologists and psychiatrists; the hidden nature of mental illness among the Japanese; the highest rate of mental illness among the Chinese in California; the highest rate of TB among the Chinese and Filipinos in San Francisco; and the highest TB death rate among the Japanese in San Francisco, Federal, State and local health agencies should take affirmative steps to combat the general apathy regarding the Asian American health concerns.[2]

---

TSUGUO IKEDA is Executive Director, Seattle Atlantic Street Center, Seattle.

[1] "The Asian American Elderly," in *Special Concerns Reports,* 1971 (Washington, D.C.: White House Conference on Aging, 1972), p. 2.

[2] *Asian Americans: a Case of Benighted Neglect and the Urgent Need for Affirmative Action,* Social Security Administration, Bureau of District Office Operations, Labor Relations and Equal Opportunity Staff (mimeographed; 1974) p. 52.

The average percentage of the elderly Asian Americans who were 65 and older with income less than poverty level in California was 13 percent, or slightly better than twice the percentage of the Blacks and Spanish-surnamed (5.8 percent). In New York, the average percentage for the elderly Asian Americans was even greater—19.6 percent which was nearly three times the percentage of the Blacks (7.1 percent) and seven times greater than the Spanish speaking (2.8 percent).[3]

The 1971 White House Conference on Aging reported:

A quick look at Asian American communities would verify that they do indeed have problems and the problems in many respects are more intense and complex than the problems of the general senior citizen population. When the Asian American suicide rate in certain areas is three times the national average, when 34 percent of Asian American aged who were studied have never had a medical or dental examination, it should be obvious that the problems facing Asian American aged are overwhelming to the point it is impossible for Asian American aged to look only to their families for help.[4]

An Asian American social worker who recently visited a home for the aged wrote about her visit:

I discovered four Japanese there, three of whom spoke very little English. Because there was no other alternative as far as a living situation was concerned, they were placed in a home for the aged and in that process, *shikataganai* (can't be helped) so far as having to conform to a different life style and pattern of social interaction. While the motivation of the institution to provide good service would not be questioned, what could be questioned would be: (1) How will communication be handled? (2) Can their dietary habits be acknowledged and honored? (3) Are there means to provide meaningful daily activities? (4) Will their health needs really be met through the institution? Will we feel that we have provided for their well-being because a responsible institution is now providing them with services? This face-to-face encounter in New York City makes me anxious to know how many more older Asians, especially those unrelated, are living here.[5]

[3] *Ibid.*, p. 56.    [4] "The Asian American Elderly," p. 2.
[5] Letter from June Shimokawa, Board of Global Ministries, United Methodist Church, Health and Welfare Ministries, New York City, Feb. 21, 1975, p. 1.

One of the biggest problems facing Asians is the following:

The assumption that most people still feel that Asian Americans
don't have too many problems and, if they do, that they pretty
much take care of their own is still evident. Furthermore, if they
have needs, they can utilize the existing resources. After all, aren't
all programs supposed to be open and not discriminate? [6]

Asians need to be involved. By involvement is meant total
involvement in the policy developments related to health issues; in the budgeting decisions of limited financial and related resources; service delivery, whether in administration,
supervision, or the delivery of service; and in the evaluation
of the services. This definition of involvement certainly
should not be new. The problem begins to develop as major
efforts are made to carry out the belief that health as well as
involvement is a right.

This resistance by the majority health professionals raises a
lot of questions. The Seattle Demonstration Project for Asian
Americans [7] is currently dealing with the question of the
hundreds of Asian health professionals (doctors, dentists,
nurses, dietitians) who have been trained in Asia but for the
most part are unable to practice in America. Most interesting
is the fact that the Philippine medical schools staffed by visiting professors from America followed approved medical
training practices in the United States.[8]

We are well aware that across this country the rural communities, poor ethnic neighborhoods, Native American reservations, and veterans hospitals, to name a few, are the least
inviting to the majority of accredited practitioners. Some
major health needs can be met by filling this gap. Certainly
this is not a simple solution but would involve screening, specialized training, and internship at various levels. In addition,
some changes will be required in law, attitudes, and practices
of health professionals. "There is nothing more difficult to
take in hand, more perilous to conduct or more uncertain in

[6] *Ibid.*

[7] Seattle Demonstration Project for Asian Americans, Sil Dong Kim, Project Director.

[8] Letter from Lindbergh S. Sata, M.D., Director, Psychiatric Services, Harborview
Medical Center, Seattle, March 3, 1975, p. 1.

its success than to take the lead in the introduction of a new order of things." This statement, made many years ago by Machiavelli in *The Prince,* is so very true today.

Are we really committed to the notion as health professionals that health is a right for Asians whether they be administrators, practitioners, or clients?

Over the last twenty-five years the National Institute of Mental Health has poured nearly $2 billion for human service training into such fields as psychiatry, psychology, and social work. The majority of these therapists were trained to meet the mental health needs of the middle class.[9] This assessment of training subsidies has done little for Asians and Pacific Island peoples. If this nation is to be really committed to health as a right for all of its citizens, then a major change in policy by the federal, state, local, and private sectors is required. Training funds must be allocated so that Asians committed to their communities may be provided equal assistance.

Some assessment of mental health counseling services for the purposes of helping has consistently been found to be ineffective in a variety of settings and by various health professionals.[10] Obviously, some of our health professionals need help, and more of the same will not provide the direction required. As Peter Drucker said: "Perhaps what we need is new perception. It is putting together things that no one had thought of putting together before, things that, by themselves, have been around a long time." [11]

Asians have a different perspective of viewing life, death, and stress and how to deal with them. Perhaps a review and inclusion of an Asian perspective may complement the Western perspective so that health, besides being a right, is also effective.

[9] Robert M. Vidaver, *Developments in Human Services Education and Manpower,* I, No. 4 (New York: Behavioral Publications, 1973), p. 390.
[10] William C. Berleman and Thomas W. Steinburn, "The Execution and Evaluation of a Delinquency Prevention Program," *Social Service Review,* XLVI (1972), 323–46.
[11] Peter F. Drucker, *The Age of Discontinuity* (New York: Harper and Row, 1968), p. 47.

# The United States Economy Today

*GARDNER ACKLEY*

Assessing the economic health of the nation, diagnosing its ailments, and prescribing remedies is never an easy task. Like the practice of medicine, the practice of economic policy rests on fundamental scientific knowledge but is itself as much an art as a science. When—as today—the national economy suffers from a number of simultaneous ills, diagnosis and prescription are particularly difficult.

To describe in one sentence the nature of our current economic ills, let me put it this way: the U.S. economy suffers primarily from a serious case of recession, considerably exacerbated by an earlier faulty diagnosis and incompetent prescription of remedies. You can see that I am very unhappy with the care the patient has received in the earlier stages of his illness. I would not classify it as malpractice, because the symptoms were somewhat unusual, there were complications which tended to obscure the main problem, and there is not complete agreement in the profession itself about how such cases are to be treated. But I am severely critical.

My prognosis? Ultimate complete recovery, without permanent impairment of function. The convalescence must necessarily be gradual; but like some other outside consultants, I regard the officially prescribed regimen for recovery as excessively and unnecessarily cautious.

I recognize that some observers (mainly persons who, however learned, seem to have few professional qualifications for practice) hold that the disease is chronic, and probably progressive; and that only radical surgery—if even that—can re-

GARDNER ACKLEY is the Henry Carter Adams Professor of Political Economy, University of Michigan, Ann Arbor.

store reasonable health. Others suggest that the patient has contracted some rare and mysterious disease never before diagnosed and for which the cure is unknown.

Obviously, such possibilities can never be completely ruled out; but my study does not support any of these fearful prognoses. To me the symptoms of common recession are clear and unmistakable, even though the attack is the most severe I have seen in almost forty years. Naturally, the patient is not so young as he once was; and he has acquired some habits not very conducive to good health. But with proper attention, I believe he will achieve full restoration of his normally robust functioning.

I have now worked the medical analogy into the ground. So at this point I doff my white laboratory coat and begin to talk like an economist.

ALTERNATIVE DIAGNOSES

Let me begin by discussing—briefly, and necessarily quite inadequately—some of the alternative, more frightening diagnoses and prognoses. It is not surprising that they have emerged. The combination, especially during 1974, of double-digit inflation with sagging production and high and rising unemployment is really without precedent in U.S. experience; and it was surely rather frightening, particularly when the rate of inflation was still accelerating until late in 1974. It is thus not strange that many observers, including a few economists, have been looking for, and even thinking that they see, new and more serious forces than those which have caused the recurrent business recessions of the past.

To the orthodox Marxist, of course, we are now entering the inevitable final crisis of capitalism, the outgrowth of its inherent internal contradictions. Many conservatives, on the other hand, see our current problems to be the inevitable and progressive consequence of creeping socialism; or of the decay of work incentives; or of the cutting in 1971 of the final tenuous link of our money with gold. I can only characterize these diagnoses as silly. There are two somewhat less implausible hypotheses: one, that our problems reflect escalating and irreversible shortages of energy, raw materials, and food relative to the world's population; and the alternative, that they stem from big (and growing bigger) government and the politicization of economic policy.

Recent years have seen a considerable revival of concern with a problem the analysis of which lay at the very center of the development of modern economic science during several decades at the end of the eighteenth and early nineteenth centuries. The fathers of modern economics saw an inevitable collision between the fixed stock of natural resources which earth provides—especially of arable land—and the tendency for population to grow exponentially. Fascination with the apparent inevitability of this collision, and with its consequences for human welfare, has never disappeared, even though its predicted date has kept moving forward, as production and economic welfare have expanded exponentially in all parts of the world and, in most, at a considerably faster rate than population.

Today's environmentalists combine many elements of this long-standing concern with inevitable resource scarcities, spiced by romantic nostalgia for a disappearing wilderness, and the revulsion that all of us must feel against the almost unrestrained fouling of air and water by the wastes of industrial and urban society, which prevailed until more effective limitations began to be imposed only a decade ago.

The fact that the direct source of much of the inflation of the last two years lies in sharply higher prices for energy, industrial raw materials, and farm products tempts many environmentalists and others to see our recent economic problems as the beginning stage of a progressively worsening pinch of foodstuffs, raw materials, and energy resources— signs that the ultimate collision between people and the resources which support them is now at hand.

FOOD SHORTAGES

It is my firm conviction that whatever problems may arise with respect to food supplies in the longer-term future are quite irrelevant to our current problems. Soaring food prices during 1973 and 1974 can be entirely explained by serious crop failures in several parts of the world, occurring simultaneously with an unusually rapid growth of incomes. The resulting inflation of food prices was greatly exaggerated by speculation, and compounded by earlier mistakes of policy which had permitted the dissipation of U.S. reserve stocks of basic foodstuffs, and by the more recent mismanagement of an obsolete program for subsidizing U.S. crop exports even to nonhungry people.

The prediction that the world is about to run out of food gained special currency as a result of the World Food Conference held a year or so ago in Rome, where the poorer countries quite naturally demanded increased concessionary shipments of food from the richer ones. Famine in several countries, although resulting not from shortages of food but from the inability to transport and distribute it to remote rural populations whose crops had failed, fanned the concern—which was then popularized and exaggerated by our thrill-seeking communications media. Most people probably failed to notice the recent inside-page story that reported a conference of experts commissioned by the National Academy of Sciences to study world food prospects. Their preliminary reports gave no support to fears that food production cannot be sufficiently expanded because of inherent limitations on the earth's resources of land, water, and sunshine.

Of course there is hunger and poverty. And their existence stains our consciences. But their source does not lie—not now, or for as many decades ahead as we can reasonably see—in inherent limitations on the earth's ability to produce food. It lies in ignorance, backwardness, and inefficient social and political institutions. No one who has ever visited Japan can seriously entertain fears of imminent world starvation as a result merely of resource limitations and large population. A string of mountainous islands, with a total land area smaller than California and arable land less than 40 percent of California's, supports a population five times as great—

more than 100 million people. Less than 15 percent of Japan's work force is engaged in agriculture, forestry, and fishing; yet—as the result of an educated rural work force, progressive agricultural technology, and effective social organization—Japanese eat very well. Japan could easily be self-sufficient in food;—and it nearly is, although it wisely does not try to achieve this.

MINERAL AND ENERGY SHORTAGES

On minerals and even on energy, the story is not much different. As has been the case with agriculture, even the wisest and most skilled observers never seem able to predict the future impact of technological progress on the availability and productivity of basic resources. In the case of minerals, such progress permits us both to find and to exploit resources hitherto unknown or considered worthless, and to reduce substantially the quantities of mineral products needed to support any given level of national output.

Just twenty-five years ago, the world experienced a steep and general inflation in raw material prices of a severity as dramatic as that of 1973–74. Then as now, it was tripped off by political shocks both to the supply of, and demand for, many materials, and was greatly exaggerated by speculative attempts to acquire inventories for both protection and profit. Then as now, it evoked great public concern about a possible growing scarcity of raw materials. In January, 1951, President Truman appointed the prestigious Paley Commission to study long-range problems of materials supply. After a year and a half it produced a detailed and thoughtful report, which stilled much of the alarm. As a part of its work it projected U.S. raw materials supply and demand to 1975.

The report has recently been dusted off by scholars to compare what was projected with actual results. The conclusions of one such review, by Richard N. Cooper, are fascinating.[1] In 1951, the experts projected a rate of growth of total

[1] Richard N. Cooper, "Resource Needs Revisited," *Brookings Papers on Economic Activity*, I (1975), 238–45.

U.S. production 25 percent less than has actually been achieved, and a growth rate of durable-goods production (where most minerals end up) less than half what has been realized. Yet their projections of 1975 U.S. *consumption* of twenty-four major minerals overstate actual current rates for all but seven, and in most cases very dramatically. For about half of these minerals, prices have risen over the intervening period by less than the average rise of all wholesale prices; that is, their "real" prices have fallen.

Once again, I do not mean to imply that we have no problems, and not in the future, with mineral or energy raw materials. Quite the contrary! What I am trying to say, and strongly believe, is that our current general economic problems—U.S. and world-wide—are not associated with any novel or newly escalating shortages of materials, and the current materials situation does not differ in degree or in kind from past and future situations.

EVER BIGGER GOVERNMENT

The last of the more apocalyptic diagnoses attracts considerable support in high places today. It holds that the basic source of our present ills—which are bound to multiply unless we excise that source—lies in the growth of big government and an accompanying politicization of economic policy.

President Ford, in a recent magazine interview, expressed the thesis this way:

Roy Ash, when he was head of the Office of Management and Budget, put together a study of the growth in transfer payments. If you take the transfer-payment growth for the last two decades—it is about 9 percent per year—and continue it, by the year 2000, 50 percent of the people will be living off the other 50 percent.

We have been able to get away with this because as these transfer payments have expanded, it has been taken out of the Defense Department. Roy Ash came up with the result that if this continues, and we continue to take it out of the Defense Department, there won't be enough money to buy one soldier one gun.

In other words, you just can't keep on doing that. There is a long-range danger, because despite allegations to the effect that the Defense Department is not the most economical and most efficiently run organization, you still have to have it in this world.

If that growth in transfer payments continues, we can't have the same economic system by the year 2000 that we have now. I don't think that we are over the cliff, but it is something we have to stop now. As more people get on those transfer payments, they become a political force and the programs are sort of self-perpetuating. In my opinion, the best example of how the matter can get out of hand is the situation in Great Britain today. They just don't seem to be able to stop the momentum.[2]

There are severe problems with the arithmetic of the President's projection. They are severe even in the far more qualified version of his projection which first appeared in the Budget Message in February, 1975. The more serious problem (in my view) is the failure to mention either in the original statement or in the President's more flamboyant version several important facts closely related to his concern: for instance, the fact that the rapid growth of federal income-transfer programs has been almost precisely parallelled by growing revenues from special taxes levied to finance them. I do not happen to like the complete dependence on the payroll tax for financing transfer programs. But through it, workers as a group do pay for the income transfers which retired and disabled workers and surviving dependents currently receive. These are called "income transfers" because they use no resources for public (as opposed to private) purposes: members of one group of private citizens are consuming more and members of another (larger) group are consuming less than otherwise as the result of the transfer. It does not resemble the construction, maintenance, and operation of a battleship or fleet of tanks (necessary as these may or may not be) which use resources that would otherwise be available to satisfy private needs and wants, and thus in the long run can only restrict the total of private incomes and the scope for private choices.

[2] "How President Ford Views the System," *Fortune*, April 1975, p. 80.

A second fact which this statement fails specifically to mention is that, despite the rapid growth of federal income transfers, total federal expenditures for all purposes have not increased relative to the size of our economy. Twenty years ago, in 1954, federal expenditures were equal to 19.4 percent of the gross national product (GNP); twenty years later, in 1974, they equaled 19.2 percent of the GNP. If it is reasonable to extrapolate into the future the past relatively fast growth of transfers (and it is not *obvious* that such an extrapolation is reasonable), why should it not be reasonable to extrapolate the relatively slower growth of other federal expenditures?

The President's remark that "by the year 2000, 50 percent of the people will be living off the other 50 percent" appears to refer to a projection of the growth of *total* government expenditures—including those by state and local governments as well as by the federal government—which would bring that total to 50 percent of the GNP by year 2000. That, of course, would in no sense mean that 50 percent of the people were "living off the other 50 percent," which seems to imply that *transfer payments* would reach 50 percent of total incomes. (Even Presidents have some obligation to avoid inflammatory nonsense!)

In any case, what basis is there for projecting even that total expenditures of all governments might reach 50 percent of the GNP by the year 2000? As we have seen, federal spending has remained a constant fraction of the GNP—about 20 percent—for two decades. Over this same period, however, state and local spending has risen from 7.4 percent of the GNP in 1954 to 11.6 percent in 1974; and the total of all government spending has thus increased from about 27 percent to about 31 percent of the GNP. At that rate of increase it would appear to take not twenty-five but fifty years to get to 50 percent. But no matter. (Incidentally, federal grants to state and local governments are included in federal spending, but I have deducted them from state and local spending in order to avoid double counting. They have more than quadrupled over the past ten years, far faster growth even than that of income transfers!)

Since it is state and local government spending rather than federal spending which has grown faster than the GNP, it is not clear why federal income transfers are blamed for big and bigger government. But whatever its relevance, can we forecast that the past relatively rapid growth of state and local spending will continue? Many think that it will not. Education and highways account for more than half of all state and local government expenditures. Over the past several decades, states and cities have been building and staffing new schools and universities at a frantic rate in an effort to catch up with an exploding population of children. But that is over. They have been building highways, streets, and expressways to keep up with an exploding population of cars and drivers which seems unlikely to continue.

I do not find that the record supports even a presumption that government spending in the United States will inevitably grow in relative importance. But, even if it did, there is simply nothing either in economic analysis or in our own experience or that of other countries which says that fact must doom an economy either to high unemployment or to accelerating inflation. So I reject the big-government diagnosis for our economic ill-health.

THE RECESSION AND ITS SOURCES

I stated that our basic economic problem is recession—a recession similar in *kind* to the dozens of previous ones that mark our economic history (there have now been seven since the end of the Second World War), although sharper in *degree* than any since the prewar recession of 1937–38, which interrupted the nation's tortuous recovery from the great depression.

This recession had two main sources: first, highly restrictive government monetary and fiscal policies; and second, the sharp increase in oil prices of the Organization of Petroleum Exporting countries. Fiscal policy and, to a lesser extent, monetary policy had been very stimulative in the election year of 1972; but both policies began to be tightened in 1973. Fiscal policy became progressively more restrictive throughout 1973 and 1974, and moved significantly in the direction of stimulus *only this month*[3] as the first tax refund checks were mailed out, and withholding rates were reduced. Monetary policy became drum-tight in 1974, and remained that way until late in the year; since then, some ease has been permitted to develop.

As it always does, tight money in 1973 and 1974 sent housing construction into a tailspin, which only now *may* have ended. Housing activity thus became one of the major contributors to the recession, as it will be also to the recovery. The tight fiscal policy contributed doubly to recession. Federal purchases of goods and services were allowed to grow exceedingly slowly even in dollar terms—which, with soaring prices, meant no growth at all in the government's real demand for goods and services. Meanwhile, inflation also increased effective tax rates, as many families were moved by inflation into higher tax brackets even though their real incomes had not risen; and the inevitable capital gains which accrued on business inventories were taxed as though they were operating profits. These appreciably reduced the real after-tax incomes available for consumer and business spending.

But the really big blow to consumer purchases resulted from the OPEC increase in oil prices. This sudden price jump effectively imposed an extra tax of close to $20 billion a year on American consumers' real incomes (and proportionately an even more significant tax on real incomes in most other countries). Unlike the proceeds of a domestic tax, almost none of the proceeds of this foreign tax have returned to the spending stream as a demand for newly produced U.S. output, or for the current services of American workers. It was the impact of this tax on consumer spending, coming on top of the catastrophic slide in housing, the in-

[3] May, 1975.

creased federal tax burden, and the failure of federal purchases to grow in real terms, that actually tripped off the recession.

Once a recession begins, it feeds on itself. Reduced consumer incomes from wages and profits further reduce consumer purchases. Reduced production lessens the demand for new productive facilities—plant, equipment, and inventories—and this adds to and extends the slide in demand. If the recession is unexpected, as it usually is, cutbacks in production lag behind the drop in sales, and, for a while, inventories accumulate just at the time when sellers would prefer to see them decline, requiring progressively sharper cutbacks of production before inventories can be brought into line with reduced sales.

With monetary policy now eased and money for housing thus once again available, with fiscal policy finally turned toward stimulus, and with inventories at last being brought under control, the end of the recession must be nearly here, although predicting the particular month or even the quarter in which the bottom will be reached is mostly guesswork.[4]

As I indicated, the drop in production and incomes caused by this recession is the sharpest since 1937–38. Even if it ends at midyear, it will be the longest recession since the one that began in 1929, although it does not in any respect compare with that one either in duration or severity. But it more nearly resembles the recessions of the prior century than it does the other postwar recessions. Over the next year, our national production of goods and services will run some $200 billion below what it could be with reasonably full employment; and at best, it will probably be more than another year after that before we get within hailing distance of even a cautious definition of full employment.

Why did all this have to happen? If, as I believe, recessions are—at least *in principle*—avoidable, why could we not at least have kept this one close to the dimensions of other postwar recessions?

[4] It was apparently reached in May, 1975.

I think the answer is simply that we did not try. Our national government simply failed to apply standard, tested knowledge of how to deal with recessions. Soon after the onset of each of our six previous postwar recessions, government economic policy—monetary, fiscal, or both—was quickly shifted, often toward outright stimulus to economic activity, but surely toward neutrality, in an effort to moderate the extent and shorten the duration of the recession. Usually, this shift occurred within a few months of the first clear evidence of a downturn. But this time both monetary and fiscal policy were tightened, not relaxed. Lacking resistance from government policies—indeed, with their support—recessionary forces were thus allowed to accumulate the strong momentum which exploded in last fall's collapse of production and purchases.

To be sure, almost no one could or did predict the full virulence of the infection which government policies permitted and encouraged to develop during 1974. The early stages of the recession had been mild, and while the great majority of economists quickly identified it as a recession, most were thinking in postwar, not prewar, terms; and none predicted its ultimate severity. Still, early in the year, many economists began to call for an easing of policy. It should certainly have been evident that to increase the already heavy weight of government restraint could only have the effect of worsening the recession and risk making it very much worse. Why, then, did the mistake occur?

The official explanation was that priority had to be given to fighting a peril more serious and obvious than recession, namely, double-digit inflation.

THE PRIORITY GIVEN TO INFLATION

I believe that history will harshly judge the priority given to fighting inflation. First, there is simply no comparison between the damage to the economic welfare of individuals and of society resulting from even a 15 percent inflation and that inflicted by a prolonged siege of 8 percent to 10 percent unemployment with its accompanying loss of potential out-

put. Inflation hurts many people; but it benefits about as
many as it hurts. Of course we do not like the random redis-
tributions of wealth and income which inflation imposes. But
a major recession benefits no one; and it selects as its principal victims those least able to bear its burdens. If the costs
associated with an extra 4 percent or 5 percent of unemployment were spread evenly over all members of society, they
would be bearable; but they are instead highly concentrated
upon the lowest-paid, the least-skilled, the minorities, the
young workers just entering the labor force. It is not clear
whether inflation helps or hurts the poor, as a class. But
there can be no doubt about the cruel effects of massive
unemployment on the poor.

The second reason why history's judgment will be harsh is
that the weapons chosen to fight inflation in 1974 were not
likely to have much effect on inflation, even though almost
certain to intensify recession. Double-digit inflation in 1974
was mainly the product of quite extraneous and accidental
forces and events: the quadrupling of the price of imported
oil; the second consecutive year of unusually bad weather for
crops; a world-wide competitive scramble to acquire stocks of
raw materials, making supplies of many of them seem very
much scarcer than it now appears they were; and perhaps a
last desperate attempt to fatten manufacturing margins before the recession deepened or controls were reimposed.
None was very sensitive to monetary or fiscal restraint.

It is clear that inflation will now decline substantially over
the next couple of years, partly as a result of recession, but
even more because the one-time effects of the special and extraneous events of 1973 and 1974 will have finally been fully
reflected in the price level. Prices one or two years hence will
be very little lower than if the government stranglehold on
the economy had been loosened a year sooner.

IS POLICY FINALLY ON THE RIGHT TRACK?

Taxes have now been cut by some $23 billion; and the ex-
penditure ceilings proposed by either the House or the Sen-

ate Budget Committee will allow reasonable growth in real federal spending. Although both the tax cut and the probable expenditure increase exceed the Administration's proposals, I would judge the present posture of fiscal policy to be about right, provided (which now seems assured) that some reasonable portion of what is now only a temporary tax cut becomes permanent. The danger which we must now principally avoid may be that of overkill in the effort further to speed recovery—such as through a massive new public works program. No matter what its proponents say, most of the stimulus from a new public works program would be felt two or three years down the road.

Although the deficits accompanying the present fiscal policy will be large, they will result mainly from the tremendous shortfall of tax revenues arising from shrunken incomes, not from an excessively stimulative fiscal policy. And despite fears to the contrary, I do not believe that financing these deficits need interfere with financing the needed recovery of housing construction and business investment, provided the Federal Reserve System follows a sensible policy, which I think that it will. Although I am sure that mid-course corrections of policy will later be necessary, I think we are now on about the right track. We must, of course, be vigilant lest the more cautious members of the President's economic leadership attempt to sabotage reasonable and needed recovery in a continuing effort to fight inflation at all costs.

Does that mean, then, that the nation's future economic health is now assured? I wish that it were so. But there are some nagging problems which we must learn to solve. One is inflation.

COPING WITH INFLATION IN THE LONGER RUN

It is clear—at least to me—that double-digit inflation in 1974 had special, accidental causes, and that prices will be rising more slowly at least for the next two or three years. But we cannot avoid the fact that ever since 1966 the rate of inflation has been slowly, if irregularly, accelerating. And while inflation is a far less serious matter than massive unemployment, it has now become a chronic problem which we must learn to cope with.

I have long believed that a number of important trends in the social, economic, and political structures of most relatively free-market countries have been working to make inflation an increasingly serious and difficult problem, although they are too numerous and too complex to discuss here. Many kinds of relatively accidental events, including government policy mistakes, can put temporary pressure on the price level in either direction. But in our increasingly bureaucratic and politicized economy and society, any temporary *downward* pressures on prices are now strongly resisted; yet even temporary upward pressures easily generate or accelerate a largely self-maintaining spiral, involving a reciprocal interaction between wages and prices, some wages and other wages, some prices and other prices. This spiral develops enormous inertial force, which makes it substantially immune even to sharp drops or prolonged weakness in overall productive activity. Let me summarize my recommendations for dealing with this now chronic problem.

1. We must be sure that when the time comes, expansionary fiscal and monetary policies are throttled back before expansion begins to put too much pressure on productive resources. We should be quite conservative for quite a while in judging what levels of unemployment and capacity utilization represent a safe margin.

2. Much closer attention must be paid by government to capacity expansion in basic industries; and there must be readiness to move in with special assistance and encouragement if and when the growth of capacity seems inadequate for the most plausible forecast of long-term growth of demand.

3. We need to enact a long list of structural reforms which will strengthen competition, eliminate the many governmental and private protections which directly raise or sup-

port costs and prices, increase labor mobility, and assist lagging industries to improve their productivity.

4. Finally, we must accept the necessity for a permanent and prominent governmental authority which will actively and continuously monitor important wages and prices, equipped with specific legal powers to permit it to get at the facts and to influence private decisions. It also needs limited power, in special circumstances, to impose temporary mandatory control over any wage or price.

I do not know—nor does anyone else—what the long-term future holds for the health of the American economy any more than for our social institutions, or our political life. But as we approach the 200th year of the Republic we should occasionally remind ourselves that its total output, measured in constant prices, has increased at least a thousandfold; real income per person has increased about nine times, while the variety and richness of its substance has perhaps equally multiplied.

I do not know how many more years our patient can expect. But he must be a pretty healthy old geezer to have achieved so much; and so far as I can tell, he is still going strong!

## RESPONSE

### *HERMAN D. STEIN*

For the past few years we have been having an acute case of nostalgia for previous decades in American life, and there has been a great market for entertainment that brings back the sounds, people, events, and perhaps the illusions of our younger years.

HERMAN D. STEIN is University Professor, Case Western Reserve University. During 1974–75 he was a Fellow at the Center for Advanced Study in the Behavioral Sciences, Stanford, Calif.

For most of us who came of age, or were of age, in the decade of the 1930s, however, it is not nostalgia that suffuses our memories of the state of the nation. It is the great depression, with its bread lines, Hooverville shanty towns, productive workers turned into street-corner apple venders, impoverished farmers migrating from their debt-ridden soil. We recall the depression's desolating impact on families of breadwinners turned into beaten people; many of us were part of the one third of the nation that was ill-fed, ill-clothed, ill-housed, scrounging for work and guarding our pennies. One would not know it from most of television's late show movies of the 1930s, but this was how it was.

Children who hear about the depression from their parents, especially after the twentieth time, finally tune out. It is an era that, in the perspective of the young, becomes telescoped with other times far away and long ago, with the Gold Rush, the Civil War, and Columbus discovering America.

But now that old depression is sneaking back into the news, not as a mirror image of today, of course, but as a point of reference and as a vision of a national nightmare we never want to live through again. A recession is bad enough, and it is not just a bad dream to those who are affected—it is still there when they wake up, and for them it is a depression.

For today, we have over eight million unemployed, 8.9 percent of the labor force. But the unemployed include 14.6 percent of the black labor force, and 40.2 percent are black teen-agers in the labor force, and over 20 percent are teen-agers generally.

Government economists tell us that we will have to live with a 6 percent unemployment rate for the balance of this decade, if we can get that low, to manage inflation. In 1960–61, President Kennedy expressed regret that we would have to live with an interim unemployment rate of 4 percent, and he stressed that it was interim, that 4 percent was too high.

Economists express satisfaction that though the percentage of the labor force without jobs rose last month from 8.7 percent to 8.9 percent, this is a lower rate of increase than before; that although unemployment and prices are still rising, they are doing so at considerably slower rates. If the unemployment rate flattens out and goes down to 8 percent or 7 percent, we are told so frequently that it has become commonplace, "We can live with that."

Who is the "we" who can live with that? Not the hundreds of thousands who have been laid off; not the skilled black workers and those of other minorities who finally made it in industry, at decent union wage levels, and then were dropped on the principle of last hired, first fired, plummeting from a newly gained sense of security and dignity back to poverty; not the women who support themselves and their children, who were dropped from the labor force; not the young people looking for jobs and finding closed doors; not the millions now living at miserable welfare levels, through no choice of their own—the object of chronic, well-publicized scavenger hunts to weed out the handful of ineligibles and bolster political reputations.

They cannot live with that; and we must make sure they are not forced to, that our society does not turn its back on the victims of our own policy failures, but strives to ensure full employment and to abolish poverty and hunger.

We know that there are huge complications in moving to these ends, even with the Hawkins-Humphrey bill. We have nothing against the economists who are trying to caution and measure, and predict, and recommend. Some of my best friends are economists. We feel for them, because their position on the throne of the social sciences has recently become shaky. They seem to be as prone to mistakes and bad judgment as the rest of the human race. We respect their contributions to the development of analytic and predictive models, and we would indeed be at a loss without their knowledge and skill in many fields. But we respectfully call attention to their limitations in guiding national policy. To quote a favorite economist who happens to be a medical economist:

Economics is the science of means, not of ends; it can explain how market prices are determined, but not how basic values are formed; it can tell us the consequences of various alternatives but it cannot make the choice for us. These limitations will be with us always, for economics can never replace morals or ethics.[1]

Social work is not a science. It is a battered, struggling profession, but it does have human and social values at its core. We welcome the clash of views with economists who see things differently from us, but we desperately need those with whom we can share common values. We need the economic and political understanding that can enable us to act rationally and effectively on the basis of these values, knowing that under conditions of economic constraints all choices become harder, and the prices paid dearer. But we in social work can make choices, even if we cannot always make decisions. As between tax privileges for the affluent and the interests of poor people, we choose the poor people. As between high levels of food and energy consumption for the relatively well-to-do, including those social workers who have good jobs, and raising the consumption level of the poor, we choose the interests of the poor. As between keeping taxes down for those of us who have good salaries and meeting the needs of the unemployed for jobs through public employment programs, we choose the needs of the unemployed.

Unemployment and inflation strike hardest at the most vulnerable. They contribute to family breakdown, to loss of pride, to loss of ambition and purpose, to aimlessness and bitterness. These in turn contribute to mental and physical illness and to lawlessness. Social workers in the myriad fields in which we practice represent one front line for helping people to cope, to struggle more successfully for their own survival and well-being and their rights, and social work should stand up with them and for them.

[1] Victor Fuchs, *Who Shall Live?* (New York: Basic Books, 1974), p. 29.

Such practice, directly with people, does not basically change the social, political, or economic conditions of our society that are part of the causative background of the problems of the people we help. However, without this varied field of direct practice we not only would be depriving those who need it most of human support, but we would deprive ourselves of the deepest source of our right to speak on their behalf, to engage responsibly in influencing social policy. I note this because of the recurrent refrain in social work of downgrading the practitioner in contrast to the policy- and planning-oriented social worker. There is no hierarchy of importance in this respect. We all have our work cut out and we need each other—practitioners, teachers, administrators, planners. And we can expect to be under more pressure than ever, economic and otherwise. Public social programs are attacked and cut first when there are budgetary problems. Voluntary agencies do not get their needed support, especially when there are not enough of the workers' wages available to go to the United Funds.

We will need each other's insights and effectiveness and our debates as well, more than ever, and we will need voluntary agencies joining in collaborative efforts with public ones, as far as possible, and social work will continue to require stronger coalitions with other groups based on common purposes. We need these, not to safeguard our own professional interests, but to be a greater source of strength to the most vulnerable in our society, to be a spur to national conscience and policy, and to be skeptical, watchful over the quality of care provided by our national economic doctors.

# The Challenge of Income Maintenance[1]

## W. MICHAEL MAHONEY

IT IS MY BELIEF that the theory of income maintenance has not been significantly advanced in recent years.
This is especially so in the area of income-tested, or welfare,
programs, where there has been a preoccupation with an-
cillary considerations and possible side effects. This preoccupation has caused many of us to lose sight of the real goals
and purposes of welfare and to accept rather uncritically certain assumptions about how welfare programs should be con-
structed. As both cause and effect, there has also been an unfortunate tendency to consider income maintenance as solely
an economic problem.

The purpose of welfare is seldom discussed, but the way in
which existing or proposed new programs are evaluated depends crucially on what that purpose is conceived to be. A
careful consideration of the purpose of welfare is made
timely by a recent report of the United States Congress, the
recommendations of which reflect a subtle and important
shift in philosophy.

In December, 1974, after more than two years of studying
welfare programs, the Subcommittee on Fiscal Policy of the
Joint Economic Committee recommended what for all practical purposes is a negative income tax. With a few exceptions

W. MICHAEL MAHONEY is a Social Science Research Analyst in the Social Security Administration, Department of Health, Education, and Welfare, Washington, D.C.
[1] The views expressed in this paper are those of the author and are not necessarily the views of the Social Security Administration or the Department of Health, Education, and Welfare.

coverage would be comprehensive and noncategorical, eligibility would be almost solely a function of income, and the marginal tax rate or benefit loss formula relatively moderate. But one clear lesson of the experience with the Family Assistance Plan is that it is impossible, without lowering existing assistance standards, to integrate an inexpensive negative income tax into the present welfare system and still achieve the proclaimed goals of improved work incentives and the elimination of categorical distinctions. This is so because many states provide only limited financial incentives for work and limit the coverage of their programs to certain categories of people but do pay more generous benefits than could an inexpensive negative income tax. These states would have to supplement the negative income tax if they wanted to maintain current standards, and it is the need to supplement that poses the dilemma. If the supplemental programs merely followed current practice, the incentive features of the negative income tax would be canceled out and categorical distinctions would remain. If, instead, the supplemental programs were patterned after the negative income tax, the states would incur greatly increased costs and expanded caseloads. Negative income taxes with benefits at or even near the poverty threshold are extremely expensive. This is true regardless of who assumes the financial burden, the federal government alone or the federal government and the states together.

If it is impossible to attain simultaneously moderate marginal tax rates, universal coverage, and adequate benefit levels, one solution is to redefine what adequacy requires. This appears to be what the subcommittee has done. In the past, the adequacy of welfare programs was viewed in terms of what they provided for those who were most reliant on them, namely, those with no other source of income. But the subcommittee measures adequacy in terms of what the program provides to people who have some income but not enough. The subcommittee report describes its recommended program as "fitting the vast majority of cases rather than being stretched to cover the worst possible cases of destitution." [2] The problem, however, is not so much that the subcommittee proposes benefit levels that others might consider inadequate but that it also proposes to require the states to have moderate marginal tax rates. States wishing to supplement would be prohibited from reducing benefits at a rate greater than sixty-seven cents for each dollar of earnings and eighty cents for each dollar of other income. [3] The subcommittee apparently would allow the states to limit supplementation to categories of their choosing and is silent about what should be required of the states with respect to accounting periods, treatment of resources, and other features of negative income taxes that affect program cost and recipients. But just the requirement regarding marginal tax rates would by itself require such an overhaul of general assistance and AFDC that most states would be forced to lower drastically their current benefit levels and quite possibly to forgo supplementing entirely. States wishing to pursue the goal of adequacy as it has been conventionally defined would find it prohibitively expensive to do so. This is the inescapable result of the subcommittee's conviction that providing financial incentives for work through moderate marginal tax rates is the paramount goal or objective.

It is not possible for a welfare system to be all of the things we might reasonably want it to be. This is a commonplace observation with which we are all familiar. But if we must choose among goals we should first consider carefully what these goals require, what assumptions have been made in their formulation, the criteria by which progress toward goals is to be measured, and, most important, to what extent our entire approach is colored by assumptions not made spe-

[2] U.S. Congress, Fiscal Subcommittee of the Joint Economic Committee, "Income Security for Americans: Recommendations of the Public Welfare Study," a report of the Fiscal Subcommittee, December, 1974, p. 13. On p. 181 the report cites Census Bureau evidence that only 17 percent of poor families have zero nonwelfare income. But this is a reference to an entire year. At any point in time, and over the course of a year, the number of families without income other than welfare will be much greater.

[3] U.S. Congress, Fiscal Subcommittee of the Joint Economic Committee, *op. cit,* p. 218.

cific. This is a process which I do not believe has been undertaken for a long time.

## THE GOALS OF WELFARE

That a just society should provide for all its members a meaningful opportunity to have an adequate income is probably the only proposition about income security that could command nearly universal agreement. Anybody who has a passing knowledge of welfare issues realizes that there are widely different conceptions of the purposes which welfare is meant to serve. Despite this, recent literature on the subject of welfare is typically devoid of substantive discussion of its purpose. It is true that goals are commonly listed, and there is widespread agreement that equity, adequacy, favorable incentives, least program cost, and least administrative cost should be on any list.[4] But these are goals common to all government programs and tell us nothing about welfare as such. They are evaluation criteria which can only be usefully applied if there is a full understanding of what the objectives of welfare are.

Nothing is more crucial to a rational discussion of welfare issues than an understanding of objectives. This is especially so when equity and adequacy are discussed because many arguments about what equity requires or about the adequacy of programs are basically arguments over program purpose. It may seem that the problem is simple and that I belabor it too much: the purpose of welfare is to alleviate poverty, to meet need. But this is too simple. If the purpose of welfare is to help the needy, then equity requires that welfare programs provide equal help to the equally needy. We need then only assume that persons with equal incomes are equally needy and the discussion is almost over. There should be a

[4] For example, see: U.S. Congress, Fiscal Subcommittee of the Joint Economic Committee, *op cit*, p. 29; the President's Commission on Income Maintenance Programs, *Poverty Amid Plenty: the American Paradox* (Washington, D.C.: U.S. Government Printing Office, 1969) p. 90; Michael C. Barth, G. Carcagno, and J. Palmer, *Towards an Effective Income Support Program: Problems, Prospects and Choices* (Madison, Wis.: Institute for Research on Poverty, 1974), p. 40.

single program treating all people alike except according to their income.

I advance a proposition that will make many people uncomfortable: the purpose of welfare is to provide to needy people the extent and nature of the help they deserve. We do not individually believe that our family members, friends, neighbors, fellow citizens, and fellow human beings each have equal claim to our concern for their welfare. Nor do we think that our concern should be manifested in the same way. Why should we as a society? Some will say that it is wrong to think that some are deserving and others not, that equity itself requires otherwise. But this is not self-evident. Unless it can be shown that equally needy people are equally deserving of assistance, the principle of equity that requires that people in similar circumstances be treated similarly does not itself require equal treatment of the equally needy. The premise that similar circumstances require similar treatment is axiomatic to most of us. The premise that people in equal need are necessarily in equal circumstances is not. This is so because when it comes to welfare most of us believe that among the relevant circumstances to be considered is whether and to what extent a needy person has a just claim on us.

What will bother some people about my proposition is that at this level of abstraction it means it could be fully appropriate to help some needy persons but not others. The logic is correct; whether the concern is well-founded is another matter. In any event, my proposition would also allow the possibility of different welfare programs for different purposes and for different people, which is its most important derivative.

A number of assumptions have affected thinking about welfare. Perhaps the most profound influence has been the tendency to assume that, for practical purposes if not fundamental principles, the purpose of welfare is simply to meet need, to help the needy. Often this is a useful and even a necessary simplification; but not when it comes to discussions of equity and adequacy or over-all program design. For example, reference is often made to the poverty thresholds to get a sense of how adequate programs are. But if the real purpose of a given program is to provide to some class of persons the kind of help they deserve, the real test of adequacy would be the extent to which they were getting that help. Thus, unless one assumes that the purposes of two different programs are nearly identical, one cannot assess one as more adequate than the other by a simple reference to the thresholds. Nor can one argue that it is unfair for one program to provide more generous benefits than another.

When someone says that his welfare proposal is fairer, more effective than some other proposal, he should be required to set forth what he takes the purpose of welfare to be.

ASSUMPTIONS UNDERLYING CURRENT WELFARE THEORY

Probably no assertion about welfare programs in recent years has been more common than that the goals of welfare pose certain irreconcilable dilemmas. But the dilemmas, as realistic as they can be made to appear, are not inherent in the real goals of welfare. Nor are they inherent in the criteria by which welfare programs should be evaluated. The only real dilemma is between welfare and the market place, a point elaborated more fully below. The apparent dilemmas are the result of assumptions about the purpose of welfare and also of assumptions about the requirements that welfare programs ought to meet. These assumptions lie, like girders, underneath much of current thinking about welfare programs and are mutually reinforcing.

Most of the assumptions discussed here serve to enhance the apparent superiority of the negative income tax. Some have been made explicit by one or more writers; others are more impoicit and affect the way a problem is presented or the way solutions to a problem are ranked. If these assumptions are of doubtful validity or relevance, then a negative income tax, or what are usually taken as the critical features of a negative income tax, will appear to be less desirable or necessary.

If any one assumption is at the heart of the problem, it is the assumption that income is the measure of need. No practical program of broad scope could operate under any other assumption. But when the over-all problem is initially viewed as income rather than need, the solution is already too constrained. Possible solutions are even more limited if it is also assumed that it is wrong to distinguish among people according to the reason for their need. But this perspective is not uncommon. One justification for it is the difficulty of explaining why an unemployed sixty-five-year-old should be eligible for assistance but an unemployed sixty-four-year-old should not. This is an argument with powerful logical and even more powerful emotional appeal. But it can be and often is extended year by year so that it becomes wrong to distinguish between the sixty-four-year-old and a twenty-one-year-old. And by this same logic, because in the spectrum of colors it is difficult to distingusih where orange becomes yellow, it is equally difficult to distinguish orange from blue!

Another justification is that categorization of people will create inequities by differentiating among people who are really in similar circumstances. But the converse is that people in dissimilar circumstances would be treated similarly. Those who favor less categorization rather than more must implicitly assume that the inequities thereby created are somehow less severe than they would be in the alternative.

One important result of these assumptions is that welfare funds cannot be allocated to one group of poor persons and not others nor can different programs be designed for them. In the abstract, a negative income tax proponent would likely consider a seventy-five-year-old and a twenty-five-year-old of equal incomes equally needy and divide available funds equally among them. But others may well choose to believe that the seventy-five-year-old is less able to fend for himself, more likely to have special problems, and having lived long and probably suffered much is entitled to comfort in his old age. Similarly, they may believe that the twenty-five-year-old is more capable of finding alternate sources of income, that he is able to endure more, and that he has established less claim for public support. Moreover, they are likely to believe that what the twenty-five-year-old really needs, and quite probably wants, is a job.

One possible explanation for the belief that both should be treated similarly is the tendency to assume that equality of treatment requires identical treatment. However, as one philosopher put it: "But suppose that society is allocating musical instruments to C and D, and that C prefers a banjo and D a guitar. If society gives C a banjo and D a guitar it is treating them *differently*, yet *equally*." [5] An example from medicine may have more practical relevance. Suppose that two individuals are equally ill in the sense that if treatment is withheld they are equally likely to succumb to their illness. If one required only an inexpensive injection and the other lengthy hospitalization, they could be provided equal but different treatment. Thus, it is not necessary to argue that the twenty-five-year-old is less needy in order to argue that he should be treated differently.

There is a more profound and, to some, more upsetting reason for distinguishing between people in different groups. The need for goods and services essential to basic subsistence is not the same as the need to obtain from the public treasury the wherewithal for obtaining those goods and services. In the absence of evidence to the contrary, it seems safe to assume that young persons are more capable than old in terms of meeting their own income needs, not simply by working but also by recourse to friends and parents. The concept of dependence is different from the concept of deserving. Thus, if it is contended that in a single class of persons where income will be the sole test of need should be included the young and the old, employables and unemployables, one- and two-parent families, mothers with

[5] William K. Frankena, "The Concept of Social Justice," in Richard Brand, ed., *Social Justice* (Englewood, N.J.: Prentice Hall, Inc., 1962), p. 11.

young children, and so on, it should be shown not only that each have equal original claims for public support but also that they are equally reliant on it. This is a view which, if nothing else, is difficult to persuade a skeptical general public is correct.

Another problem with the assumption that income is the measure of need is that its corollary is that providing equal benefits to persons of equal incomes equally meets their needs. But persons with equal incomes can have quite different needs when such things as health, disabilities, and availabilities of services are considered. This is an important issue for persons living at a subsistence level which is probably too little appreciated by persons of higher income. If income benefits are just barely adequate for normal basic expenses, some recipients will still face situations requiring them to forgo satisfying some basic need.

One problem with assuming that income is the measure of need is that it becomes easy to think that the purpose of an income-transfer program is simply that—to transfer income. This is one possible explanation of another important assumption, namely, the principles applicable to the positive tax system apply as well to welfare programs. One example of attempts to carry over features of the positive tax system is the accounting period.

The present welfare practice is usually to assess a family's income and requirements prospectively; that is, the question asked is whether the family will have sufficient funds for the next month. In contrast, most negative income tax plans call for a retrospective accounting period in which a family's benefit depends on its income in some previous period. Income received as much as a year earlier might reduce the family's current benefit. There are several good arguments for retrospective and long accounting periods. One is that they are less expensive and concentrate payments on families with chronically low incomes. Another is that they reduce the possibility of under- and overpayments. The argument most often advanced, however, is that the principles of equity require them.

The annual accounting period in the positive tax is often cited in support of the proposition that a twelve-month accounting period achieves equity among people with equal incomes but different income flows. Technically, this argument is flawed since the positive tax provides that income may be averaged over periods as long as five years. The positive tax system itself does not provide evidence on whether any given period is a better test of equity than any other period.

It seems obvious that a person who is regularly employed in a seasonal occupation should not receive more annual welfare benefits than someone who has identical annual earnings but works all year. But it is not so obvious that someone whose regular income stream is interrupted is required by considerations of equity to wait several months before receiving assistance. To whom is it unfair if assistance is provided when it is needed?

The issue of what accounting period is more equitable than another arises only because of the assumption that income is the measure of need. But income is a flow while need is a condition at a point in time. Income is only a proxy measure of need. This takes us back to the necessity of defining program purposes. If the program were supposed to serve two equally basic purposes, one of which was assisting needy persons and the other was assuring them a more equal share of total income, then there would be the problem which some have expressed as finding the balance between being responsive to need and treating people with equal incomes equally. But only by reference to the reason for assuring more equal income could we determine whether a month, year, or lifetime was the appropriate period for measuring income and equality. In contrast, assume that the sole purpose of the program is to meet needs, but for practical and administrative purposes income must be used as the measure of need. Then the requirement of equity is that equally needy persons be provided equal assistance, and the issue is whether differing periods of time are equally good proxies for need or what period is the best. There would be no inherent dilemma between equity and need, as commonly supposed.

Another example of assuming that positive tax principles are applicable is the belief that welfare programs must meet the test of vertical equity. There are several problems with this. The first is that just about the only widely accepted requirement of vertical equity is that government programs not capriciously alter relative positions on the income distribution. The word "capricious" is important here because government programs, including the positive tax system itself, do reverse income positions in ways that need not be considered inequitable. Social Security is one example; extra personal exemptions for the aged and blind is another. Thus, even if it were to be stipulated that the requirements of vertical equity do apply, the problem of deciding what is capricious and what is not remains.

Another problem is that things do not work quite the same way in welfare programs as they do in tax programs. There is a respectably large body of opinion that a further requirement of vertical equity is that higher income people should face higher tax rates than low-income people. This is a concept likely to be well-accepted by low-income people. Obviously, lower tax rates mean higher net income. Some people believe that the principles of vertical equity require also that welfare recipients face low tax rates or benefit loss formulas. Elsewhere it has been pointed out that this argument typically confuses average with marginal tax rates.[6] But a notion that vertical equity also requires that persons with higher relative incomes should continue to have higher relative incomes after the transfer (or tax) has clouded this point. Be-

[6] Bette S. Mahoney and W. Michael Mahoney, "The Policy Implications, a Skeptical View," in Joseph Pechman and Michael Timpane, eds., *Work Incentives and Income Guarantee: the New Jersey Negative Income Tax Experiment* (Washington, D.C.: Brookings Institution; 1975).

cause our thinking has been conditioned to do so, it is easy to think that a recipient with earnings or Social Security benefits will end up with higher income if he faces a lower tax rate or a moderate benefit loss formula. But from the viewpoint of any one recipient it would always pay if the welfare benefits going to persons with higher incomes were reallocated to him and persons of lower income. This would raise his benefits *and* his tax rate. For the recipient, the reward of a lower tax rate, the benefit of having more net income than someone with less nonwelfare income, is to receive less welfare.[7]

It is probably true that recipients of welfare feel that it is unfair for their benefits to be drastically reduced when their earnings increase. And it is probably true that people with small incomes that barely exceed welfare eligibility criteria may feel that it is unfair that their earnings or savings should be so poorly rewarded. The choice is cruel but necessary. For the recipient it is between greater benefits in the present and reduced benefits in the future should his income increase. For the nonrecipient, it is between greater net reward for his work or savings in the present and less adequate welfare should he suffer income loss in the future. Regardless of how generously welfare programs are funded this cruel choice will still exist.

Some proponents of negative income taxes believe not simply that the principles of the positive tax apply to welfare programs but that they *require* a negative income tax. This, however, is a confusion of the aesthetic appeal of pure symmetry with the requirements of pure logic. Worse, no proposed negative income tax has shared with the positive tax uniform definitions of income, accounting periods, filing units, and so forth. Thus, whatever symmetry there could be, would only be at the most abstract of levels. Moreover, there is no logical requirement that a program the purpose of

---

[7] If for some reason there were a requirement that marginal tax rates must be constant over the entire range of income eligibility, this kind of reallocation would not always be possible for *all* recipients.

which is raising revenue for the purchase of public goods and services should transfer funds to people too poor to pay taxes. There is logic in the proposition that persons too poor to pay taxes might very well deserve welfare, but that is a different matter entirely.

Some exception to this argument could be taken by asserting that the purpose of the tax, positive and negative taken together, is to alter the income distribution. In this view, money is taken from some and given to others not because they would otherwise have too much or too little in an absolute sense but because otherwise their share of the total would be too large or too small. People would pay taxes not just to support the public fisc but because their income was too large relative to someone else's. People would receive transfers not just because they were deserving but because their income was too small *relative to someone else's*. This, however, takes the discussion out of the limited field of income maintenance and into the larger field of income distribution. Obviously, cash transfers change the shape of the income distribution, but the change is the necessary correlate of achieving the end and not the end itself. Whatever the goals of income redistribution may be, I suspect that they are lower in priority than the goals of welfare and that they command far less public support. What this means is that, until we have better welfare programs, income redistribution as a goal in and of itself is only of theoretical interest.

Another assumption, like the one about the relevance of the positive tax system, affects much thinking about welfare programs: welfare programs should somehow preserve within them the features of the market place. This, however, is impossible. Welfare is the antithesis of the market place. The market place presumably rewards enterprise, industry and thrift and imposes sanctions on profligacy and sloth. Welfare only exists because the rewards of the market place are sometimes insufficient or not forthcoming, and its sanctions are thought to be too severe or inappropriate. The more like the market place a welfare program is required to be, the less like welfare will it be.

Once again it is necessary to ask what the purpose of the program is. It cannot be the purpose of welfare both to meet needs and to preserve the features of the market place. This is simply wanting it to be "both ways." If, however, the purpose of the program is to be a mix, then the obvious question is why the market place should be in the mix, presuming, of course, that we already know what the purpose of welfare is. If the answer is to meet some vague principle of fairness, then there is no way of knowing what the correct mix is, and we are left with the irony that fairness for the welfare recipient means that he receives less welfare. If, however, the purpose of the mix is to avoid providing incentives for undesirable behavior, there is a way of determining the right mix.

There has been very little discussion of how to determine the appropriate mix of welfare and market place.[8] This is partly because of two assumptions which taken together come close to being the binding force of negative income tax theory. That economists have been among their principal proponents is doubly ironic both because they are assumptions about magnitude and most economists will readily admit that economic theory predicts direction and not magnitude, and because on the basis of these two assumptions economists have proposed policies without regard to their costs and benefits.

The first assumption is: the incentive features of income-maintenance programs have a significant effect on the behavior of program participants. The second is: the preferred way of minimizing undesirable behavior is through positive incentives rather than negative sanctions.

Work incentives are perhaps the best example of these two assumptions at work. Economic theory predicts, as does common sense, that welfare programs reduce financial incentives

[8] But see Mahoney and Mahoney, *op cit.*

for work. But neither economic theory nor common sense can by itself predict how much impact the work disincentive will actually have, since there are reasons for working other than immediate financial gain, including a desire for independence, peer group pressures, and long-run career plans. It is true that considerable research into the labor supply effects of welfare was undertaken in the mid-1960s. But long before useful research results were made available, programs were being proposed based on the assumption that 100 percent marginal tax rates had unacceptable labor supply effects but 50 percent rates did not. Moreover, it was assumed on the basis of no data and without reference to cost that it was better to mitigate unfavorable labor supply effects by having low tax rates than by the use of bureaucratically administered work requirements.

Part of the reluctance to endorse the negative sanctions of work requirements is based on the belief that it is undesirable to invest the required discretionary authority in what would necessarily be low-level bureaucrats. In the absence of other considerations it would indeed seem preferable to limit severely the power of government workers over the lives of the people they serve. But what if the alternative is so expensive that at best, the program can be only minimally adequate, and at worst, would be unacceptable to the President or the Congress?

Incentives to marry, to dissolve marriages, to have children, to save, to migrate, and to cheat are all affected by the presence of income-maintenance programs. And, just as with work incentives, there has been a plethora of assumptions about the extent to which they affect behavior and a plethora of proposals that programs be designed accordingly. But there has been little attention to the amount of behavior effects the proposed incentive features would produce. If the purpose of preserving some features of the market place in a welfare program is to preserve incentives for work or saving; or, if the purpose of providing single-parent families less welfare than two-parent families is to preserve incentives for family stability, then these features should be incorporated into welfare programs in the amounts necessary to produce the desired results. Building expensive new transportation systems as an incentive for people to use automobiles less may be laudable. But building them, if people would nonetheless continue to drive, would be foolish. Providing incentives for desirable forms of behavior is expensive either in absolute dollars or in reductions of program effectiveness. Given that incentives entail costs, they should not be incorporated into programs simply because they are "nice."

At the end of our list is an assumption which may well explain why some of the others have been so uncritically accepted: simple programs are preferable to complex ones. Put thusly, it is more an appeal to one's aesthetic inclinations than a logical proposition. I doubt that many would argue that program effectiveness should yield to program simplicity. I know of none who would argue that programs should be needlessly complex. But the simplicity of programs like the negative income tax gives them a powerful appeal completely unrelated to their effectiveness. When dealing with substance proves difficult, it is all too easy to deal with form.

Perhaps assumption is not quite the right word for what in some cases may simply be operating principles or guidelines. Nonetheless, these are some of the assumptions that seem to this writer to underlie much of current thinking about welfare. If they are relaxed or rejected as invalid, then there is a possibility that a system of programs providing different types and amounts of assistance to different types of people would appear more equitable and effective than a single, national program.

The war on poverty of the 1960s caused a surge of interest in income maintenance which peaked with President Nixon's Family Assistance Plan but continues on a somewhat diminished basis to this day. With the wisdom of hindsight, it can now be seen that some of the earlier popular theorizing was far too simplistic. But if the economists who pretty much dominated the field are to be faulted for being both naïve and presumptuous as well as simplistic, the social work profession is equally to be faulted for letting them get away with it. The economists acted as though thinking about income maintenance had stopped with the Social Security Act of 1935; social workers have reason to know otherwise. The economists thought it a new realization that social insurance and the economy would not alleviate poverty; the social workers had been living with that fact for years.[9] The economists thought that complex econometric models and expensive experimentation were the only source of information about the effects of extending welfare to employed, male heads of families; the social workers were administering programs which already included this category and knew what the effects were. And so on.

A while back, I asked Mitchell Ginsberg why the social work profession had apparently abandoned the field of income maintenance to the economists. He replied that it was the economists' complex models and their seemingly precise equations with which the social work profession felt itself poorly equipped to deal. Mr. Ginsberg may be right but, if so, the social workers were wrong in their fears. Models and equations cannot by themselves meet the challenge of income maintenance. Moreover, assumptions about welfare, its purpose and effects are perfectly amenable to analysis by the social work profession.

The United States will never have a comprehensive federal income maintenance program with benefit levels high enough to justify saying that the purpose of welfare is achieved. This is true far more for programmatic reasons than political. That the cost of being as generous to all as we might like to be toward the most deserving is one reason. That administrative considerations may require using past

---

[9] Anyone who believes that it was not until the 1960s that it became apparent that social insurance and the economy would never provide adequate incomes for all is urged to read *Security, Work and Relief Policies,* report of the Committee on Long-Range Work and Relief Policies to the National Resources Planning Board (Washington, D.C.: U.S. Government Printing Office, 1942). I am grateful to my colleague James Callison for bringing this excellent study to my attention.

income as a proxy measure of need is another. And that at no feasible level of cash assistance would all recipients have sufficient funds to handle every special need and emergency is still a third. Thus, whether a comprehensive program like the negative tax is ever widely held to be desirable or not, there will still be a challenge in income maintenance. Some groups of people will deserve and need more assistance, and a basis for deciding who should be in the group and who should not will be required. Exceptions to the results of categorization will be inevitable, and procedures will be necessary for dealing with them. People will still have problems and emergencies that it would be unjust to ignore. The challenge to the social work profession is to help define the groups, to help devise the programs that will serve them, and to provide the skills for operating programs which by their nature cannot be simple cash-transfer programs, impersonally administered by a remote bureaucracy, but must respond to individual and widely varying human needs.

# Demogrants and Health Insurance: What We Can Afford, What We Value

## IRWIN GARFINKEL

I WILL ARGUE that we have the economic means to meet many constructive demands. I will readily concede that we do not have sufficient resources to do everything that we would like to do. But that concession does not imply that we cannot afford to do any one thing and, in fact, many things that we would like to do. In particular, we can certainly afford to enact a generous, universal, income-transfer system and a comprehensive national health insurance system. In my judgment, these are the two most important proposals on our social welfare agenda. The real question is not can we afford these programs, but rather do we want them? Our ability to afford them is beyond doubt. Whether we want them depends upon what we value, upon what kind of a people we are.

There are some desirable things that we simply cannot afford to do. We cannot, for example, eliminate poverty, as officially defined in the United States, in the rest of the world. We are not wealthy enough. We are not even wealthy enough to eliminate poverty in China and India alone. Even if we shared our wealth equally with these two countries, per capita income would only be equal to about $800.[1] It would

IRWIN GARFINKEL is Professor, School of Social Work, and Director, Institute for Research on Poverty, University of Wisconsin, Madison.
[1] Data on China and India were derived from *Asian 1975 Yearbook* and are for 1973. Data on the United States were derived from the 1975 Economic Report of the President.

be nice to be able to raise per capita income in China and India to at least $1,000. After all, our per capita income as of the beginning of 1975 was equal to about $5,600. But we cannot do it. Our wants do indeed exceed our resources.

A GENEROUS, UNIVERSAL, INCOME-TRANSFER PROGRAM

While we are not sufficiently wealthy to eliminate poverty in the rest of the world, we are wealthy enough to afford a generous income-transfer program that would reduce inequality and eliminate poverty in the United States. A demogrant or tax credit program like the one I describe here is clearly within our means and would do the job.

This particular program should be viewed as illustrative. My purpose is not to discuss the benefits and costs of alternative proposals designed to achieve the same end [2] but to focus on our ability to afford these kinds of programs and on the value judgments that determine our appraisal of their desirability. I chose this particular program to discuss because it is a good one for which estimates of costs and benefits are available. In order to obtain such estimates, detailed data on household income and composition must be combined with data on income tax returns. Such data is now available only for 1970. Thus, although the numbers reported here refer to 1975, they are derived from projections of estimates for 1970.[3] While small misestimates are inevitable, the projections do give reliable orders of magnitude.

Every adult in the United States, rich and poor alike, would be entitled to an annual demogrant of $2,000, and every person under age eighteen would be entitled to $400.

---

[2] For such a discussion see *Toward an Effective Income Support System* by Michael Barth, George I. Carcagno, and John L. Palmer, with an overview paper by Irwin Garfinkel (Madison, Wis.: Institute for Research on Poverty, University of Wisconsin, 1974).

[3] All estimates reported here on the effects of the demogrant program are derived from Benjamin A. Okner, "The Role of Demogrants as an Income Maintenance," in *Studies in Public Welfare,* Paper No. 9 (Part 1), Concepts in Welfare Program Design Subcommittee on Fiscal Policy of the Joint Economic Committee Congress of the United States (Washington, D.C.: U.S. Government Printing Office, 1973).

For a family of four that would amount to $4,800 annually or, as of the beginning of 1975, about 90 percent of the poverty level. Checks could be mailed to everyone on a monthly or biweekly basis. The personal exemptions and deductions in the personal income tax would be eliminated. Tax loopholes like the exemption of income from state and local bonds, deductions for homeowners' mortgage interest and real estate taxes, and reduced rates on capital gains would be eliminated. Federal contributions to the Aid to Families with Dependent Children program, the Supplementary Security Income program, the Food Stamps, program and housing assistance programs would be eliminated. Social Security beneficiaries would be given the choice of paying taxes on their Social Security benefits and receiving the demogrant or neither paying taxes nor receiving benefits. All income aside from the demogrant itself (and in some cases Social Security income) would be taxed at a rate of 42.3 percent.

Forty-two and three-tenths percent is the average tax rate that would be required to finance the demogrant and all other federal government expenditures currently paid for out of the federal income tax, if all tax loopholes were eliminated.[4] There is, of course, no necessary reason to tax all income at the same rate. A progressive rather than a proportional tax rate structure is possible. That is, higher incomes could be taxed at higher rates than lower incomes.

The progressivity in a demogrant-tax credit system with a proportional tax rate comes from the demogrants or tax credits rather than from higher tax rates on higher-income people. As I will show, the demogrant system proposed here is much more progressive than our current income tax transfer system. But I would still prefer a demogrant system with a tax rate somewhat lower than 42.3 percent for the poorest 75 percent of the population and higher than 42.3 percent for the richest 25 percent of the population. Unfor-

[4] Okner's estimates for the tax base, other federal expenditures, and population in 1975 were used to derive the estimate of the tax rate.

tunately, I do not have estimates of costs and benefits to losers and gainers for such a system. So, I will discuss a program for which we do have such estimates.

In order to know whether we can afford a program, we must know how much it costs. But there is a great deal of confusion about how the costs of such a program are measured. Thus, before considering the appropriate way to measure the costs of the program, it would be useful to dispose of a common, but very inappropriate, way of measuring costs. When Senator George McGovern proposed a demogrant of $1,000 per person in the 1968 Presidential primary campaign, Senator Hubert Humphrey asked him if it was not true that the program would cost $200 billion. McGovern answered that he was not sure what the program would cost.

Would such a program cost $200 billion? There are 200 million Americans. If you give each of them$1,000, that adds up to $200 billion. So is it not true that such a program would cost $200 billion? The answer is no.

Suppose that instead of 200 million Americans, there were only two Americans, one rich and one poor. Suppose that the government gave each of them $1,000 and taxed the rich man $2,000 in order to pay for the program. Would the cost of the program be $2,000? No. There is no cost to the poor man. He actually gains $1,000. The net cost to the rich man is $1,000, not $2,000 because, while he pays $2,000 in taxes, he gets back $1,000 in benefits. What about the cost to society (both men considered together)? The cost to society is zero, since the $1,000 loss to the rich man is canceled by the $1,000 gain by the poor man.

The confusion arises because of the tendency to ask what is the cost to the government rather than what is the cost to all the people or to particular groups of people. Governments never ultimately pay for anything. People do. Thus, neither the McGovern demogrant proposal nor the one presented here will cost anyone anywhere near $200 billion. What, then, are the real costs?

There are three important kinds of costs to any income-transfer program. First, there is the monetary cost to individuals and families who pay more in added taxes than they receive in new benefits. Second, there are costs that result from reductions in work effort induced by income-transfer programs. Finally, there are the administrative costs.

The administrative costs of the kind of program proposed here would be small—on the order of magnitude of the current income tax system; in fact, if adopted, the program would reduce some of the administrative costs of the personal income tax by eliminating most of the features of the tax that complicate filing and processing of returns. It is worth noting that simplification of the income tax system was one of the features of the tax credit approach that led the British Conservative Government to issue a Green Paper [5] in 1972 advocating the adoption of such a program just as Senator McGovern was being forced to withdraw his support from this so-called "radical and unworkable idea."

The net cost to losers from the program would be about $58 billion.[6] On average, each millionaire (in a four-person family) would pay about $176,000 more in taxes than he would receive in benefits. Those making between $50,000 and $100,000 would pay about $5,000 more in taxes; those making between $25,000 and $50,000 would pay about $2,500 more in taxes; those making between $20,000 and $25,000 would pay about $800 more in taxes.[7] The average family of four with an income below $18,000 would receive more in benefits than it would pay in additional taxes.

[5] See "Proposals for a Tax Credit System," Cmnd, 5116, London HMSO, 1972; Howard Glennister, "A Tax Credit Scheme for Britain—a Review of the British Government's Green Paper," *Journal of Human Resources,* VIII (1973), 422–35. The program differs from a straightforward demogrant in that those with zero income are ineligible for aid unless they are eligible for benefits from one of the social insurance programs.

[6] This figure is equal to 1.337 times Okner's estimate for a demogrant of $1,500 per adult and $300 per child in 1970. It should be very close to the appropriate figure for the 1975 demogrant of $2,000 per adult and $400 per child because the 1975 demogrant is approximately equal to the 1970 demogrant times 1.337, the rate of inflation from 1970 to December, 1974.

[7] These estimates were derived from Table 7 in Okner, *op. cit.,* with adjustments to update them to 1975.

Can those who would lose from this program afford it? Or, more accurately, since many if not most of us would, on balance, have to pay more in new taxes than we would receive in benefits, can we afford it? Of course *we* can. This is not a cavalier or flippant statement. Nor do I mean to imply that to people earning between, say, $20,000 and $25,000 that $800 is an insignificant amount. I do not believe that I spend money frivolously. Moreoever, I am sure that hardly anyone believes that he or she spends money frivolously. Before we buy something most of us think: Can I afford it? Do I really need it now? And yet, we are quite wealthy. Most of us have many more things and do many more things than our parents did when they were our age. Although they could not afford as many things as we can now, they managed. Thus, it is impossible to avoid concluding that while it would hardly be painless, we and others who will lose from this program can afford it. Some of us may prefer to spend the money on ourselves rather than increasing the incomes of people poorer than ourselves. Not wanting to spend money on something, however, is very different from not being able to afford it.

There is another way of viewing the cost. The cost to the richest one percent of the population would be that, after tax, their share of total income in the country would drop from 7.25 percent to 6.5 percent.[8] The share of total income going to the richest 5 percent of the population would fall from 19 percent to 17 percent; the share of the richest 20 percent would fall from 47 percent to 43 percent. Can they or we afford it? Once more, the answer is yes. Even if such a program were enacted, the share of total income accruing to those at the top would remain disproportionately large.

Finally, what about the costs that result from reductions in

[8] The estimate of the redistributional effect of the program is taken directly from Okner's estimate for a demogrant of $1,500 per adult and $300 per child in 1970. It is somewhat too high because incomes increased between 1970 and 1975 by a higher rate than the percentage increase in the 1975 demogrant vis-à-vis the 1970 demogrant.

labor supply induced by the program? This is an important question. Economic theory predicts that those who gain from the program are likely to work less both because their incomes have been increased and because the relatively high tax rate required to finance the program will reduce the reward to them of working. Similarly, theory predicts that those who lose from the program are likely to work less because the high tax rate will also reduce the reward to them of working. On the other hand, economic theory also predicts that those who lose from the program are likely to work more *because* their incomes are reduced. In the previous decade we have spent millions of dollars on experimental and nonexperimental research in an attempt to obtain empirical estimates of the effects of income and tax rates on labor supply.

Although our ability to predict with a high degree of precision and certainty is still limited, in these last ten years we have learned a great deal. We have learned that while prime-age males would reduce their work effort very little in response to an income-transfer program, married women, female heads of households, and retirement- and school-age men and women would, or in fact now do, reduce their work effort by more substantial amounts in response to income-transfer programs. Thus, for example, married males in the New Jersey income maintenance experiment worked only 6 percent less than the control group, while married women in the experimental group worked about 20 percent less than the control group. Note, however, that the groups of people who would have the largest percentage reductions in work effort contribute much less to the total output of goods and services than do prime-age males.[9]

More important, from these labor supply studies we have learned that the demogrant program proposed here would not lead to a disastrous reduction in the output of goods and

[9] For a summary and critical review of the literature see Irwin Garfinkel, "Income Transfer Programs and Work Effort: a Review," in *Studies in Public Welfare*, Paper No. 13 (Washington, D.C.: U.S. Government Printing Office, 1974), pp. 1–32.

services. Quite the contrary, a crude calculation indicates that reductions in labor supply on the part of both those who would gain and those who would lose from the program would result in about a 2.5 percent reduction in our gross national product (GNP).[10] Of course this reduction would be offset, at least in part, by increases in nonmonetary activities. Even so, this is by no means a trivial amount. But good things are rarely free.

In addition to the economic costs which arise out of the labor supply effects of a transfer program, there are potential noneconomic costs as well. If an income-transfer program does not have a work test for people who are expected by society to work, then these people will be able to live off the transfer payment alone. This would constitute a flagrant violation of the Puritan work ethic. I believe that this moral cost is at least as important as the economic cost to many if not to most Americans. While work tests are not likely to reduce the economic costs of a transfer program, they would substantially reduce the noneconomic costs. Work tests are unlikely to reduce the economic costs by much because most reductions in labor supply on the part of prime-age male heads of families that would result from an income-transfer program would take the form of reduced hours of work per year rather than complete withdrawal from the labor force. While married women and retirement-age workers are more likely to withdraw from the labor force, it is doubtful that a work test would be applied to them. Female heads of families are also much more likely to withdraw from the labor force, and a work test might be applied to them. But they constitute a very small proportion of the total labor supply, and their earnings represent an even smaller proportion of total earnings in the country. But work tests can prevent people from

[10] The estimate is based upon the income and substitution elasticities reported in Irwin Garfinkel and Stanley Masters, "The Effect of Income and Wage Rates on the Labor Supply: of Older Men and Women; of Young Men and Women; of Prime Age and Older Males; of Prime Age Women," Institute for Research on Poverty Discussion Papers Nos. 227–74; 226–74; 193–74; and 203–74, respectively (Madison, Wis.: University of Wisconsin, 1974).

quitting work entirely and simply living off the demogrant. As such, they prevent a flagrant violation of the Puritan work ethic. The work test is a symbolic reaffirmation of this widely held value. In my judgment, this value is so widespread in our society that we will never get a demogrant program without a work test. And only perverse logic can lead to the conclusion that not having a demogrant program is better than having a demogrant program with a work test. Consequently, despite the fact that the economic benefits of having a work test are small, to me a work test is acceptable.

If we want to make sure that certain people cannot quit work to live on demogrants, we can administer them in such a way as to preclude that. We could pay out demogrants directly only to certain groups, like the aged and disabled, and perhaps to female heads of families whom we did not expect to work. Other groups would normally receive their demogrants through the income tax withholding system. If their weekly, biweekly, or monthly tax liability exceeded their tax credit, they would have a portion of their earnings withheld. If their tax credit exceeded their tax liability, their pay check would include a government payment as well as their earnings. The government would reimburse the employer instead of collecting the withheld tax from him. People who were expected to work, but for one reason or another did not have a job, would receive their demogrants from the Unemployment Insurance Service so long as they were willing and able to work at suitable employment.[11] Thus, a work test could readily be built into a demogrant-tax credit system.

Work tests or no, we can afford a generous demogrant program. There are, of course, costs. The program would reduce the incomes of upper-income people by about $58 billion. Total output of goods and services would probably fall by about 2.5 percent. In addition, there would be some administrative costs. But everything good has costs. And we have the ability to pay for these costs. Whether we should

[11] This is very close to the system of administration proposed in the British Green Paper.

adopt a generous demogrant program, therefore, depends upon whether the benefits exceed the costs.

What are the benefits? Well, to begin with, the incomes of lower-income people would increase by $58 billion. The share of total income going to the poorest fifth of the population would increase by 33 percent, from 5.3 percent to 7 percent. The shares of the second poorest fifth and the middle fifth of the population would also increase by 22 percent and 10 percent. Poverty as officially defined would be virtually eliminated. About 80 percent of poor families would have their incomes lifted above the poverty line. The remaining 20 percent would have their incomes raised to nearly the poverty level.

We can afford a generous demogrant program. But should we adopt such a program? Do the benefits exceed the costs? How does one weigh the benefit of an increase of $58 billion in the incomes of lower income people against a decrease of $58 billion in the incomes of higher income people? Technicians cannot provide the answer. Nor can economists. The answer involves the most basic human values and emotions.

There is an old debate in philosophy and economics as to whether society is best off when all people are equally well off. The debate has been cast in terms of whether or not it was possible to prove that society is best off with perfect equality. At times the debate became quite technical, so technical that analytical geometry, algebra, and calculus were employed in the debate. Of course, the debate has been resolved in favor of the position that one *cannot prove* that society is best off when all people are equally well off. The issue depends upon value judgments. But the resolution of the debate and, in a sense, the debate itself are beside the point. For the important question is what value judgments are consistent with the advocacy of more equality and what value judgments are consistent with opposition to more equality. An examination of this debate demonstrates how attitudes toward a generous income-transfer program are determined

not so much by technical considerations of cost as by such values and emotions as modesty and generosity.

Although the debate got quite technical at times, the differences between the sides are quite easy to understand. On
the one hand, those who believed in equality said that if we
take a dollar away from a richer man and give it to a poorer
man, the increase in the poorer man's well-being will exceed
the decrease in the richer man's well-being. Total well-
being—the sum of the two men's well-being—will have increased. The opponents answered: Your argument assumes
that one more dollar means less to a person if he has a lot of
income than if he has a little income. But this is not always
the case. There are contrary examples, like the following.
Suppose that you have lots of income, and if you had one
more dollar, you could buy a very good stereo system. On
the other hand, suppose you had much less income, and with
one more dollar all you could afford would be a used portable high-fidelity phonograph. Surely this is a situation in
which you would get more pleasure out of an additional
dollar if you were rich than if you were poor. For a good
stereo system is surely better than a portable high-fidelity
phonograph.

The only problem with this argument is that hardly anyone believes it. The examples are exceptions that prove the
rule. Every example is a bizarre and unusual case. Introspec-
tion convinces most people that an extra dollar means less to
them the more dollars they already have. Most of us make
more money as we grow older—at least up until some age. If
you ask yourself, am I quite as careful now when I spend a
dollar as I was a few years ago, you will probably answer no.
But if you are less careful about how you spend that dollar,
then it must mean less to you. If so, like most people you
simply do not believe that, on average, a dollar would mean
as much to a man when he is rich as when he is poor.

If that had been the only argument of those who were opposed to equality, they would clearly have lost the debate.
For which is more believable? That an additional dollar

means more to a man when he is poor than when he is rich? Or that an additional dollar means as much to a man when he is rich as it does when he is poor?

But those opposed to equality had another argument. This argument was more convincing because it explicitly invoked the blessing of science. The opponents said that we cannot know if the increase in the poor man's well-being exceeds the decrease in the rich man's well-being when we transfer a dollar of income from the rich to the poor, because it is impossible to compare the well-being of one person with that of another person. And, of course, they were right. A scientific comparison is impossible. But the issue is ethical, not scientific. The belief that all human beings have an equal capacity to experience satisfaction, to experience joys and sorrows, is an ethical belief. When Thomas Jefferson asserted in the Declaration of Independence that all men are created equal he was not setting forth an empirically verifiable or refutable proposition. Rather, he was expressing a moral sentiment shared by most of his compatriots.

This belief is also widely shared today. It is a basic part of our cultural and religious heritage. Imagine a relatively well-off person saying, "Yes it's true that a dollar means less to me now than when I had less money. But I don't believe that it would mean as much to a poorer person because his capacity to derive pleasure from goods and services is less than mine." Today most of us would label such an attitude as arrogance. If we were less secular, we would probably call it pride. Arrogance and the biblical notion of pride are clearly not attributes that are widely admired in our society.

The belief that the poor are undeserving is a more subtle version of arrogance and pride. In part this belief is based upon the myth that poor people are poorer than the rest of us because they do not work as hard as the rest of us. The facts are at variance with this myth. In a recent study Robert Haveman and I discovered that if one compares actual family earnings with an estimate of how much the family could earn if the adult members worked full time, full year—a concept we call "earnings capacity"—the ratio of actual earnings to earnings capacity is virtually the same for those with high and low capacity.[12] This is not to say that some poor people are not lazy. Undoubtedly, some are. But no more than rich folks. What distinguishes richer people from poorer people is not effort, but rather earnings capacity. In our society some people are lucky enough due to inheritance or environment to have the ability to earn a great deal of money, while other less fortunate people can earn very little.

Why does it require a serious recession or a depression for us to recognize this obvious truth? It appears that most of us need to know personally someone we love and respect, like a relative or close friend, who has had the misfortune to lose a job before we are willing to admit how important luck is, and how lucky rather than how deserving we are.

The myth that the poor are poor because they do not work hard enough is a very convenient, albeit false, rationalization for the belief that the poor are undeserving. The rationalization is convenient because it helps keep people who believe it from consciously recognizing the arrogance and pride that underlie the belief that the poor are undeserving. For implicit in the notion that the poor are undeserving is the idea that "I" am more deserving.

But even if our imaginary relatively well-off person were not guilty of arrogance or pride, he might still be unwilling to give money to the poorer person. He might say, "Yes, I believe that as you transfer money from me to a poorer person, his well-being will increase by a greater amount than my well-being will decrease, but I've got to look out for number one." Selfishness! Of course selfishness plays a role in shaping people's attitudes toward generous income-transfer programs. How could it be otherwise? Some people are lucky enough to have more income than others. Some do not want

    [12] Irwin Garfinkel and Robert Haveman, "Economic Inequality and the Utilization of Earnings Capacity," Institute for Research on Poverty Discussion Paper No. 300–75 (University of Wisconsin-Madison, 1975).

to give up any of it. Some are willing to give up some of it. But who among us is willing to give up all of our income and wealth?

All of us are selfish to a greater or lesser extent. At times, many of us are also arrogant. But most of us seek to strike a balance between arrogance and modesty and selfishness and generosity. Societies must strike the same sort of balance. In my judgment, we would be striking a better balance if we enacted a generous income-transfer program like the demogrant program that I have proposed. Others may disagree. But at issue is not our ability to afford such a program, but rather the degree to which we value what it would achieve.

## COMPREHENSIVE NATIONAL HEALTH INSURANCE

The story about national health insurance is similar to the demogrant story. We can afford a comprehensive national health insurance program. Such a program would be costly, but not nearly so costly to anyone as the estimates of federal budget cost suggest. And finally, whether we should have such a program depends upon whether the values achieved by the program are judged to exceed the costs.

Unlike the demogrant proposal, comprehensive national health insurance has some influential congressional support. Forty years after the inception of the Social Security Act we appear to be on the verge of enacting some kind of national health insurance program. The major question now is what kind of program. The Kennedy-Griffiths plan [13] would pay for all medical care costs with the exception of certain prescription drugs, extended psychiatric care, and adult dental care. In addition to the comprehensive Kennedy-Griffiths plan there are numerous other proposals which differ in cost, comprehensiveness of benefits, coverage of the population, financing, administration, and costs control provisions. An excellent summary of the major differences can be found

[13] Now sponsored by Representative James C. Corman since Martha Griffiths has retired.

in the February, 1975, issue of *Consumer Reports*.[14] I shall
focus here on the costs and values or ends that would be
achieved by the Kennedy-Griffiths plan.

How much would the Kennedy-Griffiths plan cost? Again,
the question of how to measure costs is confusing. Again, we
must ask, costs to whom? And once more, if we ask what are
the costs to the federal government, we will get an answer
that is very misleading. The annual cost to the federal government of the Kennedy-Griffiths program would be about
$100 billion. But 90 percent of this money is now being spent
anyway by consumers, or health insurance companies, and by
federal, state, and local governments. And anything that
health insurance companies or governments spend on medical care must ultimately be paid for by people. The appropriate questions to ask, therefore, are: What is the cost to all the
people? What is the cost to particular groups of people?

The cost to all the people is the additional resources that
must be devoted to health care to meet the additional demand for health care that is generated by the program.
While the exact magnitude is uncertain, the Department of
Health, Education, and Welfare has estimated that this
would amount to about $13 billion. As a people, can we af-
ford to spend an additional $13 billion on health care? Of
course we can. Our GNP exceeds a trillion dollars. The question is ludicrous.

The costs of a comprehensive national health insurance
program are well within our means. Should we incur these
costs? The answer to this question depends upon how much
we value the objectives that would be achieved by such a program.

Two frequently cited objectives for national health insurance programs are: eliminating financial catastrophes that

---

[14] Estimates of cost are derived from an HEW report to Congress in July, 1974, as
reported in *Consumer Reports*, February, 1975. For another excellent but brief discussion see Karen Davis, "National Health Insurance," in *Setting National Priorities: the
1975 Budget* (Washington, D.C.: Brookings Institution, 1975).

result from high medical care expenditures and achieving equal access to medical care.[15]

One rationale for government action to insure people against financial catastrophe is that the free market cannot provide such protection at reasonable prices.[16] If all individuals are free to choose whether or not to buy catastrophe health insurance, those who are most likely to need it are the ones who would be most likely to buy it. Premiums would have to be high enough to pay for the medical costs of this self-selected high-risk group. Some low-risk people would choose to forego the purchase of catastrophe insurance, making the insured group even more high-risk on average, which in turn would raise premiums and lead more low-risk people to forego purchase of the insurance. This self-selection process which leads to very high premiums helps to explain why so few Americans voluntarily purchase catastrophe health insurance.

Government provision of *compulsory* catastrophe health insurance, in contrast, obviates the self-selection problem. The average tax per covered family required to finance the program would be much less than the private health insurance premium that would prevail under free-market conditions because all low-risk as well as high-risk families would be covered.

A second reason that the market cannot provide catastrophe health insurance is that what constitutes a catastrophic medical bill depends upon one's income. To a family with a $20,000 income, a $2,000 medical bill is a heavy blow. To a family with a $4,000 income, a $2,000 medical bill is a financial catastrophe. Even if private insurance companies could set up separate insurance systems for a large number of income classes, the lower the income class the higher the pre-

---

[15] There are, of course, other objectives, including reducing the cost to society of medical care. See Davis, *op. cit.*, and Victor R. Fuchs, *Who Shall Live?* (New York: Basic Books, 1974), p. 97, for a good discussion of these objectives.

[16] See Kenneth J. Arrow, "Uncertainty and the Welfare Economics of Medical Care," *American Economic Review*, LIII (1963), 941–73.

mium would have to be. Many, probably most, low-income families would not purchase such catastrophe medical insurance. This problem would be exacerbated by the self-selection process just described.

When very large financial bills are incurred in the absence of catastrophe insurance, they become an income-maintenance problem. The income-related feature of catastrophe insurance may, therefore, be thought of as an efficient way of dealing with this income-maintenance problem. It avoids the need to tailor a general income-maintenance program to respond to individual needs that arise out of large medical bills.

Thus, because the market cannot efficiently provide catastrophe health insurance in general, and because income-related catastrophe health insurance performs an income-maintenance function which cannot be efficiently performed by a general income-maintenance program which is not tailored to individual need, the case for government provision of catastrophe health insurance is quite persuasive.

Before examining whether the case for equal access is as persuasive, equal access must be defined. The objective of equal access is frequently stated in terms of removing income as a barrier to the consumption of medical care. As such, equal access can be defined as a situation in which medical care consumption would be identical for all income classes to the extent that health status, knowledge, and tastes for medical care and risk aversion did not vary systematically with income. (To the extent that the poor have poorer health than the rich, equal access would imply proportionately greater consumption for the poor.)

The argument for equal access derives from two qualities of medical care and one ethical judgment. The first quality is that in some cases the difference between receiving and not receiving medical care has profound effects on the quality of life, and in some cases makes the difference between life and death. Second, the efficacy of medical care in any particular case is, from the patient's point of view, highly uncertain.

Given this uncertainty, whether or not individuals who have symptoms of illness will seek medical care depends upon their knowledge, tastes, risk aversion, and, most important for present purposes, upon their income. The more income a person has, the greater his ability to afford the cost of medical care; consequently, other things being equal, the more likely he will get medical care. In cases where early medical care makes the difference between life and death, more poor people will die simply because they had less income. A society in which one's chances of survival depend heavily on one's income is, in many people's judgment, unacceptably unjust. This is the ethical judgment. In a society such as ours where equality of opportunity is such a widely held value, most people must share this ethical judgment. For surely nothing could be more basic to equality of opportunity than an equal opportunity to survive. Note that the equal access case does not rest upon the belief that our judgment about what is good for a particular poor person is better than his judgment. Quite the opposite. I assume that we would behave exactly the same way as a poorer person when confronted with the same symptoms. Rich and poor behavior differ only because the rich are more able to afford to not take a chance. So long as incomes remain substantially unequal this will be the case. Even if the demogrant plan proposed here were adopted, incomes would remain substantially unequal, and the probability of survival would continue to depend upon income.

But inequalities in income may affect the probability of survival in other ways besides its effect on medical care consumption. As a consequence, in order to make an informed judgment about how far we ought to go in achieving equal access to medical care consumption, we need to know how much the achievement of equal access to health care would reduce inequalities by income class in the probability of survival. A complete analysis would also require knowledge about the efficacy and cost of alternative policies designed to reduce these inequalities.

Thus, whether we ought to have a national health insurance program and what kind of a program it should be depend not only upon the costs of such programs, but also upon how much we care about helping people to achieve security against large medical bills that cannot be achieved efficiently through the market, and how much we care about achieving equal access to medical care.

While we cannot afford to do everything that we would like to do, we are wealthy ènough to afford both a relatively generous demogrant-tax credit program and a comprehensive national health insurance program. These programs have costs. But to say that something has a cost is not to say that we cannot afford it or that we should not have it. Because our wants exceed our resources, everything has a cost. It is important to know what the costs of achieving something worthwhile are. Frequently, the real costs of programs like universal demogrants and national health insurance are not clearly understood. Frequently, opponents exaggerate the costs while proponents minimize the costs. I have tried to give a clear and accurate picture of the costs of these programs. But the debate does not end with an accurate estimate of the economic costs of a program. Rather, accurate estimates of economic costs are a prerequisite to intelligent debate. Once the costs are known, the question becomes: what do we value?

# The Wages of Neglect: Death and Disease in the American Work Place

## THE WALTER REUTHER
## MEMORIAL LECTURE

*ARNOLD MILLER*

THE OPPORTUNITY TO SPEAK in memory of a labor giant like Walter Reuther is a rare privilege indeed, and I would like to express my appreciation to the United Auto Workers of America for inviting me to deliver the Walter Reuther Memorial Lecture.

I am not a health professional. I am president of a union of coal miners. And for most of my working life I was a coal miner, too. So I shall discuss health problems from a miner's point of view, for I think they are similar to the problems millions of other American workers face every day in factories, farms, mills, and foundries across the nation.

I worked for twenty-four years in the coal mines of my native state of West Virginia until 1970, when I was forced to quit because of my health. I was just forty-seven years old at the time and I could not qualify for a pension for another eight years. But I had no choice. My lungs were filled with coal dust, and my bones were stiff and numb from arthritis brought on by years of work in knee-deep water and the cool, damp mine air.

My experience was not unique. If a roof fall or an explosion did not get them first, coal miners in my day could count

ARNOLD MILLER is President, United Mine Workers of America, Washington, D.C.

on having their health destroyed as a price for working in the mines. It was the miners' lot, and nobody really thought that anything could be done about it.

It was not that miners lacked the will or the courage to try to change their condition. Hundreds of miners had endured long and bitter strikes, and many had died organizing our union. What we lacked was an understanding of what was destroying our health.

During my years in the mines, the bosses always told me that coal dust was not harmful. Company doctors said the same thing. In fact, several claimed that coal dust was good for us. And they always threw in some four-syllable scientific mumbo jumbo to support their claims.

Silicosis was the only lung disease miners suffered, we were instructed, and it was mainly found among hard-coal miners in the anthracite region of eastern Pennsylvania, and a few hard-rock drillers. All we soft-coal miners needed was a good chew of tobacco, the doctors said, and we did not have a thing in the world to fear from coal dust.

Miners who complained of shortness of breath were regularly diagnosed as having anxiety problems or psychological disorders. Or they were accused of trying to get out of working by winning a disability award. The companies mockingly called it "compensationitis."

We did not know at the time we were being fed this medical snake oil that 3,000 miles away in Great Britain the National Coal Board had identified black lung as a major occupational disease. We did not know that in the early 1940s the British had set up a program of compensation awards for black lung victims and later instituted dust standards in the mines.

But we did know that something was badly wrong in the coalfields.

Silently, without warning, miners would begin to feel the first faint signs of shortness of breath. A lifelong hunter could no longer carry his rifle. A walk up a hill became an ordeal. Young men with only ten or fifteen years in the mines would awake from their sleep to spit up clumps of black material. In every coal camp and hollow in Appalachia one could find coal miners hacking and coughing, unable to catch their breath, unable to work, and unable to quit working lest they descend into poverty.

Coal dust was good for you, they told us, and everywhere you looked in the coalfields you saw dying men.

In late 1968, three West Virginia doctors became alarmed at the staggering number of coal miners who were disabled by breathing difficulties. Coal miners were dying from respiratory disorders at five times the rate of the general population. And autopsies of miners revealed their lungs to be little more than masses of dead, coal-encrusted tissue. Coal dust was the killer, the doctors concluded, and they set out to let the miners know.

With the help of some interested miners, Vista Volunteers, and poverty agency lawyers, the three doctors toured the coalfields, meeting in schools and local union halls with groups of both working and disabled miners, their wives and widows. The county medical associations passed resolutions condemning the doctors and threatened them with disciplinary action. But the doctors were unmoved, and the crowds grew. Black lung is killing you, the doctors preached, and the message spread throughout the coalfields like lightning.

In early 1969 a number of miners organized the West Virginia Black Lung Organization and asked a sympathetic state legislator to introduce a bill which would recognize black lung as a compensable, occupational disease under state Workers' Compensation. As the bill ran into opposition from the coal-dominated legislature, miners spontaneously walked off their jobs throughout the state until every mine was shut down. In all, 40,000 miners joined the strike, and a good number of them marched on the state capitol in Charleston, demanding passage of the Black Lung bill. In the end, with miners packing the galleries of the legislature and refusing to work, the legislature relented. The miners then made sure the Governor signed the Black Lung bill into law. Only then, did they go back to work.

The three-week black lung strike in West Virginia was probably the largest strike over occupational health issues by American workers, and its effects were far-reaching. Congress passed a federal black lung benefits program covering disabled miners and their widows as part of the 1969 federal Coal Mine Health and Safety Act. And it established maximum permissible dust levels for the first time in American coal mines.

Since then, there has been a good deal of study and research on this disease, and we know much more about it. What we have learned is truly frightening.

Black lung is one of the most widespread and deadly occupational diseases in the country. It kills more than 4,000 miners each year. Many of these men die when their hearts collapse from the strain of pumping blood through coal-ravaged lungs. At least 200,000 former coal miners are totally disabled by black lung disease today. And it is estimated that as many as one out of every five working miners is also a victim.

Black lung cripples and kills coal miners in this nation in epidemic proportions. What is even more frightening is that black lung represents only the tip of the iceberg of occupational diseases that are crippling and killing American workers throughout the nation.

No accurate statistics exist that truly portray the dimensions of the problem because we have never thought enough about workers' health problems to require national record keeping. But the studies which have been done show the American work place to be a chamber of horrors and the eight hours a worker spends on the job to be the most dangerous eight hours of his day.

He may be exposed to cancer-causing radiation or breathe air polluted with deadly carbon monoxide. Toxic chemicals like mercury or lead seep into his bloodstream. His lung tissues are gradually eaten away by exposure to cotton dust or asbestos dust or dust from rock or glass or stone. He works surrounded by deadly machinery which can tear off an arm or leg in an instant. The crash and roar deaden his hearing. The heat of a coke oven or a blast furnace blisters and peels his skin.

Lest you think I am exaggerating listen to these findings:

A survey of one million workers in Chicago found that nearly half of them are exposed to "urgent and serious health hazards" on the job.

Another study revealed that half of the 1,115 asbestos workers tested suffered from asbestiosis, a killer lung disease for which there is no cure.

One hundred out of 145 workers in a lead plant were found to have lead contamination in their bloodstreams.

Steelworkers who work around coke ovens contract cancer at three times the rate of other steelworkers. Workers employed in refining nickel die from cancer at five times the rate of the general population. Workers in the chromate-producing industry die from cancer at twenty-five times the rate of the general population.

The average sample of air from 691 work places was found to contain sulphur dioxide at four times the highest level recorded in the killer smog in London which claimed 4,000 lives in 1952.

Fourteen million workers are exposed to noise levels higher than 80 decibels, the level at which hearing loss occurs.

Just the other day, a study of 908 farm and factory workers in Oregon and Washington found that at least 31 percent of the medical disorders which they suffered—from cancer and lung disorders to skin disease and high blood pressure— were job-related.

More disturbing was the finding that 90 percent of the job-related health disorders had never been recorded by the government. Up to now, the best federal estimate has been that 400,000 workers contract occupational diseases every year.

This study suggests that the number is at least 4,000,000. Recent evidence seems to indicate that on-the-job injuries probably exceed 20 million rather than the reported 2 million, and deaths may be nearly twice the reported 14,000.

One would think that the slaughter and slow poisoning of millions of American workers every year would be considered a major social crisis and the government would long ago have mobilized to fight it. But that has not happened.

The average state budget allocates forty cents per worker per year for occupational health—less than a penny a week. A survey of twenty-five states showed that they employed one and one-half times as many fish and game wardens as health and safety inspectors. And what few inspectors there were, were mostly assigned to elevators and boilers. Eight thousand chemicals are commonly used in the industrial work place; so-called "safety levels" for worker exposure have been set for only 450 of them. About 40 percent of the fines levied against coal companies for violations of the federal Coal Mine Health and Safety Act have been collected.

The system of Workers' Compensation as administered by the states is a miserable failure. The average payment for full disability is less than federal poverty standards. Moreover, many occupational diseases are not even recognized by the states and, therefore, are not compensable.

What is worse is that a worker covered by Workers' Compensation loses his legal right to sue his employer for negligence. So the system, in effect, protects the employer more than the worker. Clearly, we need a federal system of Workers' Compensation with uniform payments that adequately compensate a victim. And if that system is to act as a deterrent, a worker must be given the right to sue his employer for additional damages in cases of negligence or outright violations of the law.

Our Constitution says there is equal justice under the law. But in the area of job health and safety, one has to wonder if it is so. If a factory worker drives his car recklessly and cripples a factory owner, the worker loses his license to drive, is heavily fined, and could spend some time in jail. But if a factory owner runs his business recklessly and cripples 500 workers with mercury poisoning, he rarely loses his license to do business and he never goes to jail. He may not even have to pay a fine.

Frankly, I do not understand why. If a few factory owners or coal mine operators received stiff jail sentences when their workers are killed and maimed because of unsafe conditions, one would be amazed at how fast working conditions at other mines and factories would be improved.

We are faced with a paradox. Occupational diseases infect this nation like a plague. Yet there is no sense of public urgency about the problem. There are a number of reasons for this.

First, I think the dimensions of the problem are hard to grasp. If an asbestos plant explodes and 500 workers are killed, it is instant news. But when 500 former asbestos workers die a cruel and hopeless death in 500 separate hospital rooms and nursing homes, the grief is private. It is rarely the stuff of headlines. No television cameras record the scene.

The organized medical profession also bears some responsibility for this lack of urgency. Company doctors all too often act as apologists for industry rather than as physicians concerned about the health of their patients. The American Medical Association helped lead the fight against the 1970 Occupational Health and Safety Act. And less than 10 percent of the medical schools in the country teach occupational health and safety.

The so-called industrial hygienists, who should be leading the fight, are usually too busy denying that any problem exists. One industrial hygienist was quoted a few years ago as saying that "occupational diseases don't produce a wiggle in the general death rate any more." [1] The same year he made that statement 1,700 coal miners died from black lung in the state of Pennsylvania alone.

[1] "Industry Doctors Try New Approach," *Business Week*, May 13, 1967, pp. 80–91.

If we ever hope to eliminate the terrible health hazards workers face on the job, there has to be a fundamental change in public attitudes about the problem of occupational health. Changing public attitudes is never easy, but we can take heart from the success of the environmental movement.

Only a few years ago, the only people talking about saving the environment were a handful of conservationists. Then more citizens became involved, students took up the cause, and the media began to document the pollution of our lakes and streams, our air and water. Today, as every politician knows, the environmental movement represents an idea whose time has come.

Surely, if the nation can become aroused by the pollution of our natural environment, we can become equally aroused by the pollution of our work environment. For they are really one and the same issue. There is no more precious natural resource than people. And if there was ever an endangered species, it is the American worker today.

Workers in the social welfare field, particularly those who work in health-related areas, can play a crucial role in this effort. Extensive health studies and medical research need to be performed on workers and on the work environment and their findings brought to wide public attention. Those who work in public health can insist that job health become a major ingredient of every public health program, and that workers and their unions be involved to the maximum.

As citizens and members of organizations in the social welfare field, social workers can join forces with those who are fighting for enactment and strict enforcement of health and safety legislation. They can demand that every candidate for public office take a stand on the issue of job health and safety.

They can call their governor and write their Congressman. They can picket an unsafe factory alongside the workers. They can protest company practices at a shareholders' meeting. They can make speeches and write letters to the editor. But do not expect miracles.

All of us know that the goal of a safe and healthy work place will not be won overnight. We are talking about a long and difficult fight. But what is essential is that we begin now—because time is not on our side.

There is a common misconception that the more we modernize and automate the work place, the healthier it becomes. The opposite is often the case. The high-speed labor-saving machinery now used in coal mining, for example, produces much greater quantities of coal dust in the air than mining done by manual labor alone. The same is true in textile factories, glass manufacturing, stone cutting, and many other industries.

Every twenty minutes, we introduce a new chemical substance into the work place.[2] We have little idea of its effects as it seeps into the bloodstreams of thousands of workers and fouls their lungs. We cannot even guess what its genetic effects might be on future generations. We dare not wait to find out.

The job of cleaning up the work environment will be costly and difficult. But what it comes down to in the end is not a question of cost but of priorities. If this society can devote millions of dollars and thousands of trained workers to the goal of landing a man on the moon, surely we can devote equal resources to making it safe for a man or woman to earn a living here on earth. What we need is the will to make it happen.

The task we face is great, but I am not discouraged. I am confident that the will we need is there.

[2] *Occupational Disease . . . the Silent Enemy* (Washington, D.C.: U.S. Department of Health, Education, and Welfare, Public Health Service, 1974), p. 6.

# Utilization in the Health Care Delivery System

## HENRIK L. BLUM

IN ORDER TO DISCUSS the health care system it must be seen as one critical but inseparable and interacting ingredient of the process of utilization.

### FOUR KEY SETS OF FORCES

The utilization process has been visualized as the interaction of three major sets of forces: the person or potential user, the carer or care system, and the society with its institutions and mechanisms in which the first two are embedded. Alternatively, utilization has been perceived as the outcome of the meshing of these three sets of forces, with an appreciation that the act of utilization as an outcome in turn affects the three sets.[1] Thus the triad can be said to create a fourth major force, the process of utilization, which takes on a dynamic of its own that affects each of the others.

The following diagram attempts to visualize the concept of a dynamic and complex set of forces that enters into the process of utilization. Each set not only acts and reacts with the other three but is in itself the expression of an equally complex set of an historically based and currently activated flow

HENRIK L. BLUM, M.D.; is Professor of Health Planning, University of California, Berkeley.
[1] Ronald Anderson and J. Newman, "Societal and Individual Determinants of Medical Care Utilization in the United States," *Milbank Memorial Fund Quarterly,* LI, No. 1 (1973), 95–124; Aaron Antonovsky, "A Model to Explain Visits to the Doctor: with Specific Reference to the Case of Israel," *Journal of Health and Social Behavior,* XIII (1972), 446–54; Reed Geertson *et al.,* "A Reexamination of Suchman's Views on Social Factors in Health Care Utilization," *Journal of Health and Social Behavior,* XVI (1975), 226–37; Earl L. Koos, *The Health of Regionville* (New York: Columbia University Press, 1954).

of forces which helps determine the posture of that set in a given interaction of user-care system-society. Thus, the current state of affairs in each set determines whether engagement will be attempted, whether it will be continued, and whether it will be successful.

FORCES WHICH DYNAMICALLY INTERRELATE THE FOUR SETS

There are many ways to classify these forces. McKinlay, in the classic work on the use of services,[2] provides six frames of reference by which to categorize forces or determinants. He appears to locate the determinants as operative at one of two sets, the person or the care system. More careful consideration of these determinants will make it clear that in a given situation each of the four sets is likely to react to each force that is present (see diagram). And how the four sets behave to one another in relation to each of the forces and to the aggregate of those that are operative in the situation will determine the success of the utilization process.

The first six classes of forces are taken from McKinlay:

1. *Economic forces.* The financial cost to the potential user of services, whether direct or indirect, implicit or explicit, includes often disputed forces such as: cost of service; the user's economic assets; facilitating devices, such as insurance, prepayment, and so on.[3]

2. *Sociodemographic force.* The age, sex, race, education, income, religion, family size, and urbanity types of user at-

[2] John B. McKinlay, "Some Approaches and Problems in the Study of the Use of Services: an Overview," *Journal of Health and Social Behavior,* XIII (1972), 115–52.

[3] Emil Berkanovic and Leo G. Reeder, "Can Money Buy the Appropriate Use of Services? Some Notes on the Meaning of Utilization Data," *Journal of Health and Social Behavior,* XV (1974), 93–99; David Coburn and Clyde R. Pope, "Socioeconomic Status and Preventive Health Behavior," *Journal of Health and Social Behavior,* XV (1974), 67–78; Karen Davis, "Financing Medical Care: Implications for Access to Primary Care," in S. Andreopoulos, ed., *Primary Care: Where Medicine Fails* (New York: John Wiley and Sons, 1974), Chap. 4; Irving Leveson, "The Demand for Neighborhood Medical Care" (New York: Rand Corporation, 1968; mimeo.); Lois Montiero, "Expense Is No Object: Income and Physician Visits Reconsidered," *Journal of Health and Social Behavior,* XIV (1973), 99–115; Milton I. Roemer *et al., Health Insurance Effects,* Bureau of Health Economics Research Series, No. 16 (Ann Arbor, Mich.: School of Public Health, University of Michigan, 1972).

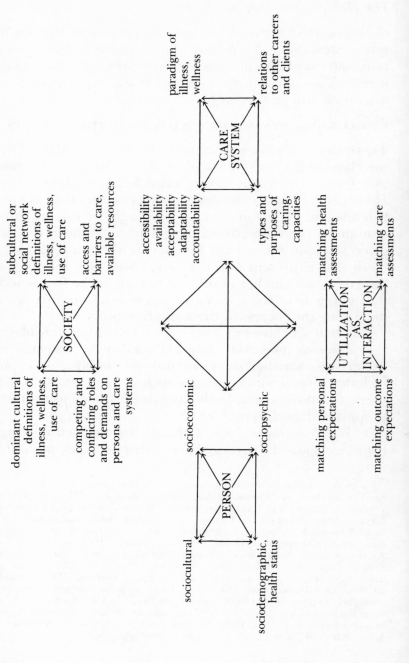

FORCES AT WORK IN
THE UTILIZATION PROCESS

SOCIETY

subcultural or
social network
definitions of
illness, wellness,
use of care

access and
barriers to care,
available resources

dominant cultural
definitions of
illness, wellness,
use of care

competing and
conflicting roles
and demands on
persons and care
systems

CARE
SYSTEM

paradigm of
illness,
wellness

relations
to other careers
and clients

accessibility
availability
acceptability
adaptability
accountability

types and
purposes of
caring,
capacities

PERSON

socioeconomic

sociopsychic

sociocultural

sociodemographic,
health status

UTILIZATION
AS
INTERACTION

matching health
assessments

matching care
assessments

matching personal
expectations

matching outcome
expectations

tributes correlate significantly with use of services. These determinants do not of themselves explain the degree of usage, but when they indicate significant differences they suggest causality, or at least indicate where to investigate further.[4]

3. *Geographic forces.* These cover the proximity of sources of care.

4. *Sociopsychological forces.* These are factors of motivation, perception, beliefs, knowledge, learning, alienation, feelings, and cues that trigger action.[5]

5. *Sociocultural forces.* Factors of class, ethnicity, culture, family relationships, social networks, and so on are included here.[6]

6. *Delivery system forces.* These include the means of entry, organization, organization goals, professionalism, personnel, skills, behaviors, facilities, nature of coverage and financing, style of engagement with the client, and adaptability to multiple types of clients.[7] Even the relative availability of beds compared to other services determines hospitalization.[8]

7. *Interaction process.* This comprises the factors of prior experience, satisfaction, and expectations on the part of both the user and the care system, and the meshing of user and carer assessments of the patient's health status, the type of

[4] James G. Anderson, "Demographic Factors Affecting Health Services Utilization: a Causal Model," *Medical Care*, XI (1973), 104–20.

[5] Chester W. Douglass, "A Social-psychologic View of Health Behavior for Health Services Research," *Health Services Research*, VI, No. 1 (1971), 6–14; David S. Gochman, "Some Correlates of Children's Health Beliefs and Potential Health Behavior," *Journal of Health and Social Behavior*, XII (1971), 148–54; John Stoeckle *et al.*, "On Going to See the Doctor; the Contributions of the Patient to the Decision to Seek Medical Aid," *Journal of Chronic Diseases*, XVI (1963), 915–89.

[6] C. J. Schumaker, Jr., "Change in Health Sponsorship: II. Cohesiveness, Compactness and Family Constellation of Medical Care Patterns," *American Journal of Public Health*, LXVI, No. 7 (1972) 931–41; Clarissa S. Scott, "Health and Healing Practices among Five Ethnic Groups in Miami, Florida," *Public Health Reports*, LXXXIX, No. 6 (1974), 524–32.

[7] Raymond Fink, "The Measurement of Medical Care Utilization," in Merwyn R. Greenlick, ed., *Conceptual Issues in the Analysis of Medical Care Utilization Behavior* (Washington, D.C.: DHEW, PHS, HSMHA, 1969). Conference Series.

[8] M. Shain and M. L. Roemer, "Hospital Costs Relate to the Supply of Beds," *Modern Hospitals*, XCI (1959), 71–73, 168.

care to be applied, the interpersonal relationships to be maintained, and the outcomes to be anticipated.[9]

8. *Intercultural stress.* This might be considered a subset of either psychosocial or psychocultural determinants. It includes the degree of difference or incompatibility between the demands placed on a given user by his subcultural, family, or social network definitions and expectations and those placed on him by the dominant culture and the caring system, which until recently only reflected the dominant culture.

9. *Social goal conflict.* This set of forces could be a subset of the delivery system.[10] Included are the degree of competition or incompatibility between the various demands on the care system, such as individualized care versus efficiency, health promotion versus treatment, prolongation of life versus patient well-being, or certifying and sorting for societal purposes of control rather than meeting patient needs.

10. *The care system paradigm of health.* The generally somatic orientation of most medical care organizations ignores: (a) the interrelationships and transmutability of social, psychic, and somatic illness; (b) the social and psychic precursors of somatic disease; and (c) the nonsomatic reasons that bring persons to medical care settings which may be the only available or acceptable supporting institutions.[11]

11. *The person's health status.* Finally, there is the nature of, and the person's perception of, his wellness or illness. This force seems too obvious to deserve comment, but it is often overlooked. A certain level of good health is no doubt as-

[9] Eliot Freidson, "Client Control and Medical Practice," *American Journal of Sociology,* LXV (1960), 374–82; Eliot Friedson, *"Patients' Views of Medical Practice* (New York: Russell Sage Foundation, 1961); David Hayes-Bautista, "Patient and Practitioner: the Interaction of Assessments" (Berkeley, Calif.: University of California, 1974; mimeo.); B. S. Hulka *et al.,* "Satisfaction with Medical Care in a Low Income Group," *Journal of Chronic Diseases,* XXIV (1971), 661–73; Julius Roth, *Timetables* (New York: Bobbs-Merrill Co., 1963).

[10] Kenneth E. Boulding, "The Concept of Need for Health Services," *Milbank Memorial Fund Quarterly,* XLIV, No. 2 (1966), 202–23.

[11] Alfred Childs, "The Functions of Medical Care," *Public Health Reports,* XC, No. 1 (1975), 10–14; J. T. Shuval *et al., Social Function of Medical Practice* (San Francisco: Jossey-Bass, 1970).

sociated with many other capacities, one of which is the ability to make the effort to get care. Another is the general association of good health with other attributes that tend to be associated with more usage of ambulatory care. At the other extreme, it is the persons with demanding illnesses, particularly the chronic ones, who are driven to extensive use of all kinds of care. Sickness may cause confusion in the user's selection, and specific illnesses tend to influence the choice of services. The reverberations of experience and satisfaction with services (interaction process) are probably key forces in affecting care-seeking and using behavior.[12]

Examination of almost any aspect of these eleven categories reveals that each force typically affects utilization by involving a matching or meshing process at and between the three primary sets and with feedback from the utilization process. For example, cost, a so-called "barrier" to use, is not a barrier to wealthy users, no matter how high it is; the significance to them is quite relative, as it is to everyone else. But a person who has literally no means at his disposal will certainly postpone costly, or even inexpensive, care until he has no other survival choice. Preventive care is particularly susceptible to cost barriers.[13] At the same time, a philanthropic care system may accept him without charge, while a university system may admit him for teaching or research purposes. Society may set up far-reaching national health insurance so that neither monetary, social, nor travel costs are

[12] Lu Ann Aday et al., "Development of a Framework for the Study of Access to Health Care," Preliminary Report No. 1., Center for Health Administration Studies, University of Chicago (1973; mimeo); Lu Ann Aday, "Economic and Noneconomic Barriers to the Use of Needed Medical Services," *Medical Care*, XIII (1975), 447–56; Lu Ann Aday and Ronald Anderson, "A Framework for the Study of Access to Medical Care," *Health Sciences Research*, Fall, 1974, pp. 208–20; Merwyn R. Greenlick et al., "Determinants of Medical Care Utilization," *Health Services Research*, Winter, 1968, pp. 296–315; Oscar C. Stine and Constantino Chuaqui, "Mother's Intended Actions for Childhood Symptoms, *American Journal of Public Health*, LIX, No. 11 (1969), 2035–44; Thomas T. H. Wan and Scott J. Soifer, "Determinants of Physician Utilization: a Causal Analysis," *Journal of Health and Social Behavior*, XV (1974), 100–108.

[13] "An Ounce of Prevention: "How Much Is It Worth?" *Health News*, California Department of Health, II, No. 2 (1974), 6.

involved. It may set up special categories or devices that remove his personal cost barrier to service, but it may provide
this care at some sacrifice of his social standing or personal
pride. In addition, the intensity of care, nature of service,
and ways of using services such as phone calls, visits, or hospitalization, interact differently with different forces.[14]

How the patient is treated if he has Medicare or Medicaid,
has other insurance or unlimited personal resources, or has
no resources, is no small factor in altering the health care system's practices, the user's self-image, and further user-carer
interaction.[15] Thus the cost of service reacts with other determinants in the person set, such as the cost of taking time
from work or traveling, feelings about how one is likely to be
cared for given his economic and social status, his sociocultural and sociopsychic willingness to brave the care system
and to face the implications of illness.[16] Similarly, the issue of

[14] Roger M. Battistela, "Utilization of Preventive-diagnostic Services among Late
Adulthood Persons," (Ithaca, N.Y.: Center for Housing and Environmental Studies,
Division of Urban Study, Cornell University, 1969; mimeo); Irving D. Goldberg *et
al.,* "Effect of Short-term Outpatient Psychiatric Therapy Benefit on Utilization of
Medical Services in a Prepaid Group Practice Medical Program," *Medical Care,* VIII
(1970), 419–28; Robert F. L. Logan *et al.,* "The Liverpool Study into Use of Hospital
Resources," London School of Hygiene and Tropical Medicine, Memoir No. 14
(1972), pp. 135–44; Lawrence Podell, "Studies in the Use of Health Services by Fam-
ilies on Welfare: Utilization of Preventive Health Services" (New York: Center for
Study of Urban Problems, Graduate Division, Bernard M. Baruch College, City Uni-
versity of New York, 1969; mimeo); Richard Pomeroy *et al.,* "Studies on the Use of
Health Services by Families on Welfare: Utilization by Publicly Assisted Families"
(New York: Center for Study of Urban Problems, Bernard M. Baruch College, City
University of New York, 1969; mimeo); Clyde R. Pope *et al.,* "Determinants of Med-
ical Care Utilization: the Use of the Telephone for Reporting Symptoms," *Journal of
Health and Social Behavior,* XII (1971), 155–62.
[15] Raymond S. Duff and A. B. Hollingshead, *Sickness and Society* (New York:
Harper and Row, 1968); Anselm Strauss, "Medical Ghettos," *Trans-Action,* May,
1967, pp. 7–25; Bruce Stuart and Ronald Stockton, "Control Over the Utilization of
Medical Services," *Milbank Memorial Fund Quarterly,* LI, No. 3 (1973), 341–94.
[16] T. F. Kelley and G. J. Schieber, *Factors Affecting Medical Services Utilization: a Be-
havioral Approach* (Washington, D.C.: Urban Institute, 1972); Selma J. Mushkin ed.,
*Consumer Incentives for Health Care* (New York: Prodist, 1974); K. J. Rogham and E.
A. Powell, "Impact of Medicaid and an OEO Health Center on Use of Dental Ser-
vices in an Urban Area," *Public Health Reports,* LXXXIX, No. 4 (1974), 325–29; Kerr
L. White and Jane H. Murnaghan, "International Comparisons of Medical Care
Utilization," National Center for Health Statistics, Series 2, No. 33 (Washington,
D.C.: HEW, PHS, HSMHA, 1969).

cost reaches the care system set and interacts with feelings about the aged, the poor, ethnics, prognosis, and societal interactions such as peer review of utilization and quality. The utilization process also forces the cost issue to spill back into the societal frame of reference, where it is confounded with issues of rights, deterrants to use, efficiency, alternative schemes, and concepts of prevention at environmental and behavioral levels.[17]

Unfortunately, it is obvious that total removal of all blocks to satisfactory utilization of care cannot be achieved by any direct interventions mounted solely from the societal locus. Societal inducement, penalties, or structures are unlikely to be well-enough engineered to overcome the blocks faced by each individual whose impasses to utilization may vary even over the period of care for a single siege of illness.

This realization suggests a mixed strategy. The major common barriers can be set aside by societal agreement and actions, such as national health insurance to overcome costs; organized comprehensive systems to provide convenient primary care and whatever secondary and tertiary care is needed; sickness insurance to permit taking time from work; outreach to educate and follow up individuals with excessive problems, and so on. Responsibility for overcoming unusual and unique blocks must, however, be assigned to the caring system itself. By demanding that health professionals become knowledgeable about and adept at recognizing and penetrating the complex dynamics of unfavorable utilization for any given individual, we can expect major improvements in care and utilization.

WHAT IS THE CARE SYSTEM EXPECTED TO GENERATE?

The health care delivery system is very likely to reflect the broadest aspirations of the larger society. At the same time, it is imperative to note that the aspirations of individuals are

[17] Henrik L. Blum, *Planning for Health* (New York: Human Sciences Press, 1974), Chap. 10.

more likely to reflect those of smaller social networks, such as families and subcultures, and thus may differ fundamentally from those of the larger society. In fact, individual roles may reflect family needs. It is not unusual for a father to aspire for total disability as a means of maintaining his family in a worn-out mining community. It is hard for a member of the caring system to work with such a user. The desire of a family to maintain its balance by avoiding therapy for a schizophrenic child is also a trying experience for the helping professions.

Clearly, potential recipients may have roles assigned to them by society and family that are not always congruent with better health for the individual. Moreover, the health professionals, who tend to identify with a specific individual, may have tremendous difficulty in mobilizing the necessary forces which will allow a higher level of resolution among a user's conflicting roles so that his health can be aided at the same time that his family or social group can be helped to a healthier level of functioning.

*What society requires of the care system.* It has been pointed out that the medical care system is in fact not expected to promote health, that it is most specifically expected to diagnose and treat illnesses, and that a large part of its efforts are directed to categorizing, certifying, and sorting for social purposes.[18]

A significant portion of the health care system's efforts are spent on sorting and categorizing persons for legal and forensic purposes. These may be examinations for: (1) admission or athletic eligibility for schools; (2) pre-employment for jobs generally and government services; (3) for licensure; (4) verification of illness or incapacity to work; injury; ability to return to work; (5) eligibility for benefits; (6) ability to testify or be at liberty, and so on. Only exceptionally do such categorizing efforts have caring or curing as their avowed goal. For example, the health screening of Medicaid eligible and

---

[18] Alfred Childs, *op. cit.*

other children. Often the goal is social stabilization.[19] These sorting efforts may constitute a quarter or more of the system's efforts.

The proportion of the health care system's efforts devoted to promotion of well-being is by contrast very small, of these the "annual physical" is probably a misguided ritual rather than a service. When well-person examinations serve as the basis of "prospective medicine" [20] we may have a socially useful product. Then a person will be evaluated for genetic and environmental (including occupational) impacts, health-affecting behavior, and evident deficiencies in well-being. These will then be used as the basis from which to formulate a health-promoting regimen specifically for that person. This is a new field, rarely tilled.

The bulk of medical care remains devoted to diagnosing and treating sick people. The leaders in the field are the physicians, and they have with society's approval and support made themselves into one-organ, one-tissue, or one-procedure specialists. They have not been prepared to deal with or promote clients' well-being, nor would they be able at present to earn a living doing so.[21]

It is of special interest that not until recently, and then only ambivalently, has our society felt that it might be important to have organized systems of care so that a user could be assured of a continuity of services, all covered by his subscription to that given system (P.L. 93-222, the Health Maintenance Organization Act of 1973). As a result, the health care services are, with few exceptions, the creation of isolated entrepreneurs acting as individuals, groups, or institutions, each providing their chosen services and, typically, failing to relate to other necessary service elements. We have a veritable jungle of unrelated, overlapping, and unmatching ser-

[19] Howard Waitzkin, "Latent Functions of the Sick Role in Various Institutional Settings," *Social Science and Medicine,* V (1971), 45–75.

[20] "Prospective Medicine: Improving the Patient's Survival Odds," *American Medical News,* September 2, 1974, pp. 17–19.

[21] Richard M. Bailey, "An Economist's View of the Health Services Industry," *Inquiry,* VI, No. 1 (1969), 3–19.

vices in some urban and suburban areas, often little or nothing in others, and generally little in rural areas.[22]

FROM WHAT CONCEPTUAL BASE SHOULD
THE SYSTEM OPERATE?

Presumably, it is health that the caring system is to affect favorably, and that is exactly what carers are led to believe, that they and they alone are doing, as they learn their skills through long and arduous training. Unfortunately, their paradigm of the forces that affect health is a very skewed one as we shall see.[23]

The relative importance of the health-affecting forces— heredity, environment, behavior, and medical care—is not what physicians seem to believe. Medical care is the least, genetics somewhat more, behavior several times as important, and environment, including the physical and socioeconomic cultural factors, more important than all of the three preceding.[24]

*Interrelationships and transmutability of somatic, psychic, and social health.* It is once more being perceived that social, psychic, and somatic well-being are inextricably tied together, that failure at any one level is likely to lead to disturbances at others.[25] It is also now overwhelmingly confirmed that social forces can result in psychic and somatic ill-health; somatic damage, in psychic and social perturbations; and psychic illness, in social and somatic ones. These forms or aspects of

[22] Ruth Roemer *et al., Planning Urban Health Services: from Jungle to System* (New York: Springer Publishing Co., 1975).

[23] George L. Engle, "The Best and the Brightest: the Missing Dimension in Medical Education," *Pharos,* XXXVI (1973), 129–33.

[24] Robert J. Haggerty, "The Boundaries of Health Care," *Pharos,* XXXV, No. 3 (1972), 106–11; John Powles, "The Medicine of Industrial Man," *Ecologist,* II, No. 10 (1972), 24–36; Warren Winkelstein, "Epidemiological Considerations Underlying the Allocation of Health and Disease Care Resources," *International Journal of Epidemiology,* I, No. 1 (1972), 69–74.

[25] Howard Brody, "The Systems View of Man: Implications for Medicine, Science and Ethics," *Perspectives in Biology and Medicine,* Autumn 1973, pp. 71–92; Alan Sheldon, "Toward a General Theory of Disease and Medical Care," in Alan Sheldon *et al.,* eds., *Systems and Medical Care* (Cambridge, Mass: Massachusetts Institute of Technology Press, 1970), pp. 84–125.

well-being are inseparable. Problems, particularly severe ones, in any of the three areas are therefore likely to involve or disturb the other two areas as well, perhaps showing up as one or more repeated failures.[26]

We must be prepared to accept that a health-caring system must be much more than the traditional somatic or medical one. In fact, satisfactory utilization in the sense of providing meaningful and helpful intervention cannot be limited to a traditionally therapeutic or a somatically based system of care. The tragically comparable isolation of social and mental health support services has been commented on.[27]

ATTRIBUTES NEEDED TO OVERCOME THE BARRIERS

By taking a more discerning look at the present caring systems we may be able to find out why they so often either fail to overcome barriers to utilization or proceed to erect new ones.

*Overcoming socioeconomic and mechanical barriers.* I automatically put the burden of removing geographic and financial barriers on society. However, even if these barriers were in essence totally removed by national health insurance and guaranteed to every citizen by a type of delivery system, there would still be barriers for many individuals. The time costs when other things are more pressing, loss of income by absence from work, lack of care for children, lack of mobility, and so on, are examples of barriers which society can partially but never completely overcome for all individuals.

[26] Lester E. Hinckle, Jr., *et al.,* "An Investigation of the Relationship between Life Experience, Personality Characteristics and General Susceptibility to Illness," *Psychosomatic Medicine,* XX (1958), 278; Thomas H. Holmes and Minoru Masuda, "Psychosomatic Syndrome," *Psychology Today,* April, 1972, pp. 71–72, 106; R. H. Rahe *et al.,* "A Longitudinal Study of Life Change and Illness Patterns," *Journal of Psychosomatic Research,* X (1967) 355–66; Alfred Slote, *Termination: the Closure of Baker Plant* (Indianapolis: Bobbs-Merrill Co., 1969); Harold G. Wolff, *Stress and Disease* (Springfield, Ill.: Charles C. Thomas, 1953).

[27] John Hastings, *The Community Health Center in Canada* (Ottawa, Ont., Canada: Information Canada, 1972); Jonathan P. Leopold, "Organization of Mental Health Programs," Program Notes, AUPHA, LXIII (1975); 18–35; John T. McLeod, "Consumer Participation," Regulation of the Professions; and Decentralization of Health Services," a report submitted to the Minister of Health, Regina, Sask., Canada, 1973.

The care system itself must be given the responsibility for finding out when such factors are operative and the resources to reach out, whether by home visit, ambulance, supplementary income, baby-sitting, and so on to allow necessary utilization. For example, care in the home may call for a hydraulic jack, a nurse twice weekly, a monthly ambulance trip, friendly ʌneighbors, training family members or other persons in various procedures so that utilization is satisfactory and at the same time a family is enabled to remain together.

*Overcoming sociocultural barriers.* It seems unrealistic if not downright undesirable to expect our society to homogenize. Evidence seems to be accumulating that our nation creates ever new subcultures rather than functioning as an effective melting pot. Among the more spectacular points of differentiation between our subgroups are their concepts of health, what should be done about it, and who should do it. For many, there is an interesting convergence of old beliefs that good health results from a happy relationship with nature and new beliefs about the importance of harmonious ecologic or systems relationships to achieve the holistic oneness of social, psychic, and somatic well-being.

What can the care system do about eliminating the barriers that people from so many old cultures as well as new subcultures encounter in dealing with somatic-oriented, Western medicine? The first requirement, of course, is that Western medicine bring itself abreast of the newer scientific knowledge that behavioral and environmental inputs of a social, economic, and physical nature are indeed the major determinants of health. The care system then has to become a force for promoting health, quite an interesting state of affairs for organized medicine and a great number of practitioners whose social outlooks are a bit frightening.[28]

[28] E. Cray, *In Failing Health: the Medical Crisis and the A.M.A.* (Indianapolis: Bobbs-Merrill Co., 1970); Pierre deVise, "Misused and Misplaced Hospitals and Doctors," Commission on College Geography Resource Paper No. 22 (Washington, D.C.: Association of American Geography, 1973), pp. 51–57; Rosemary Stevens, *American Medicine and the Public Interest* (New Haven, Conn.: Yale University Press, 1971).

The second major advance will be for practitioners of Western medicine to appreciate the inseparability of somatic, psychic, and social wellness. Many practitioners have begun to nudge the care system into providing all basic human support resources in primary care settings near to people.[29] Each user with apparent psychic, social, or somatic imbalances would have a major therapist at a primary well-being center who would also be his advocate or convener to see that he obtained the services really needed at the primary, secondary, and tertiary levels of care.

These primary service centers close to people should be kept small to minimize bureaucratic tendencies and should service no more than 10,000 persons. People indigenous to various segments or subcultures served would be drawn into employment at the unit. In all but very sparsely populated areas there would be many such units from which to choose. In this way almost everyone would find one center with workers with compatible culture, language, health beliefs and practices. *Curanderos,* medicine men, transcendental meditators, and so on can be well-absorbed into centers with appropriate clientele. Consumers would also have the opportunity to relate to many kinds of servers so that they could find one suitable key server who would become their convener or advocate.[30]

If any or all of these changes are to take place, society must allocate major decision control to the users of each primary center. At the same time, society must "allocate" to each citizen his share of dollars to sign over to the service system he joins. Open enrollment and an opportunity to change from one center to another can probably take place quarterly, and

[29] Hastings, *op. cit.;* Leopold, *op. cit.;* McCleod, *op. cit.;* Alberta W. Parker, "The Dimensions of Primary Care: Blue Prints for Change," in Spyros Andreopoulos, ed., *Primary Care: Where Medicine Fails* (New York: John Wiley and Sons, 1974), Chap. 1.

[30] Henrik L. Blum, "The Multipurpose Worker and the Neighborhood Multiservice Center," *American Journal of Public Health,* LVIII, No. 3 (1968), 458–68; David L. Cowen and John Sbarbaro, "Family-centered Health Care—a Viable Reality?" *Medical Care,* X (1972), 164–72.

certainly annually. In this way the consumer can express his approval by staying at his chosen center or his disapproval by taking his health dollars elsewhere.

More specifically, we need to select and educate our practitioners differently. They must learn to care and be anxious to become familiar with the beliefs and cultural requirements of each client and extend the capacities of the system so as to make a useful connection with the patient that he perceives as sensible and dignified. This too calls for more resources at the point of primary contact than a one-physician office. It calls for many skills; for both sexes; often for several races and religions; for an openness to training; for the use of volunteers; and for an extensive commitment to health promotion. Health promotion essentially means working with clients to use self-help and be guided by an outlook that relates behavior to one's environment and one's capacities, and thus helps determine how to live to enhance one's well-being.

*Overcoming sociopsychic barriers.* The care system needs to develop a sensitive awareness of the various utilization patterns that result from the interplay of cultural, educational, economic, and other forces on the individual's personality, beliefs, perceptivity, motivational and behavioral make-up, and capacity to trust the honest and relevance of carers. It no longer is (and never really was) axiomatic that the Parsonian notion about the role of a patient is so well-defined by society that an ill person cutomarily seeks and accepts appropriate care; not only do subcultures and the smaller social networks, such as families, have more determining power about the use of care, but highly individualized psychosocial factors determine the form of illness as well as the need for an acceptable type of care. Freidson, Hayes-Bautista, Roth, and others [31] have recently worked out elaborate patterns of how patients and careers independently assess what seems to be wrong,

---

[31] Freidson, "Client Control and Medical Practice"; Freidson, *"Patients' Views of Medical Practice;* Hayes-Bautista, *op. cit.;* Roth, *op. cit.*

compare opinions, attempt convergence if they are aware of differences, get into conflict, resolve them or part company. As a result, a client, may use different carers for different types of problems because each offers a better match with his perception of a particular aspect of his wellness or illness.

Again, the major capacity to compensate for, and relate to, an individual's incapacity to use care must lie with the members of the health care system. They have to be alert and study failures. In every case, by sincere reaching, even if not based on full understanding, they must elicit patient partnering.

*Overcoming other sociodemographically demonstrated barriers.* By reasonably maintained evaluation and use of sociodemographic descriptors, the care system will learn that such characteristics as age, sex, religion, number of children, education, and social status will be seen as distinguishing some users who react unsatisfactorily. Awareness on the part of the caring system as to who does or does not use various services in a reasonable manner enables the system to explore the failures.

Sometimes nonutilization may be simply explained as use of competing, subrosa, or illegal systems which may also be dangerous. The elucidation of forces which interfere with utilization by any category of user allows the care system to adjust its own operations to enable it to serve the special cases. Even if cause and effect are not perceived it is possible to experiment empirically with ways of establishing acceptable contact and health-promoting behavior.

PRINCIPLES ON WHICH TO BUILD HEALTH CARE SYSTEMS

It is inconceivable that any society can be healthy if it predicates that all health guidance and activities are to be initiated by designated health workers. It is also inconceivable that any society could afford the personnel required by such an approach. Yet, we have until recently moved more and more in the direction of professionalizing support services and making each individual less and less capable of helping himself.

Under the guise of technicians "knowing best," we give individuals little if any say about governing their own health, their health care expenditures, or the institutions that serve them.[32]

*Consumer control.* Consumer control of health care institutions is an educational tool and a means of introducing social direction above technical imperatives. It is the only real means of forcing attention on unsatisfactory utilization and the barriers to improvement. Consumer control offers the place and circumstances where the nonusers, the overusers, and the mal-users can be identified and efforts made to reach them and their problems with a sufficient diversity of resources.

*Self-help.* The self-help principle [33] extends from the governance level to health promotion and to the care process itself. The maiming and killing diseases of our times will only respond directly to changes in our dietary, smoking, drinking, recreational, and driving habits and indirectly to our ecologic and social behavior brought on in response to our environment. The front-line, first-point-of-contact, or well-being centers have to learn how to attract their subscribers while they are well to participate in what might be called "personal and social survival wisdom." [34]

*Share-care.* The caring attendant on illness must also be shared by the client. Otherwise, he will continue the insane practice of paying for care and then undoing it by failing to have his prescriptions filled, or to take them. He has to become a real partner who can express his misgivings, fears, or miscomprehension and know that he will be respected for his honesty in revealing his feelings. He has to know that consumers control the caring system if he is going to work with the carers.

---

[32] Ivan Illich, *Celebration of Awareness: a Call for Institutional Revolution* (Garden City, N.Y.: Doubleday, 1971); Ivan Illich, *Deschooling Society* (New York: Harper and Row, 1970).

[33] Walter S. Strode, "Primary Care and a Changing Medical Model" (Honolulu: Strode Clinic, 1973).

[34] Jonas Salk, *The Survival of the Wisest* (New York: Harper and Row, 1973).

*Volunteers.* A client's involvement in helping others as a volunteer at home or in the center will help him understand his own needs as well as bring outreach, translation service, and support for the needs of other clients.

Future professionals recruited from such health care environments, and receiving much of their training in such settings, should on their employment be able to raise the mutually supportive ambience of an environment that is built on client governance, self-help, and share-care with technically and socially competent professionals. Such centers have been hypothesized and some are now in existence.[35]

## THE NEED FOR COMPREHENSIVE, PREPAID CARE SYSTEMS

The sustained growth and evident over-all consumer satisfaction with prepaid, comprehensive, health care programs that offer primary, secondary, and tertiary services despite generalized medical opposition has led to the HMO act of 1973 (P.L. 93-222). In spite of its unrealistic premises, it probably was the opening wedge for giving every person in the United States the opportunity to be covered by such a system. In fact, the Health Planning and Resources Development Act of 1974 (P.L. 93-641) and the "Executive Summary of the Forward Plan for Health for FY 1976–1980" from HEW (1974) indicate that every citizen is indeed going to have an opportunity to escape the jungle of piecemeal services and financing in the near future.[36] Similar expectations have been faced elsewhere in the world and in many cases have been met.[37]

The kind of caring system that encompasses the consumer and provides partnering in psychic, somatic, and social sup-

[35] Seymour S. Bellin and Jack H. Geiger, "Actual Public Acceptance of the Neighborhood Health Center by the Urban Poor," *Journal of the American Medical Association*, CCXIV (1970), 2147–53; Blum, "The Multipurpose Worker . . ."; Marc Lalonde, *A New Perspective on the Health of Canadians* (Ottawa: Government of Canada, 1974); La Santé, "Rapport de la commission d'equete sur la sante et la bien-être social, gouvernment du Quebec (1970); McCleod, *op. cit.*

[36] Leopold, *op. cit.*; Roemer *et al.*, *op. cit.*, *Planning Urban Health Services: from Jungle to System*.

[37] Hastings, *op. cit.*; McCleod, *op. cit.*; Roemer *et al.*, *op. cit.*

port services is also one that must operate under a public policy umbrella. It also has to respond to publicly developed policy and laws, be under public agency evaluation and planning, and under public agency inspection and control.[38] This seems to be the only plausible approach to an industry which in no way responds to the so-called "market place." [39]

[38] Blum, *Planning for Health*, Chap. 7.
[39] Kenneth Arrow, "The Welfare Economics of Medical Care," in H. M. Cooper and Arthur J. Culyer, *Health Economics* (Harmondsworth, England: Penguin Books, 1973), pp. 13–48; Arthur J. Culyer, "Is Medical Care Different?" in *ibid.*, pp. 49—74; Victor Fuchs, "Health Care and the U.S. Economic System: an Essay in Abnormal Physiology," *Milbank Memorial Fund Quarterly*, L (1972), 211–37.

# Protection of Privacy and
# Fair Information Practices[1]

## JOHN P. FANNING

THE DEPARTMENT OF HEALTH, Education, and Welfare (HEW) has been centrally involved in the over-all federal effort on behalf of fair information practice in personal data record-keeping. In 1971, former HEW Secretary Elliot L. Richardson appointed an Advisory Committee on Automated Personal Data Systems, which was given a mandate to study the problems arising from the application of computer technology to record-keeping about individuals. The Committee completed its report in 1973, and it was released by Secretary Caspar Weinberger. The basic concepts developed in this report, *Records, Computers, and the Rights of Citizens,* are being used within the federal government to understand and deal with a wide variety of issues in record-keeping and personal privacy beyond those springing directly from the impact of computerization.

Late in 1974 Congress passed and President Ford signed the Privacy Act of 1974 (P.L. 93-579). One portion of this act establishes a set of rights for individuals with respect to individually identifiable data about them maintained by the federal government. This act embodies the major principles of the recommendations in the HEW advisory committee report. This portion of the act goes into effect on September

JOHN P. FANNING is Director, Task Force on Health and Medical Records, Office of the Assistant Secretary for Health, U.S. Department of Health, Education, and Welfare, Rockville, Md.
[1] The opinions expressed in this paper are those of the author and are not necessarily expressions of policy of the U.S. Department of Health, Education, and Welfare.

27, 1975. (Other portions of the act establish a Privacy Protection Study Commission to study the issue further, with particular attention to the question of applying the principles of the Privacy Act to information systems not affected by the act. Another element of the act is a restriction on the use of the Social Security number by federal, state, and local government agencies.)

The Domestic Council Committee on the Right of Privacy, established in February, 1974, under the chairmanship of then Vice-President Ford, has launched a series of initiatives to further refine and focus federal activities in the area of privacy. One of its projects, assigned to HEW, is to develop recommendations for the application of fair information practice principles to health and medical record-keeping. The task coincides with the obligations, under the Privacy Act, to apply such principles to all federal data systems, and the department's own commitment to apply the principles to all record-keeping which it can reach, such as the activities of grantees and of service providers compensated under third-party payment programs. It is anticipated that the recommendations of the HEW task force on this subject will be available in late 1975.

All these various efforts are to apply the principles of "fair information practice" to record-keeping and use. These principles spring from, and are designed to implement the concept of, "mutuality." Collection and use of information inevitably involve some sort of interaction between the data subject and the data user. Abuses of data can occur when the data user arrogates to himself the exclusive power to decide when and for what purposes information will be used. The concept of mutuality in data use stresses the data subject's participation in deciding how information pertaining to him will be used. In setting forth mutuality as a basis for dealing with data, we hope to provide a more positive theoretical base for making decisions about data than one of mere secrecy or concealment. Traditional approaches to medical data have been ones of simple confidentiality—concealment—and of professional judgment about what may be revealed about patients.

The demands for information created by new and complex systems of medical care, together with the increasing sophistication of the consumers of medical care, make imperative a flexible, subject-centered approach to the handling of data. An approach based simply on confidentiality is not functional in a situation where more and more persons and institutions need data about patients for legitimate purposes connected with the well-being of the data subjects and of society generally. A brittle insistence on secrecy will either thwart patient care and medical research, or fail completely to protect the rights of individuals by reason of its unrealistic demands. An approach based on subject involvement provides a basis for the data transfers necessary in new complex systems of care, while assuring that the data transfers do not harm the individual through either deliberate misuse of data or through uncontrolled, system-serving dissemination.

The code of fair information practice which we see as assuring this mutuality has essentially five components:

1. There should be no personal record-keeping system whose existence is secret.

2. There must be a means by which an individual can find out what information about him is in a record and how it is used.

3. Perhaps the most basic element is that there must be a way for an individual to prevent information about him that was obtained for one purpose from being used or made available for other purposes without his consent.

4. An individual must be able to correct or amend a record of information about himself.

5. Finally, any organization creating, maintaining, using, or disseminating records containing personal information must assure the reliability of data for their intended use and must take precautions to prevent misuse of the data.

The application of these principles to medical record-keeping (or any other kind of record-keeping) is not a simple, automatic process. The principles provide a framework, but are not meant to answer many of the substantive questions dealing with the use of data. That is left, even under the Privacy Act in many instances, to decision, legislatively or administratively, in the context of specific types of records. For example, the requirement that there be a way for an individual to prevent information about him obtained for one purpose from being used for other purposes without his consent is not conceived as absolute. The data subject involvement in decisions about use of data need not be on an individual basis. Participation may be on a general societal level, as in the statutory establishment of requirements for transfer of data. We are still left with many difficult questions, which must be resolved either generally or on a case-by-case basis, in light of principles appropriate to the type of record under discussion. For example, the desire to encourage healing by making it safe to discuss one's condition with a physician without fear of disclosure is a strong basis for the general rule of medical confidentiality. At the same time, the societal interest in preventing the spread of illness, or in preventing the abuse of children by their parents, does support such requirements as those for the reporting of communicable diseases and suspected child abuse without regard to the desires of the individuals involved. The mutuality in the latter instances is obviously of a very different character from that in the more routine medical situation, and does involve a governmental decision to act without an individual's consent in matters affecting him. (Even in instances of obligatory data transfer, awareness by the data subject of course remains a crucial requirement which serves his need for involvement as best it can be served in such a situation.)

On the other hand, the requirement for the subject's consent in certain instances of data transfer cannot be seen as solving the entire issue of mutuality. Not every consent is evidence of complete mutuality, and decisions about the value of consent must also be made with an eye to the specific issue involved. A consent to use of data which is effectively forced because it is necessary to obtain a needed service (medical care, generally) or enrollment in a payment program (health insurance), or reimbursement under a payment program (private health insurance, Medicare, or Medicaid) is not necessarily bad, but it does present certain problems, and is perhaps more realistically handled if we see it as an aspect of obligatory data transfer.

Thus, some of the basic issues about the use of data remain to be solved, on a wide policy basis, or on a system-by-system basis, or on a case-by-case basis. The concept of mutuality, and its policy offspring such as the Privacy Act of 1974, is an important beginning point for substantive decisions about the use of information about individuals, and a good reference point when it comes time to make decisions. But it merely provides the framework.

I suggest that the framework is one which is most appropriate for the handling of medical information in its acknowledgement of the paramount role of the individual in the decisions about use of data.

Many particular demands for confidentiality that are needed in individual fields, such as health and medical records of all kinds, must be asserted constantly. The need for transfer of data must be examined and documented. The visibility provided by the Federal Privacy Act and the principles of mutuality generally aids this process. In particular, the demands for accountability with respect to the need for, and quality and cost of, medical care create special data needs. The specifics of these needs must be looked at carefully. There can be no question of the need for accounting for individual health expenditures under public payment programs such as Medicaid and private health insurance programs. But we must look hard at the particular data needs in all of these instances. Is each patient's name really necessary? Conventionally, of course, it is. But are there not other techniques for determining whether payment has been made properly? Is sampling of no value? What about exchanges of data for serving individuals? Is the subject of the data part of the process? Is the data transferred truly necessary to the decision involved? These are issues that must be worked out for each use of data.

Uses for research must be examined from the same perspective. Our framework allows several approaches. The use of treatment data for research can be seen as another use for which individual, specific consent must be obtained in each instance. At the same time, it is possible to make research uses of a record as basic as treatment uses, and avoid obtaining individual consent for each use. Under the Privacy Act, the subject must be informed of such uses, and an accounting kept of the disclosures. The framework to involve the data subject is there; it still must be decided how this particular use is to be handled within this framework. It is entirely possible that we will feel comfortable in some instances in making data more available than it was before. The notice and accountability assure a data subject involvement that can make us more flexible in permitting the use of records about individuals.

We think the basic concept and the principles of fair information practice are useful at any level of decision-making about data. Full implementation of such an approach requires a statutory base, with penalties for data transfers and other behavior not in conformance with the principles, as is found in the Privacy Act. However, the principles are a good starting point for making decisions about policy at the level of the service-providing agency.

In conclusion, it might be good to note again that "starting point" is the right description for the concept of mutuality and the principles of fair information practice. The concern for the confidentiality of personal information that has characterized the medical and social work professions must be asserted continually to assure that decisions about the use of data are based on the values of freedom and autonomy that we cherish. It is to be hoped that the framework provided by the principles of fair information practice and legislation implementing the principles will make it easier to make such decisions.

# Transition from Mental Hospital to Community

STEVEN P. SEGAL
and
URI AVIRAM

$D$URING THE PAST twenty years the population of state mental hospitals throughout the country has been declining. The responsibility for care of the mentally ill is moving into the local community. In California, the community is now the locus of service effort. Yet, one must observe that there has been little change in the needs of the mentally ill population. Although we must be aware of the problems of defining mental illness and measuring its rate in the population,[1] it seems that the incidence of psychosis in the eighteen to sixty-five age group has not varied in the past century.[2] We have found no miraculous cure for this disorder. Though the introduction of psychoactive drugs has been credited for enabling a community care emphasis, the decline in the hospital population began before the introduction of these medications,[3] and there have been successful

STEVEN P. SEGAL is Assistant Professor and Cochairman, CMH Sequence, School of Social Welfare, University of California, Berkeley. Dr. URI AVIRAM is a Lecturer, School of Social Work, and Head of CMH Program, Tel-Aviv University, Israel. This project was supported by the California State Department of Health and the National Institute of Mental Health.

[1] Bruce Dohrenwend and Barbara Dohrenwend, "The Problem of Validity in Field Studies of Psychological Disorder," *Journal of Abnormal Psychology*, LXX (1965), 52–69.

[2] Herbert Goldhammer and Andrew Marshall, *Psychosis and Civilization* (New York: Free Press, 1953).

[3] George Brown, "Length of Hospital Stay and Schizophrenia: a Review of Statistical Studies, *Acta Psychiatrica Scandinavica*, XXXV (1960), 414–30.

community care efforts carried on without drugs.[4] It therefore seems reasonable to conclude that while the needs of the
mentally ill have not changed, what has changed is our perception of how these needs might best, or at least more economically, be met.

The necessity for a sheltered living arrangement has not
disappeared with the closure of some state hospitals. In fact,
a full third of the formerly mentally ill living in sheltered
care in California have not been institutionalized in the sense
of being socialized into a state hospital life style but were admitted to the state hospital system following the passage of
the Lanterman-Petris-Short legislation in 1969 and have
stayed short periods of time in a hospital environment. Their
primary experience, therefore, has been in community-based
sheltered care facilities.

Glasscote, Gudeman, and Elpers define "halfway house" in
terms which are broad enough to encompass all types of sheltered care living arrangements:

A halfway house for the mentally ill is a non-medical residential facility specifically intended to enhance the capabilities of people who
are mentally ill, or who are impaired by residuals of or deficits
from mental illness, to remain in the community, participating to
the fullest possible extent in community life.[5]

While these authors looked only at halfway houses, our
research group studied the total system of sheltered care facilities which has developed in California in the past thirteen
years. Facilities in this system include not only professionally
operated halfway houses and certified family care homes but
also former boarding houses, old hotels, converted apart-
ment buildings, expanded single-family homes, and other
types of living arrangements which have come to provide
board and care to the released hospital patient.

Our study involved a sample census of all nonretarded individuals with a past history of mental illness between the

---

[4] Loren Mosher, "Soteria: an Alternative to Hospitalization for Schizophrenia,"
paper delivered at National Institute of Health Conference, 1974 (mimeo.).
[5] Raymond Glasscote, Jon Gudeman, and J. Richard Elpers, *Halfway Houses for the
Mentally Ill* (Washington, D.C.: Joint Information Service, 1971), p. 11.

ages of eighteen and sixty-five living in sheltered care facilities in California. Interviews were conducted with 499 residents and the operators of the 234 facilities in which they lived. The results indicate that sheltered care, at least in the foreseeable future, is here to stay and along with it a set of five major issues which, as much as we try to ignore them, continue to be of primary importance.

1. Should we focus our help on the traditional categorically defined patient groups or emphasize the necessity to provide residential care for all socially dependent groups?

2. Should we emphasize rehabilitation or the prevention of social deterioration?

3. Whose rights have priority—the former patient or the community?

4. How do we insure the individual's right to treatment, not merely maintenance, in the community?

5. How do we take up the responsibility to insure, or even begin to assess, quality care in community facilities?

1. *Traditional categorical need as compared to the needs of the socially dependent.* At issue is whether there should be joint care of the mentally ill, mentally retarded, aged, drug abuser, physically handicapped, and other traditional categories of clientele under the same roof, as part of a generalized, socially independent population.

The sheltered care service system in California was only in part developed to provide traditional categorical care. Primarily, it developed in an *ad hoc* fashion to serve the socially dependent as an aggregate. Glasscote and his colleagues in a nationwide sample found that only 47 percent of the halfway houses they studied catered solely to the mentally ill.[6] Our study results indicate that in California approximately 68 percent of the facilities now serving the mentally ill also serve other groups, such as alcoholics, mentally retarded, dependent aged, and transients, on more than an occasional basis. As a general policy such care represents a return to the poorhouse approach, emphasizing aggregate care for all those unable to "make it" in our society.

[6] *Ibid.,* p. 15.

In this situation it is not simply a choice between a negative labeling process and a beneficial shedding of a stereotype. We are, in fact, exchanging one label for another—"mental illness" for "totally disabled"—or, perhaps worse, burdening the individual with the negative stereotypes associated with several labels. The public reaction could well be to generalize all the negative characteristics associated with the categorical groups in a given facility to each individual in the facility. This seems to be the situation in San Jose, California. Moving from the traditional categorical approach to the current situation limits the application of specific helping strategies to specific groups by submerging their special needs in the more general and variable needs of the larger group.

2. *Social rehabilitation as compared to preventing social deterioration.* At issue is the emphasis placed on reintegrating the former mental patient into the community and the practicality of such a goal, considering the extensive social and psychological handicaps of this group.

In an achievement-oriented society, it is difficult to focus on the goal of preventing deterioration. Success is "movement," and work with the chronically mentally ill—the primary mandate of the psychiatric social worker—is perhaps less rewarding because of what appears to be client intransigence or, at best, limited movement. The basic problem is that in order to be rehabilitated one must first be habilitated.

Our data raise serious question as to whether the residents in our sample were ever qualified participants in society. Almost half of the population of concern are between fifty and sixty-five years of age, and 59.8 percent have never been married. One third have never had steady employment for a year or more. In addition, the level of psychological disturbance was found to be a significant handicap in current social interaction. Given this population, a selective use of the rehabilitation model seems more realistic and an emphasis on preventing further deterioration, crucial.

3. *Individual or community protection.* At issue is the current emphasis on protecting the rights of the former mental pa-

tient versus community fear of sickly people. How real *is* the danger posed by what one newspaper called "a mass invasion of mental patients"?

In the past five years communities throughout the country have reacted strongly to the influx of former mental patients. Community reaction has primarily focused on the most visible members of the group—those individuals living in sheltered care. While few communities have gone so far as Long Beach, New York—passing an ordinance which in effect bars former mental patients from registering in local hotels—zoning ordinances, fire clearance regulations, and bureaucratic stalling have been employed as effective exclusionary devices throughout California.[7] One rationale for these procedures is the threat to property values perceived as a result of locating community care facilities in a given neighborhood. In fact, those neighborhoods which have actually experienced a large influx of community care facilities were already in a stage of decline, and the addition of a single community care facility has not depressed prices in high property value areas. This rationale for excluding the sheltered care facility, however, seems to be of only secondary importance in the community's fear of the mentally ill.

The popular conception of the mentally ill is the "raving maniac" whose acts have no rational basis and are, therefore, unpredictable.[8] Such unpredictable individuals are viewed as always posing a potential threat. While it is realized that questioning the validity of this stereotype will have only minimal impact in changing behavior, it is important because the stereotype is used to justify continued denial of patient rights.

The evidence comparing violent crime in the released hospital population with violent crime in the general population is equivocal. Although a recent study in California found

[7] Uri Aviram and Steven P. Segal, "Exclusion of the Mentally Ill: Reflection of an Old Problem in a New Context," *Archives of General Psychiatry*, XXIX (1973), 126–31.

[8] Shirley Starr, "The Public's Ideas about Mental Illness," paper delivered at Annual Meeting of the National Association of Mental Health, 1955.

higher conviction rates in the total released patient population than in the general population,[9] previous reports have indicated little difference between the two groups, or a lower rate in the released patient group.[10] One finding, however, consistent in all these studies, is that the older people in both groups have the lowest rates of violent crime. This is significant in that almost half the adult, nonaged residents in sheltered care are between fifty and sixty-five years of age. These facts indicate that the community's fear of the sheltered care resident is misdirected. If any released patients pose a serious threat to the community, it is those who "fall through the cracks," who are so disintegrated that they are unable to establish themselves in a more settled sheltered care environment. Yet, even if these individuals were in sheltered care, our current ability to predict "dangerous behavior" would hardly justify their involuntary detention over a long period of time. Even though the best known predictor of the commission of a violent act is the threat of such an act, McDonald found that out of 100 "threat-to-kill" admissions to a Colorado Psychopathic Hospital, only three patients eventually took the lives of others and four committed suicide.[11] This represents only a 9 percent accuracy rate in predicting violent behavior. We wonder if the results would have been much different had he studied serious "threats to kill" among the so-called "normal" population.

Thus the continued peremptory exclusion of sheltered care facilities from residential zones in violation of state law has dubious justification. While the community is entitled to protection, such protection cannot be guaranteed at the expense of the civil liberties of the released patient population.

[9] Larry Sososky, "Putting State Mental Hospitals Out of Business— the Community Approach to Treating Mental Illness in San Mateo County" (Berkeley, Calif.; University of California Graduate School of Public Policy, 1975; mimeo.).

[10] George Gulevich and Peter Bourne, "Mental Illness and Violence," in David Daniels, Marshall Gilula, and Frank Ochberg, eds. *Violence and the Struggle for Existence* (Boston: Little, Brown and Co., 1970), pp. 309–27.

[11] John McDonald, "Homicidal Threats," *American Journal of Psychiatry*, CXXIV, No. 4 (1967), 475–82.

4. *Right to treatment.* At issue is the right of the formerly hospitalized patient in a sheltered care facility to receive treatment on the same basis as any other member of the community, as opposed to relying on a separate treatment system to meet his needs.

The *Wyatt* vs. *Stickney* (Civil Action No. 3195 N.M.D.) decision in Alabama and similar court rulings have emphasized the right of the chronic hospital patient to receive treatment in state hospitals and have defined this right in terms of improved institutional financing and patient-staff ratios. Although there was a precipitous transfer of patients to community care placement following this decision, community care rather than hospital care does not change the treatment needs of these individuals; on the contrary, it raises additional problems in providing care. The degree of psychological disturbance found in our surveyed population emphasizes the necessity for treatment of a more interpersonal nature than mere supervision of medication.

The first problem in the provision of community-oriented treatment programs is that hospital programs are competing with community care programs at a time when resources are becoming tighter; [12] in other words, is it to be institutional treatment or community treatment? By institutional treatment we mean the development of self-contained treatment facilities in local areas—chronic "mini" hospitals similar to those which have developed in Wisconsin in the past hundred years. By community treatment, we mean a system to meet the treatment needs of individuals in sheltered care on an outpatient basis in the same fashion as the needs of other community members are met. In this type of system the hospital would be used more directly as a "prosthetic" device.

The pressures mounting around attempts to provide community treatment are well illustrated by the effort of the

[12] Charles Cleland and Gary Sluyter, "The Alabama Decision: Unequivocal Blessing?" *Community Mental Health Journal*, X, No. 4 (1974) 409–13.

Hoch Psychiatric Treatment Center in Long Beach, New York, to provide outpatient care in a central location. According to the physician in charge of the aftercare unit, this effort was blocked by community interest groups who wanted psychiatric care to be provided in the facilities where released patients lived. Such an approach can result in the creation of a small hospital within the community and raises question about how services can be offered in the small facility. If the resident has a "right to treatment," will this force the small facility out of existence or lead, perhaps, to a "home visit" type of treatment? At least one demonstration project providing services to the aged in small facilities is currently underway in California. One must question whether this type of service delivery enhances a sense of exclusion and apartness. If former patients are to live in the community, they should not have to sneak in the back door of the local community mental health center.

5. *Assessment of quality care in community facilities.* At issue is the ability of the community and its state representatives to monitor the quality of care in the sheltered care facility system. In the past we have failed to maintain a high level of care in a small number of state hospitals in California. How can we expect, even with a licensing system, to assess and insure the quality of care in more than a thousand community facilities?

A partial solution to this problem is currently built into the sheltered care system. Although it has not been so named, since the enactment of the 1963 California welfare regulations, a voucher system for the provision of sheltered care to the adult socially dependent population has been in effect. The Supplemental Security Income check at the special board and care payment rate is the sheltered care resident's voucher. In theory, though not in practice, he acts in a consumer role in choosing his residence. Unlike a cash grant, the level of payment to the resident is tied to the use of a specific service and is reduced accordingly when it is determined that the resident is no longer in need of this service. This type of organization rests on the implicit assumption that an approximation of a free-market economy will develop whereby low-quality service providers will be forced out of the market. The free-market concept, however, is a fragile one and needs safeguards built in to protect its functioning. In the case of the former mental patient, these safeguards can, perhaps, most effectively be exercised by service providers who have already adopted the role of resident advocate—for example, the placement workers. An even more desirable addition, of course, is the development of an active consumer organization among the residents themselves.

The need to structure consumer input as a safeguard in a voucher system is particularly important when the individual concerned is both the commodity and the consumer; that is, both an object of barter and the recipient of a service. The extent to which an individual adopts the recipient role is determined by his level of participation in the decision-making process relating to his care. Yet here we face a situation where the resident is powerless in terms of his ability to organize, in terms of his dependence on the facility operator and other service providers, and in terms of his lack of funds to invest in consumer activity. Given these obstacles, patient organizations to act as third-party participants in the negotiations between a resident and his service providers are needed. Implementing or at minimum supporting this participative action is crucial in order to enhance the resident's role as a community participant and to insure higher quality care.

SOCIAL WORK AND THE SHELTERED CARE SERVICE SYSTEM

In its role as a provider of service to the released mental hospital patient, social work occupies a unique position—a position which can be central in making the community care system a constructive step forward. As the primary placement officers, social workers have a strong influence on the referral system. In encouraging a resident to take a more active role in choosing facilities and in maximizing their information on facility vacancies, the social worker can begin to exercise effective sanctions against poor-quality facilities. Such a strategy, however, will not be effective in a system where there is a lack of facility placements. Social workers must therefore, in addition, promote laws to attract new facilities into the market to provide a choice among available beds.

There currently is empirical evidence supporting the utility of hospital-based social work service in reducing the community burden and enhancing patient outcome.[13] In an effective community-based service, social workers must join with their clients in a facilitative role to maximize the fit between facility characteristics and resident need, to prevent the resident's social deterioration, and to insure the individual's right to treatment. Such action will result in less community burden, less justification for the social exclusion of this population, and more assurance of a continued emphasis on the civil liberties of former patients.

[13] Jacquelin Grad, "A Two-Year Follow-up," in Richard Williams and Lucy Ozarin, eds. *Community Mental Health: an International Perspective* (San Francisco: Jossey-Bass, Inc., 1968), pp. 429–54.

# Darlings, We Are Growing Old

## HARRIET MILLER

It was in the 1870s that the American composer Hart Danks bought a handful of poems from a Wisconsin farm magazine editor for three dollars a piece. The one he decided to set to music was "Silver Threads among the Gold," with its repeated refrain of "Darling, I am growing old."

Now, a century later, more and more Americans are, indeed, "growing old." Both the numbers and proportions of older people in the American population have been increasing steadily since records were first kept, but the increase has been most rapid in this century. In 1900, some 3 million Americans were age sixty-five or over, representing 4 percent of the total population. Today the number is more than 21 million. They now represent 10 percent of the population. In this century the proportion of older people in the total population has increased two and one-half times. The 1970 census found that nearly 7 million Americans were seventy-five or older and that more than a million were eighty-five or over.[1] Within the next fifty years, the number of Americans in the sixty-five-and-over group will have doubled to more than 40 million.

It is estimated that at any given time as many as 12 percent of the older population, more than a quarter of a million persons, are in need of supportive services for their major

HARRIET MILLER is a board member, National Council for Homemaker-Home Health Aide Services, Inc.
[1] James D. Manney, Jr., *Aging in American Society* (Ann Arbor: Mich.: Institute of Gerontology, University of Michigan-Wayne State University, 1975) pp. 54–55.

daily activities. Among low-income groups the proportion is probably 20 percent.[2]

So, there we have it. More of us are growing older, more of us *will* be old, and a significant number of us will need help to carry on our daily lives. What kind of help will we receive? Will we receive the kind and quality of supportive services we will want and need? An article in *Modern Maturity* has this to say:

Older patients often stay in the hospital longer than is medically necessary. Often they go to a nursing home instead of going home. The reason: they cannot receive adequate care at home. This is particularly the case with older patients who live alone or with a spouse who is unable to care for them properly. They are not acutely ill, but they may need to receive an injection once a day, have a bandage changed or receive weekly physical therapy. Or they may simply require help in taking a bath, preparing meals or performing general housekeeping chores.

A government study shows that 25% of patients in hospitals and nursing homes are being treated in facilities that provide a higher level of care than they need.[3]

This is not to say that hospitals and other out-of-home facilities should be done away with. They are indispensable for those who need them. But because they *are* indispensable we must make sure that the care provided within institutional walls is compassionate, humane, and skilled. What is wrong, however, very wrong, is that each year between one-quarter and one-half million men and women end up in costly institutions for reasons *other* than medical care. A quarter to a half of the $2 billion spent each year for nursing home care is spent for patients who have no medical reason for being in a nursing home.[4]

Why are they there, then? They are people who *do* need help, who are frail, perhaps, or who have various infirmities

[2] Louis E. Gelwicks and Robert J. Newcomer, *Planning Housing Environments for the Elderly,* (Washington, D.C.: National Council on the Aging, Inc., 1974), p. 16.
[3] Cyril F. Brickfield, "Why Not Go Home?" *Modern Maturity,* February–March, 1975, p. 30.
[4] Robert Morris, "Alternatives to Nursing Home Care: a Proposal," prepared for Special Committee on Aging, U.S. Senate, 1971, pp. 5, 7.

which prevent them from getting out to shop for groceries or from performing the other necessary routines of daily living. Often all these older persons need is just a little help, someone to shop, to help with the meals and with the household tasks on a part-time basis.

It is easy to understand that most people prefer to live in their own homes and to continue to be as independent as possible. For some, perhaps, the opportunities for socialization in a congregate living arrangement may be appealing, but socializing opportunities can be made available outside institutions, too.

The National Council for Homemaker-Home Health Aide Services receives many letters from older people, and from others on their behalf, pleading for the kind of help which will allow them to remain in their own homes. It is not much to ask—or to give—to allow an older person to remain in his own home in dignity and safety. Such services provided to older people in their own homes are available in many communities, but they are *not* available in most.

It is the goal of the Council to have services available in *every* community in the nation, for people in all economic brackets, who may need them at some time in their lives. In pursuit of this goal the Council is implementing the first phase of a national advocacy project aimed at developing and expanding homemaker-home health aide and supplementary services for all age groups while affording older persons new volunteer and career opportunities.

Unfortunately, money is much more readily available today for services that take people out of their homes than it is for those which help them to remain at home. Less than one percent of all the dollars paid out under Medicare and less than one half of one percent paid under Medicaid go for home health services. Our laws (and the regulations which implement them) are heavily slanted toward institutional care. That this should be so is downright strange when one considers that our national policy, as voiced by our national leaders, is a commitment to the dignity and worth of every individual and to policies at all levels of our national life which will permit each individual the right of choice as to how and where he shall live.

At the 1961 White House Conference on Aging, the delegates said: "The need to expand institutional facilities should not discourage noninstitutional alternatives, particularly treating the individual in his own home." Ten years later, President Richard Nixon told the 1971 White House Conference on Aging: "The greatest need is to help more older Americans to go on living in their own homes."

The statements are clear, but the program decisions currently on the books give them a hollow ring. Without enabling legislation, regulations, and, above all, adequate funds, the services to prevent or postpone institutional care simply do not and cannot exist in anywhere near the numbers required to meet the need.

How many older Americans *do* need such services? This question was answered in an introductory report prepared by the subcommittee on Long-Term Care of the Senate Special Committee on Aging:

Agnes Brewster, consultant for the Senate Committee on Aging, estimates that 2.6 million individuals over 65 need in-home services; 300,000 who are now in institutions and another 2.3 million in the community.

Commenting on this report, Elaine Brody of the Philadelphia Geriatrics Center characterized the 2.6 million figure as an understatement. Ethel Shanas, professor of sociology at the University of Illinois, arrived at a figure of 4 million home health beneficiaries by adding the institutionalized, bedfast, homebound and those who walk with difficulty. By this estimate, one out of every five older Americans is a potential candidate for home care.[5]

The Senate committee report concludes that:

There is no firm national policy with respect to alternatives to institutionalization. Home health care receives a very low priority in the United States. . . . This glaring lack of policy is all the more

[5] "Nursing Home Care in the United States: Failure in Public Policy," introductory report, December, 1974, pp. 58–59.

evident when American health delivery services are compared with some European systems where home health is a full partner in a genuine continuum of care.

One result of this failure is that the United States does not take advantage of the significant cost savings inherent in a viable home health program.[6]

The concept of a "continuum of care" *includes* institutional care when it is needed; *includes* congregate living when that is the arrangement of choice, and for many it is; *includes* day-care facilities; *includes* recreational and socialization opportunities; *includes* a whole variety of community supports. But the most important single characteristic in a genuine continuum of care is that it does not lock the individual into any single mode of care when that mode is no longer appropriate to his needs.

The American Nurses' Association Task Force on Options for Health Care Services has put it very well:

In-home services must be developed as a network of many community services, health, social and supportive. . . . The network must allow freedom of movement back and forth between facilities, hospital and home. . . . Planning for these services should be accomplished by a consortium of the total community: consumers of service, third-party payers, providers, planners, industry and government.[7]

Here is one innovative example of the kind of service which can be provided to allow for that freedom of movement. Montefiore Hospital in New York City has experimented successfully with the use of a minibus capable of transporting from four to six persons in their wheel-chairs from their homes to the hospital to receive occasional specific services. During these visits the patients may receive physical, occupational, recreational, or speech therapy and they have access to physicians, nurses, social workers, podiatrists, laboratory examinations, beauty or barbershop services, and the

[6] *Ibid.,* p. 64.
[7] Report of Task Force Sub-group on In-Home Services presented to Committee on Skilled Nursing Care, American Nurses' Association, 1974.

library. The hospital estimates that at least half of the patients cared for at home could participate in this program.
Of course, the basic services needed by the bedfast, the
homebound, and those whose mobility is seriously limited are
provided in their own homes. One interesting "fall-out" development is that many patients on a low priority for physical
therapy who had not received it at home are now able to get
it through this program of hospital visits.

The construction and sound operation of a genuinely comprehensive health care system calls for a high degree of commitment, and intrasystem cooperation; a good deal of management sophistication, and the absolute conviction that
there must be a rational balance between in-home and out-
of-home care.

Dr. Philip G. Weiler suggests that our health care system is
geared essentially to acute-care problems and that although
we are spending nearly $16 billion on health services to the
aging, our efforts may be counterproductive. He estimates
that for 25 percent to 50 percent of the people the institutional setting is inappropriate and/or detrimental.[8] He also
says that because we are almost entirely locked into the acute-
care model, "health services have been provided for the elderly as though these were their dominant need." [9] Of
course the elderly do sometimes become acutely ill, but 80
percent of them have chronic problems which call for long-
term rather than short-term care.

Dr. Weiler calls for a fundamental strategy of long-term
health care for the aged in a continuum of services: residential services (room and board); personal support services
which include care for chronic ailments, geriatric nursing
supervision, intermittent technical nursing services, psychosocial activities, and assistance with daily living; as well as
medical, dental, and psychiatric services when needed. "Pri-

[8] Philip G. Weiler, M.D., "Cost Effective Analysis: a Quandary for Geriatric
Health Care Systems," paper delivered at annual meeting of the Gerontological Society, 1973; printed in *The Gerontologist,* October, 1974, pp. 414–17.
[9] *Ibid.,* p. 415.

mary emphasis must be on strengthening the patient's potential to function in the social, professional and family spheres of his life." [10]

The Council also proposed the continuum of services concept in its testimony on national health insurance. Without acceptance of this over-all concept of health care it is doubtful that homemaker-home health aide service will ever be accorded its proper role in the health delivery system of the nation or be used to the maximum of its very considerable potential.

A "right" need not, as some of my legal friends might believe, be enforceable in a court of law. Webster agrees that a "right" is that which belongs to a person by law or by nature or tradition. Under both definitions, home care *is* a right.

What are some of the implications for homemaker-home health aide services to help assure that this right is extended to *all* those elderly persons who wish to remain at home and could if services were available to them? Of course, the first implication is the most obvious one: the number of agencies providing in-home services must increase. The Committee on Home Health Care reported to the Health Insurance Benefits Council on September 10, 1974, that about half of the counties in the nation had *no* home health agencies. Only slightly more than 2,200 home health agencies, including homemaker-home health aide agencies, are certified for Medicare.

As we move to increase the number of services, we must assure from the outset the quality of those services so that we can safeguard the vulnerable. We believe that the following principle must be adopted and implemented: every agency providing home health service or homemaker-home health aide service must have its standards of service reviewed by an objective third party—either governmental or voluntary nonprofit—which is recognized by governmental and other third-party payers.

[10] *Ibid.*, p. 415.

Standard-setting was among the basic charges given to the National Council when it was established by the National Health Council and the National Social Welfare Assembly in 1962. A code of standards was developed in 1965 and in 1972 the Council established a program to approve evaluated homemaker-home health aide programs that complied with the recommended standards.

This is not a program of certification for individuals, but of the entire program of services. This was a decision consciously taken because we do not believe that paraprofessional personnel who care for the most vulnerable of our people ought to be individual entrepreneurs. Rather they are part of a service team, which includes professionals to assess the person's needs, determine the plan of care, and supervise the aides. There are fourteen basic standards for agencies to meet. All are important to the quality of the service provided, but the most crucial are those which require a high quality of training and supervision of the homemaker-home health aides.

We believe that the decision to have the service accountable rather than the individual was a wise one because it provides the best protection against inadequate or inappropriate service. Surveys in San Francisco and Washington, D.C. indicate that agencies providing professional assessment and ongoing case management tend to have lower costs per case although they may have higher costs per hour. Such findings suggest that carefully planned, tailored-to-the need homemaker services are effective in ways that tend to shorten the length of time service is required.[11]

This brings us to still another implication for the service, as we strive to make it readily accessible to all who need it. Having recruited and trained homemakers who will perform the often complicated and sometimes unpleasant tasks required with good will, dedication, and skill, let us value them as full partners in this unique team service. They are the heart and hands of this service which could not function without them.

[11] Eugene B. Shinn and Nancy Day Robinson, "Trends in Homemaker-Home Health Aide Services," *Abstracts for Social Workers*, X, No. 3 (1974) 6.

Personnel policies and benefits accorded to any member of the team should be accorded in equal measure to all. Unfortunately, in some agencies, this is not the practice. And it lowers the quality of the service when there is a constant turnover of aides because their salary and benefits are not commensurate with their responsibilities.

These last implications have dealt with the internal systems of the agency. There are others that have to do with community relationships. Linkages must be formed to connect all agencies providing various kinds of services, or "umbrella" agencies should be formed through which large numbers and varieties of services are available.

Every person must be able to obtain the *kind* of help needed *when* it is needed. This means that the service continuum—from acute-care inpatient services to the essentially nonprofessional in-home services, such as friendly visiting— must have open lines of communication and a steady flow of information to bring about the needed care. Many families and individuals are able to function with the help of a single supplementary service, while others may need several services, often in conjunction with homemaker-home health aide service, to maintain or return to independent living.

The National Council recognizes its special obligation to assist in the development of in-home services and to assure an interlocking relationship between homemaker-home health aide service as a core program and those which can be considered supplementary to it, such as the Meals on Wheels program, help with chores, friendly visitors, telephone reassurance, escort service, shopping services, and transportation. Acting on this concern, in March, 1974, the National Council adopted a policy statement encouraging this trend.

The expansion of in-home services will require additional funds. Since we are all keenly aware that there is no such thing as a continually self-replenishing money tree, we must face the question of where the money is to come from. The answer lies in highly competent community planning so that urgently needed services will be accorded the dollars needed from the supply that *is* available. This may well result in the reallocation of funds according to priorities so that, for instance, some of the vast amounts spent now for institutional care may be spent for in-home care.

Now that the "new federalism" is becoming more and more the style for getting things done, we who care about services for people must increase our involvement at state and local levels where the decision-making process is coming to rest. If state and area agencies on aging, health systems agencies, and state and local social service departments do not recognize the need and make allocations for homemaker-home health aide services, there is very little hope for changing the service *status quo.*

The *status quo,* incidentally, also includes the fact that while some funds are channeled to services for the poor—though, as we all know, not enough and often not in ways that preserve human dignity—it is the middle-income people who find that their home care and supportive services are burdensomely expensive. Third-party payers are needed to help them get the services they need. Unless those who wish this aspect of the system changed will let legislators and the insurance industry (both nonprofit and for profit) know of their concerns, it will be a "frosty Friday in the nether regions" before the needed services are available to all.

Another barrier which we must somehow hurdle is the fact that the training of human service workers today is almost completely institution-oriented. We must mount a concerted campaign to reach nurses, therapists, social workers, physicians, and others during their training periods to instill in them a recognition that there is another way to care for people. This might be accomplished by providing field work placements or a summer work experience in homemaker-home health aide agencies or by conducting orientation courses or planned home visits for health and social service students. While we are educating the coming generation of workers, we must also see to it that those now practicing become aware of the value of services provided to people in their own homes.

Homemaker-home health aide services should also work closely with such consumer groups as associations of retired persons, cancer groups, heart associations, multiple sclerosis societies, and others at all community levels—local, state, and national—so that people who need homemaker-home health aide or other supportive in-home services may know what their options are and what they could be. For instance, the American Cancer Society's board of directors passed a resolution in October, 1974, strongly urging the growth and development of local comprehensive home-care programs for cancer patients. This landmark statement offers an excellent opportunity for follow-up with local chapters of the Society. Opening avenues of communication and interpretation will lead to increased understanding of these services and more service through added funding opportunities.

Let me summarize the actions which must be taken to assure that home care is available as a right.

1. In-home services must be increased.

2. Funding sources, including third-party payers, must be expanded.

3. Objective evaluation and monitoring of the quality of service are essential to safeguard the vulnerable.

4. Increased status and benefits must be assured to all members of the service team, including the paraprofessionals.

5. Cooperative relationships and open lines of communication must be established among all community resources to assure a genuine continuum of services.

6. Supplementary nonprofessional services, complementary to homemaker-home health aide services, must be developed to help older persons remain safely in their own homes.

7. Sound community planning is required to reorder priorities and reallocate funds to reduce overemphasis on institutional care.

8. Middle-income groups, consumer groups, and human services personnel must be informed about the options for care which are, or should be, available.

# Self-Help Groups
# and the Professional Community

## ALFRED H. KATZ

To one who has been interested in self-help phenomena and their relationship to social welfare and health services for many years, the recent surge of professional interest in them is striking and gratifying. Professionals in various fields and disciplines are now discovering the potentials and potency of self-help forms of care and treatment, and coming to realize that "natural" or "spontaneous" support systems have unique values in offering an alternative or adjunct form of helping to the formalized structures of professional agencies and practitioners. Research, which for many years had hardly looked into these phenomena, has now begun to consider different aspects of self-help groups—their history, operations, structure, dynamics; their effects upon member participants and on the professional community. Hardly an issue of a professional journal in social work, psychology, psychiatry, nursing, or other fields appears without some discussion, specialized or general, of self-help groups.

The reasons for this surge of interest are manifold and interactive, but not hard to define. They represent, first, social movement factors arising in response to the perceived failures, exclusions, and discrimination of the larger society: the failure of its institutions to provide nurturance and social support for the needy, the stigmatized, the socially isolated or nonconformist. Then there are professional develop-

ALFRED H. KATZ is Professor of Public Health and Social Welfare, School of Public Health, University of California, Los Angeles.

ments—a convergence of research, practice, and theory in education, psychology, sociology, and medicine—all of which have produced telling evidence for the importance, the value, the indispensability of involving the consumer, the client, the pupil, the patient in his own learning or relearning, and in contributing to decisions about his own destiny. These convergences have resulted in the rediscovery of the self-help form, those natural support systems of peers, relatives, kith and kin, and the like-minded which have existed immemorially but are now especially necessary and salient in a time of much social fragmentation, loss of relatedness, and alienation.

The recent flowering of self-help groups and of professional interest in them, then, is all to the good, but I have several cautions and caveats to convey to those whose interest in them has arisen more recently. My first caution lies in the area of definition; I suggest that in thinking about self-help groups we must be especially self-conscious and sensitive to the social role of professionals and to its implicit elements of social control. To this burgeoning new field there may be applied that tendency in American life which we have come to refer to as co-optation, or, "If you can't lick 'em, join 'em," or, more subtly, "control 'em." We have seen this phenomenon arise in regard to the youth culture, especially in its easily commercialized aspects, such as clothing, music, and food. It would be a tragedy if, arising from a sense of frustration about the possibilities of system change—that is, change in the particular agencies or institutions in which we work—we were to go overboard about the potentials represented by self-help groups on the one hand, or to look on them as merely some form of extension of professionalized service on the other. If from the best motives in the world we look on self-help groups as a kind of adjunct to the professional services that we have tried patiently to construct over the years, and that for whatever reasons target populations do not greet with hosannas of praise or universally use, then it is perhaps natural for us to seek to be the arbiters of *who should join and use self-help groups,* and even of what self-help groups do and how. That this is not a fictitious danger may be gauged by a few quotations from a paper given at the American Orthopsychiatric Association by Dr. Thomas Powell of the University of Michigan School of Social Welfare. In discussing the relationship of professionals to self-help groups Dr. Powell states:

With a client for whom it is important to remain involved with the dominant community and continued treatment with the professional, it is important [for the professional] to weigh carefully the probable effect of affiliation with groups, such as Synanon or various patient liberation groups. Likewise affiliation with a group, such as the Gay Liberation Front (depending on the extent of politicization in the local group), may also tip the balance in favor of opposition to participation in larger community activities including formal human service agencies.[1]

In other words, Dr. Powell believes that professionals should decide for clients whether or not they should participate in self-help groups in which they might be interested. The analysis in his paper is careful, compassionate, and professional in the best sense, and *his* cautions include the possibility that for a client to participate in self-help groups may "magnify the difference" or otherwise "tip the balance" against the client's participation in mainstream "larger community activities." Powell goes on: "Membership in a group like Parents Anonymous, given its built-in feature of a professional sponsor, is likely to strengthen whatever existing inclination there is to participate in treatment."[2] In other words, if a self-help group *does* intensify the likelihood that a particular client will then seek out or participate in professionalized services, then participation in that self-help group is viewed as good and useful. Dr. Powell is thus arrogating to the professional the responsibility for making life decisions for clients in support of values or behaviors which the pro-

---

[1] Thomas J. Powell, "The Use of Self-Help Groups as Supportive Reference Communities," paper presented at annual meeting of the American Orthopsychiatric Association, 1975, p. 3.

[2] *Ibid.,* p. 4.

fessionals judge as useful or constructive for the client. It does not take much sophistication to understand that such a suggestion contravenes quite precisely the very definition of self-help groups, as well as the impulses that led some people to have formed them in the first place and others to join them. These are purely and simply impulses for finding in the like-minded forms of support and nurturance otherwise lacking "in the larger community," including the institutionalized panoply of professional services.

DEFINITION AND ATTRIBUTES OF SELF-HELP GROUPS

Perhaps it will advance this discussion and clarify the picture to quote the definition of self-help groups that Eugene Bender and I employ in our book:

Self-help groups are voluntary, small group structures for mutual aid and the accomplishment of a special purpose. They are usually formed by peers who have come together for mutual assistance in satisfying a common need, overcoming a common handicap or life-disrupting problem, and bringing about desired social and/or personal change. The initiators and members of such groups perceive that their needs are not, or cannot be, met by or through existing social institutions. Self-help groups emphasize face-to-face social interactions and the assumption of personal responsibility by members. They often provide material assistance, as well as emotional support; they are frequently "cause"-oriented, and promulgate an ideology or values through which members may attain an enhanced sense of personal identity.[3]

Please note that self-help groups have several characteristic attributes that flow from this definition:

1. They are patterned small-group or face-to-face interactions.

2. They are spontaneous in origin.

3. They may have a variety of functions and characteristics.

4. There is personal participation. Mere formal membership or financial support (as in belonging to and con-

[3] Alfred H. Katz and Eugene Bender, *The Strength in Us* (New York: Franklin Watts; 1976).

tributing to a conservation or neighborhood improvement group) does not define the individual as a true member or participant.

5. The groups supply a reference group, a point of connection and identification with others, a baseline for activity, a source of ego reinforcement, a value system by which the individual's tasks, joys, sorrows, accomplishments, and frustrations can be evaluated and dealt with.

6. The members agree upon and engage in some actions.

7. Typically, self-help groups start from a condition of powerlessness. No matter what they may later achieve, their initial resources are always limited, and the exercise and control of power are not among their objectives.

DIFFERENCES AMONG GROUPS

These attributes point to a second caution: self-help groups are not all the same. They need to be differentially evaluated and analyzed in order to be understood by professionals, and enthusiasm for them may be tempered thereby. A couple of years ago *Social Work* published a rather rhapsodical article by Dr. Anthony Vattano,[4] which made some rhetorical claims for self-help groups, and in effect put them all in the same box, as representing a form of countercultural protest and a political stance which Vattano broadly classed as "power to the people." But such a claim does not stand a moment's analysis, for example, of the philosophy, values, or internal operations of groups like Alcoholics Anonymous (AA) or Recovery, Inc., two of the largest, most influential, and, in many respects, most useful of the self-help groups organized to serve special categories of needy people. Investigation would have convinced Dr. Vattano that the aim of groups like AA (and its many spin-off "anonymous" groups, such as Narcotics Anonymous, Overeaters Anonymous, Gamblers Anonymous, etc.) is exactly that of assisting their members to conform to the values of the dominant, middle-class society.

[4] Anthony J. Vattano, "Power to the People: Self-Help Groups," *Social Work,* XVII, No. 4 (1972), 7–15.

Their members are viewed as being outside the mainstream of that society because of their particular addiction or behavior problem. To suggest that groups whose major aim is to keep an alcoholic dry, to help obese persons overcome a compulsive food addiction, or to give emotional support to persons who define themselves as "nervous" (the Recovery member) are exponents of "power to the people" is to distort the evidence; the aims of such groups are clearly those of adapting to, and not challenging the values of, the dominant society. As such, in my opinion, they do useful work, but they should hardly be confused with the Black Panthers or Maoist cells.

No, the analysis needs to be sharper than this. We first have to understand the phenomena with which we are dealing in their many-sidedness, and to develop some taxonomies for ordering and classifying them, before we can usefully discuss any of their aspects—whether it be their relationships with professionals, their probable future, their relationship to the "organized society," and so on. In our book,[5] we attempt a fivefold classification of self-help groups as follows:

1. *Groups that are primarily focused on self-fulfillment or personal growth.* These are often referred to by themselves and others as "therapeutic" (as in the American Federation of Therapeutic Self-Help Clubs). A good example of this type of self-help group is "Recovery, Inc."

2. *Groups that are primarily focused on social advocacy.* We use this term rather than the more usual "social action" because it is broader. Advocacy includes agitating and education directed at existing institutions, professionals, the public; confrontation, muckraking, and social crusading. It can be both on behalf of broad issues, such as legislation, the creation of new services, change in the policies of existing institutions, and so on, or it can be on behalf of individuals, families, or other small groups. Typically, such groups as welfare rights organizations and the Committee for the Rights of the Disabled use both kinds of advocacy.

[5] Katz and Bender, *op. cit.*

3. *Groups whose primary focus is to create alternative patterns for living.* Group solidarity provides a foundation for society's changing social institutions and attitudes. These groups may start new living and working alternatives of their own. Individual growth and self-fulfillment are obtained in the process, but are not the primary group goals. Examples are Women's Liberation, Gay Liberation, Operation Bootstrap, many communes.

4. *"Outcast haven" or "rock bottom" groups.* These groups provide a refuge for the desperate attempting to secure personal protection from the pressures of life and society, and thereby save themselves from mental or physical decline. This type of group involves total commitment in a living-in arrangement (a sheltered environment), with close, if not twenty-four-hour-a-day, supervision by peers or persons who have successfully grappled with similar problems of their own. An example of this type of group is the X-Kalay Foundation in Vancouver, British Columbia, and, in its beginning, but in our view not at present, the Synanon Foundation.

5. *"Mixed" types.* We resorted to this variant because some groups did not fit neatly into any of the above, such as Parents Without Partners and some groups of former prisoners.

When viewing self-help groups through even this primitive classification scheme it becomes apparent that they cannot be forced into a single box like "power to the people" or any other simplistic categorization. In fact, analysis and study of them need to pursue, in our opinion, a number of dimensions which we have only briefly touched on in the book, but which, it seems to us, hold suggestive implications both for their relationships with professionals and for research. Among the dimensions that need consideration and study is, first, that of the groups' ideology. Do they, for example, have a belief in God or a higher power, on which their adherents ultimately depend for the solution of their problem behavior? Many self-help groups, particularly AA and its spin-offs, do have such a philosophy, and it is characteristic of these groups that they maintain a tight control over members, expect frequent participation in meetings, and regular consultation with a "sponsor" or "buddy" more experienced than themselves. Such groups believe, in fact, that the problem behavior is never "cured" but may only be controlled through close involvement with the group. In practice, without relying on the notion of a higher power, and without as well worked-out a set of procedures and rituals as is found in AA and its imitators, Synanon has a similar approach. Anyone who has visited or participated in Synanon activities knows that an underlying belief is that "once a Synanon member, always a Synanon member"; members are not encouraged to "split" or outgrow the sheltering self-help group. In fact, this kind of self-help group often assumes a messianic and universalistic character; it proselytizes actively and sees itself as providing a truly alternative and total way of living. This dimension, then, of the kind and extent of philosophy or ideology, and the consequent tightness of social control of members, is a very important one to keep in mind in considering how to work with particular self-help groups; or in thinking about the degree to which their members may attain liberated self-awareness and social competence.

The importance of ideology as an influence upon structure, group life, and member adaptations is observable among communes or "intentional communities," as social scientists like to call them. Those communes endure which have a strong ideology as a binding tie. Examples are the Hutterite and other religious groups which live communally and therefore have rules of behavior, procedures, and internal system-maintaining regulations, but which are found much less frequently in the rapidly appearing and equally rapidly disappearing rural and urban communes formed by the alienated or disaffected or by proponents of particular life styles in our population.

So, professionals do have to take into account these specifying, differentiating characteristics, the presence or otherwise of ideology, and of system-maintaining regulatory procedures and behaviors in attempting to understand these groups as organizations *sui generis,* and in understanding as well their potential meaning and helpfulness to clients, and also, more broadly, in speculating about their probable future and durability as social institutions.

DEPENDENCY

A point that often troubles professionals about self-help groups is their perceived role in promoting, maintaining, intensifying, or prolonging dependency. About this there are both general and specific things to say. Dependency on others is of course as natural to the human species as breathing or metabolizing one's food. Such dependency on those to whom one is, or can feel, close is lifelong and constructive; effects of the lack of reliable interpersonal supports on which to depend are documented in the annals of human misery that social workers daily compile. And the securing or extension of reliable support systems is one of the latent but obvious motives people have in establishing and joining self-help groups, even though the manifest motives may be to obtain concrete services or engage in social action.

Here again, differential analysis is required in order to understand that in their concrete particularities various self-help groups approach the problem of dependency in different ways. To take a striking example, that of organizations of former drug addicts, Synanon, as we have seen, socializes its members to believe that affiliation with it is indeed a lifelong affair. But other organizations of former addicts and "refuge haven" self-help groups, such as X-Kalay in Canada which in other respects is close to the Synanon model, approach the matter of lifelong affiliation quite differently. They not only encourage independence and their members' growth to the point that they no longer need the continuous sheltering environment provided by the group, but they have ingenious graduation or *rites de passage* ceremonies to mark the coming of age, as it were, of member participants, their reentry or entry into the wider social world. In self-help groups which do not involve such a total commitment or life style—Parents Without Partners is an example—the question of prolonged dependency for their members does not really arise.

The whole complex question of the role of professionals vis-à-vis self-help groups, then, merits much further thought. In my opinion, the first requirement for professionals is to understand that these groups are a natural phenomenon, that they are here to stay, as a permanent and probably growing feature of the social landscape; that they can provide for many people who themselves choose to go that way a resource for life support and sometimes life change that has qualities different in kind from and in some ways transcending those available from professional sources. Among these, to repeat, are opportunities for peer support, for identity establishment, for personal change and self-validation, as well as for simple socialization and an array of concrete benefits. They achieve these through group contacts and group life that simulate "real" life—the stuff of living social reality—in ways that professional relationships and contacts can never duplicate. Above all they offer the status of reciprocal equality in social relationships. Whatever else we may think about professionalism, it can never really supply a climate or status of egalitarianism. Professional relationships always imply and carry the burden of super- and subordination, of "authority," while in the self-help group the relationship is a horizontal one between equals and peers—peers in the possession of a common problem, but also peers in the possession of a common social status. As I have written elsewhere,[6] professionals have many contributions to make, arising out of their training, their personal sense of justice and their sensitivity, their technical skills, their anxiety to do good in the world. It would be a mistake to regard self-help groups as operating in exactly the same way and in the same universe of assumptions as professionals, for in that way we would tend to

[6] Alfred H. Katz, "Self-Help Organizations and Volunteer Participation in Social Welfare," *Social Work*, XV, No. 1 (1970), 51–60.

regard them as mere untrained and therefore presumptuous competitors and would see them as mainly a threat or danger. There is plenty of work to do in this world to help needy people, and self-help groups for some time have been doing it, often with success, sometimes with professional support and understanding, often without it. Professionals should have humility and open-mindedness, learn what they can about and from them, cooperate with them when they can, but should not regard the groups either as panaceas or nostrums for every social ill, or as undisciplined, threatening rivals.

What professionals can occasionally contribute to self-help groups is expertise in the form of knowledge and resources of all kinds; professional knowledge regarding effective programmatic approaches, sources of funding and political strategies. Sometimes this may take the form of teaching or consultation or even supervision, but it is clear, harking back to that hoary social work principle of self-determination—much more honored in the breach than in the observance—that professionals in no way can dominate self-help groups and that they should only intervene in them when asked. If they are instrumental in their initial creation, then professionals should withdraw gracefully from the scene as early as possible. If an individual social worker wishes to be a member of a self-help group, he should be just that, expect no special status, and relate to its other members on a basis of equality.

That there are gains for "clients," members of the community, the disenfranchised and dispossessed, the stigmatized and needy in affiliation with these new or rediscovered forms for mutual aid and caring in social life seems to me indisputable. That some of them can occasionally undertake and accomplish larger effects upon the social environment, upon social policy, that they can be factors in system change to bring about more human living conditions for all, I also do not doubt. But in order to accomplish the latter, it is clear that they cannot go it alone, that they need friendly support, understanding, and friends and potential allies. I include in the latter group the most concerned and flexible, the least bureaucratically minded, among professionals—those whose greatest commitments are not to professional or personal status and to system maintenance but to human welfare and the full flowering of human potential.

# Humanization of Prisons and Corrections[1]

## ECFORD S. VOIT, JR.

T HE TERM "HUMANIZATION," or one of its variants, has predictably infused the rhetoric of correctional reform for almost two centuries. Usually employed in a relative sense, it will be recalled that imprisonment *as* punishment was considered a "humane" alternative to the barbarisms of the pre-Enlightenment period, while reformation and rehabilitation, during the latter part of the nineteenth century, came to be viewed as a "humanitarian" advance over retribution. Currently, with the concept of rehabilitation under attack and the concerned public in the midst of a "sporadic fit of attentiveness" to the role and conditions of prisons in our society, to use Martinson's cynical little phrase,[2] it is not surprising to find the concept again in the vanguard of our benevolent repertoire. But apart from purifying our intentions and conveniently precluding empirical assessment, it is unclear, at least to me, what we mean by "humanization." Yet if we are to take seriously the apparent increasing emphasis on the "humanization" of corrections and especially of our prison system, it would seem entirely appropriate and reasonable to contemplate briefly the substance or content of this term.

ECFORD S. VOIT, JR., is Special Assistant to the Chief, Center for Studies of Crime and Delinquency, National Institute of Mental Health, Rockville, Md.

[1] The views expressed in this paper are the author's and do not necessarily reflect those of the National Institute of Mental Health.

[2] Robert Martinson, "What Works—Questions and Answers about Prison Reform," *Public Interest*, Spring, 1974, p. 22.

THE CONCEPT OF "HUMANNESS"

It is interesting to note that in the behavioral and social science literature, so far as I could determine, the words "humanization," "humanism," "humaneness," "humanitarianism," and so forth, are for the most part used interchangeably but with no effort at definition or clarification. Similarly, although a cursory review of the philosophical literature, where one would expect to find a conceptual dissection of these terms, revealed several scholarly discussions, these analyses produced so many questions about so many questions that their value, at least for my purposes, was somewhat constrained. As a consequence, I decided to turn to that old reliable, *Webster's Dictionary.*

According to Webster, the word "humanization" means simply to "endow with human character." But what is "human character?" "Humanitarianism," denoting the promotion of human welfare, sheds little added light on the issue. "Humaneness," often used synonymously with "humanization," suggests sympathy, compassion, or consideration for other human beings or animals, and connotes, it seems to me, a condition of relative inferiority or difference on the part of the recipient. (One is "kind" to animals, for example, or compassionate toward the sick.) Thus to be "humane" toward others does not necessarily mean that they will be treated as human beings or as equals. Meanwhile, the word "humanism," by asserting the "dignity and worth of man and his capacity for self-realization through reason," seems to come closest to the meaning of "human character." But what does this tell us about the concept of "humanness"?

In exploring this self-imposed query, I discovered that several writers in the field of biomedical ethics have become interested in explicating humanness, or as one author put it, "what it means to be a truly human being." [3] Based on these readings and a little speculation, it would appear that a sense

[3] Joseph Fletcher, "Indicators of Humanhood: a Tentative Profile of Man," *The Hastings Center Report*, III, No. 5 (1972), 1.

of dignity and personal worth *derives* from the capacity for
self-realization through reason, which in turn suggests the
capacity for self-control and a measure of personal autonomy.[4] Thus, it is *not* the nature of man to be helplessly
subject to the blind workings of physical or physiological forces. Furthermore, through his capacity for reason, man is
likewise capable of rational choice among alternative courses
of action (which vary, of course, to restrict the *range* of
choice), for which he is responsible. As Fletcher notes, to the
degree that man lacks control over his environment, "he is
not responsible, and to be irresponsible is to be sub-per-
sonal." [5] Similarly, Robert Burt, in a recent discussion of informed consent in the Kaimowitz psychosurgery case, suggested that man's "capacity for self-conscious, purposeful
control of his physical environment [is what] basically dif-
ferentiates him from other animals." [6] Thus, it appears that
to be human is to possess reason, the corollary capacity for
rational choice, a measure of control over one's existence,
and responsibility. In his analysis of "postive liberty," Isaiah
Berlin puts the matter this way:

I wish my life and decisions to depend on myself, not on forces of
whatever kind. I wish to be the instrument of my own, not other
men's, acts of will. I wish to be a subject, not an object; to be moved
by reasons, by conscious purposes, which are my own, not by causes
which affect me, as it were, from outside. I wish to be somebody,
not nobody; a doer—deciding and not decided for, self-directed
and not acted upon by external nature or by other men as if I were
a thing, or an animal, or a slave incapable of playing a human role,
that is, of conceiving goals and policies of my own and realizing
them.[7]

If this, then, is essentially what it means to be human and if
"to humanize" is fundamentally to foster "humanness," it

[4] Peter Steinfels, "Individualism—No Exits," *The Hastings Center Report,* II, No. 3
(1974), 3–10.
[5] Fletcher, *op. cit.,* p. 2.
[6] Robert Burt, "Why We Should Keep Prisoners from the Doctors," *The Hastings
Center Report,* V, No. 1 (1975), 31.
[7] Isaiah Berlin, *Four Essays on Liberty* (New York: Oxford University Press, 1969),
p. 131.

would seem that our correctional policies and programs should attempt, through the process of humanization, to recognize and support these qualities in offenders—whether in the community or confined to institutions.

CORRECTIONS AND RETRIBUTION

Against this backdrop it is to be noted that correctional ideology of the late eighteenth and early nineteenth centuries, which resulted in the amelioration of physical punishment and created the idea of punishment as restraint through imprisonment,[8] was largely consistent with the aforementioned rationalistic conception of man. In effect, this ideology maintained that natural law rather than the divine right of kings provided the foundation for the social order, that man was endowed with knowledge of right and wrong (reason), that he possessed a free will, and that he operated on the principle of hedonism in pursuit of pleasure and the avoidance of pain. In this view, crime was perceived as a *deliberate* act, the result of malicious intent and a perverse will for which the perpetrator was deemed morally responsible. In short, criminals were no longer seen as possessed of evil, but as persons who had deliberately *chosen* to violate the law.[9]

Given this conception of man, an effort was made during this period to establish an equitable and rational system of justice. Relying heavily on the Pennsylvania Code of 1682 and on the Becarrian principles embraced by the so-called "classical" school of penology, criminal statutes introduced the definite-sentence system "with its emphasis upon equality and certainty of punishment expressed in the establishment of prescribed sanctions for every crime according to its seriousness." [10] Thus, an offender's fate was sealed the mo-

[8] Clarence Schrag, *Crime and Justice: American Style* (Washington, D.C.: Department of Health, Education, and Welfare, 1973).
[9] President's Commission on Law Enforcement and Administration of Justice, *Task Force Report: Corrections* (Washington, D.C.: U.S. Government Printing Office, 1967).
[10] Paul Tappan, "Sentencing under the Model Penal Code," *Law and Contemporary Problems,* Summer, 1958, p. 529.

ment his guilt was established in accordance with the motto, "Let the punishment fit the crime." [11] And since imprisonment was the primary mode of punishment, prisons were a necessary adjunct to the statutory reform and to the realization of this correctional ideology. Under this system, furthermore, any character reform which might have occurred in the offender through penitence was considered entirely *his responsibility*.

Ohlin has observed that there was something "uncompromisingly honest" about the retributive justification for imprisonment prior to the 1870s. "Because crimes had been committed, offenders were to be subjected to punishment, hard labor and solitude to encourage repentant thoughts. This is what the convicted felon expected, and [this is what he] got." [12] In a similar vein, Temple some years ago suggested that punishment, "even in brutally vindictive forms," [13] does at least treat its victims as *persons* and moral agents.

CORRECTIONS AND REHABILITATION

Despite the relative compatibility of the retributive ideology with our earlier conception of humanness, emphasis began to shift during the 1800s away from the legal system and imprisonment as a means of punishment, to the offender and incarceration as a vehicle for reformation.[14] Rational criminal statutes had not reduced crime, and prisons were not fulfilling the basic task of protecting the community.[15] As a consequence, the late eighteenth-century principle that punishment should be directly proportionate to the magnitude of

[11] Schrag, *op. cit.*, p. 10.
[12] Lloyd Ohlin, "Correctional Strategies in Conflict," in *Proceedings of the American Philosophical Society*, June, 1974, p. 249.
[13] William Temple, "The Ethics of Penal Action" (1934), as quoted in Morris Ginsberg, *On Justice in Society* (London: Heinemann Educational Books, Ltd., 1967), p. 175.
[14] Harry E. Barnes and Negley K. Teeters, *New Horizons in Criminology* (Englewood Cliffs, N.J.: Prentice-Hall, Inc., 1953).
[15] David Rothman, *The Discovery of the Asylum* (Boston: Little, Brown and Co., 1971).

the crime, without reference to the characteristics of individual offenders, largely gave way to a view which stressed the "treatment" of the offender. And while some reform measures, consistent with the gradual public acceptance of more humanitarian ideologies in the provision of human services, began to be realized during the 1880s and 1890s, such as vocational training and remedial education,[16] the new treatment philosophy received its crucial impetus around 1900 from psychiatric thought, and especially from Freudian psychology.[17] To use Rothman's phrase, this period witnessed the "triumph of the medical model."

But notwithstanding the explicit concern for humanitarianism and humaneness in the handling of criminal offenders, it is interesting to reflect on the implications of this benevolent ideology for the concept of humanness. First of all, in contrast with the earlier notions of free will and rationality, Freudian psychology placed major conceptual reliance on psychic determinism, viz., that nothing in the psychic life of man is a function of rational processes, but rather that all behavior follows lawful and determined paths over which man has little control.[18] By extending the concept of determinism, long recognized and accepted in the physical realm, to psychological phenomena, behavior came to be explained in terms other than volition. Thus, one behaves reprehensibly not through malevolent choice, but as a consequence of psychic determinants *within* the person. Accordingly, under the psychiatric influence, a constantly increasing respectability was ascribed to irrationality, with a corollary decrease in the kinds of behavior considered rational,[19] and generally resulted in the "discrediting of reason." [20]

[16] Ohlin, *op. cit.*

[17] David Rothman, "Behavior Modification in Total Institutions," *The Hastings Center Report*, V, No. 1 (1975), 17–24.

[18] Scott Briar and Henry Miller, *Problems and Issues in Social Casework* (New York: Columbia University Press, 1971).

[19] Frank Hartung, *Crime, Law and Society* (Detroit: Wayne State University Press, 1965).

[20] Erich Kahler, *Man the Measure: a New Approach to History* (New York: Pantheon Books, 1943), p. 485.

Given this new conception of man, the impact on the correctional process was far-reaching. Clearly, if behavior is viewed as a function of causes beyond a person's rational control, then that person is not capable of willfully violating the law. And since a person can only be held responsible for acts done voluntarily (or which could have been avoided) with some understanding of their consequences and insight into their rightness and wrongness, the notion of responsibility is called into question.[21] Similarly, if responsible moral agents alone are liable to punishment, then the concept of retribution is rendered of dubious moral validity. (It has been argued, for example, that the distinctive feature of retribution is its exclusive emphasis on a specific past act rather than on the personality of the offender.) Consequently, instead of fitting the punishment to the crime, which now made little sense, the new motto for corrections became: "Let the treatment fit the needs of the individual offender." [22] The allure of this approach was understandable; surely it was far more humanitarian (humane?) to treat individuals according to their needs than to group them artificially and improperly under inflexible legal rules and remedies.

CONSEQUENCES OF THE MEDICAL ANALOGY

In light of this rehabilitative ideology, with its underlying deterministic conception of man and corollary medical analogue, a number of critical practice and policy consequences evolved in the correctional process. Although integrally related, they will be artificially isolated here to permit greater conceptual clarity.

*Discretion.* First and foremost, the medical analogy of treatment fostered a vast increase in discretionary decision-making. Obviously, if the system was to concern itself not with the act of criminality but rather with the offender's state of mind (reflected in the slogan, "Treat the criminal, not the crime"), then the interventions appropriate for one type of

[21] Ginsberg, *op. cit.*     [22] Schrag, *op. cit.,* p. 11.

offender might not necessarily be appropriate for another. Officials had to have leeway to decide among them. As a consequence, in the name of treating the criminal and not the crime, the justice system became unpredictable and ultimately arbitrary. And whatever inequities occurred were simply interpreted as a necessary and proper by-product of "individualized treatment." [23] As Cohen observed,

the goals of corrections [consistent with the new philosophy could] best be obtained by the preservation of maximum discretion on the part of judicial and correctional authorities. Discretion, in turn, [was] maximized by the reduction or elimination of procedural "obstacles"; [by] minimizing the role of the offender or his representative in the decision-making processes; and [by] the maintenance of a statutory framework that [was] so broad that virtually any decisions [could] be smuggled through the mythical borders of legislative intent.[24]

*Indeterminacy.* The shift in emphasis to treatment of the offender, which as noted earlier replaced the eighteenth-century principle of proportionality between crime and punishment, also resulted in the virtual disappearance of statutorily fixed sentences and a concomitant increasing emphasis on indeterminacy. In effect, minimum and maximum limits were established for sentences to correctional institutions, such as one to three years, five to ten, and so on,[25] and were designed "to take account of individual differences among prisoners" and to provide "incentives to reformation found in a device which placed in the prisoner's power some means of shortening the duration of his confinement." [26] A link was thus created between time served in prison and the of-

[23] Rothman, "Behavior Modification . . ."
[24] Fred Cohen, *The Legal Challenge to Corrections,* Joint Commission on Correctional Manpower and Training (Washington, D.C.: U.S. Government Printing Office, 1969), p. 29.
[25] Walter Reckless, *The Crime Problem* (New York: Appelton-Century-Crofts, 1961).
[26] Thorsten Sellin, "Indeterminate Sentence," in *Encyclopaedia of the Social Sciences* (1932), as quoted in Reckless, *op. cit.,* p. 440.

fender's involvement (and apparent response to) prison treatment programs.[27]

But while indeterminacy was hailed as a humanitarian advance in theory, like so many other developments, it became something quite different in practice, like so many other developments. In fact, it has become "one of the most painful aspects of prison life." [28] Now the offender not only must pay his debt to society in the "old-fashioned way of doing time," but in addition must prove "that the modern treatment method has worked, that he is cured, rehabilitated and ready for parole." [29] Indeterminacy thus created high stakes for the convicted offender; any real attempt at rehabilitation became secondary to "playing the treatment game." As Mitford observes,

to decline to play . . . can be dangerous indeed. The prisoner who refuses to submit to therapy will find himself labeled "defiant," "hostile," "uncooperative," and the classification committee will act accordingly by confining him in a maximum security prison—not, of course, as punishment, but as the next logical step in his treatment.[30]

Moreover, indeterminacy follows the offender through the parole stage, at which point he is confronted by an agency whose "discretion is at least as broad as that of the sentencing authority (the court) and whose accountability is just as minimal." [31] While stressing rehabilitation as the basic standard for parole, wide discretion and ambiguous criteria allow parole authorities to consider numerous other factors in their decisions, such as the exigencies of overcrowding or the obverse need to maintain a given population level, which has inevitably degenerated into a tool for institutional manipulation and control; that is, the offender never knows whether

[27] Norval Morris, *The Future of Imprisonment* (Chicago: University of Chicago Press, 1974).

[28] American Friends Service Committee, *Struggle for Justice: a Report on Crime and Punishment in America* (New York: Hill and Wang, 1971), p. 93.

[29] Jessica Mitford, "Kind and Unusual Punishment," *Atlantic Monthly*, March, 1971, p. 47.
[30] *Ibid.*     [31] Cohen, *op. cit.*, p. 31.

the sentence is three years or ten, and discipline is maintained by the threat of more time.[32]

Still, given the aforementioned rationale underlying the broad discretionary powers associated with indeterminacy,[33] one might assume or suspect that, as a mitigating consideration, offenders spend *less* time in prison than they would were their sentences fixed or definite. Yet, available evidence suggests that this has not been the case. In fact, studies have shown that indeterminacy has resulted not only in the imposition of longer prison terms,[34] but also in an increase in the median time served in confinement.[35]

*Prediction.* Another manifestation of the ideology of treatment which pervades indeterminate sentencing policy is the belief that future criminal behavior can be predicted by diagnosing a given problem and observing an offender's reaction to treatment. Obviously, if there were no basis for ascertaining *when* an offender might be "ready" for release to the community, there would be little justification for indeterminate sentences. This is, of course, consistent with the deterministic notion underlying the medical analogy of treatment, which suggests that behavior, like phenomena in the physical realm, follows predictable, lawful courses. But on what basis is "readiness" for release ascertained by parole authorities?

In discussing this issue, it is instructive to note that the medical analogy of treatment presupposes a "present condition" or "state" which exists during the period of treatment.[36] In short, if there were no condition, the object of treatment would be somewhat elusive. Furthermore, in order to justify the discretion and indeterminacy of correctional sentencing,

[32] American Friends Service Committee, *op. cit.*

[33] Sellin, *op. cit.*

[34] John P. Conrad, *Crime and Its Correction* (Berkeley, Calif.: University of California Press, 1965).

[35] Gail Garringer, "Indeterminacy in the Sentencing Process" (unpublished paper, 1972).

[36] Leslie T. Wilkins, "Putting 'Treatment' on Trial," *The Hastings Center Report*, V, No. 1 (1975), 35–48.

the offender's "state" or condition must be altered to a point sufficient to warrant release. Accordingly, since the emphasis is on behavior rather than on physical illness, an implicit association is made between a prisoner's response to treatment and the likelihood of subsequent criminal conduct. However, it has been pointed out that prison behavior is *not* a predictor of community behavior.[37] Indeed, offender records (prior to incarceration), family ties, a place to live, and a job—all these and perhaps other *extra*-institutional factors—appear to be most related to postinstitutional avoidance of criminality (not to mention the aging process), over which treatment personnel have virtually *no* control.[38]

It might also be noted in passing that many writers as well as national policy-setting organizations, such as the National Council on Crime and Delinquency, who have otherwise been critical of our sentencing policies have nevertheless tended to draw distinctions between "dangerous" offenders, who should be imprisoned, and "nondangerous" offenders, who should be diverted to community-based alternatives, a distinction, of course, which implies a capability to differentiate between, or "predict," these "states." But the available empirical evidence again does not support this implication. On the contrary, even the most comprehensive prediction studies conducted to date [39] have produced error rates approaching nine incorrect predictions for every one correct prediction, hardly a level of predictive accuracy on which to base public policy.

*Coercive cure.* One final noteworthy consequence of the medical analogue of treatment clearly implicit in the foregoing discussion is a belief that psychological change can be coerced. This too is consistent with the deterministic notion regarding behavior; that is, if behavior is largely a function

[37] Morris, *op. cit.*

[38] Daniel Glaser, *The Effectiveness of a Prison and Parole System* (Indianapolis: Bobbs-Merrill Co., 1964).

[39] Ernst A. Wenk *et al.,* "Assaultive Youth: an Exploratory Study of the Assaultive Experience and Assaultive Potential of California Youth Authority Wards," *Journal of Research in Crime and Delinquency,* IX, No. 2 (1972), 171–96.

of forces beyond a person's control, then it is unreasonable to expect that person to volunteer for, or otherwise choose to be involved in, a treatment program; rather, it must be compelled "for the person's own good." However, in the prisoner's acceptance of treatment there is, to use Norval Morris's phrase, a "fatal compromise": given the indefiniteness of release and parole discretion held by correctional authorities, the hope of early freedom is inexorably tied to the prisoner's *apparent* serious involvement in treatment. Thus, prisoners hold the key to their imprisonment, but, again to quote Morris, it is a "bogus key." They must present a façade of being involved in their own rehabilitation, and building that façade may preclude the "reality of reformative effort." As a result, no one—neither the treated nor the treaters—can actually know whether the prisoner genuinely wishes to use treatment or whether he merely seeks to "con" those who can assure his release.

## THE EFFICACY OF TREATMENT

Despite the psychological hardship and other deleterious consequences for offenders resulting from practices associated with the humanitarian policy of rehabilitation, perhaps it might be argued that such practices would be justified if together they served to prevent further criminality or recidivism; that is, if treatment under the inherently coercive conditions of imprisonment were effective. However, a review of the relevant literature reveals that treatment results (as opposed to intentions) provide little justification for coercion. Without belaboring the issue, two major reports will suffice to make the point. First, Bailey analyzed over one hundred studies of many different types of correctional programs conducted between 1940 and 1959 and disclosed that those studies in which the greatest care had been taken in the experimental design reported either harmful effects of treatment or, more frequently, no change at all.[40] More recently,

[40] W. Bailey, "Correctional Outcome: an Evaluation of 100 Reports," *Journal of Criminal Law, Criminology, and Police Science*, LVII, No. 2 (1966), 153–60.

Martinson reviewed over two hundred studies spanning the period 1945–67, including programs of education, vocational training, individual and group psychotherapy, and so forth, and concluded that, "with few and isolated exceptions, the rehabilitative efforts that have been reported so far have had no appreciable effect on recidivism, the phenomenon which most directly reflects how well our present treatment programs are performing."[41] In the meantime, Wilkins sums it up this way:

It seems safe to conclude that it is extremely doubtful whether any variants of present methods of treatment of offenders make any difference to the reconviction rate. Indeed, there has been no demonstration that any activity termed "treatment" possesses the necessary characteristics to justify the use of the term.[42]

It thus appears that while the ideology of rehabilitation held out promises of self-development opportunities, they were never—and perhaps could never—be realized under the conditions of coercion which characterize our correctional system, and particularly our prison system. In effect, the philosophy of treatment created, in Ohlin's words, a "credibility gap of serious proportions."[43] Though congenial to humanitarian and professional ethics, the notion of rehabilitation has contrasted radically with the facts of everyday life experienced by most offenders. In short, despite the rhetoric, prisons and to some extent all of corrections continue to serve the ends of custody and punishment rather than treatment and rehabilitation.

TOWARD HUMANIZATION AND EQUITY

If nothing else, it would seem fairly clear, in light of this discussion, that humanization of prisons and corrections is somewhat less than synonymous with the philosophy and practice of rehabilitation. Although it may well sound "humanitarian" to associate these concepts, the *consequences* of treatment have not been particularly "humanizing." In fact,

[41] Martinson, *op. cit.*, p. 25.     [42] Wilkins, *op. cit.*, p. 39.     [43] Ohlin, *op. cit.*

if one accepts the notion that to be human is to possess inherent dignity and personal worth through reason, the capacity to make choices and to be responsible for actions taken, then the treatment approach, with its deterministic underpinning and medical analogy as practiced coercively in correctional settings, has served almost systematically to destroy the remaining vestiges of humanness in criminal offenders. Indeed, the medical analogue *required* it.[44]

To recapitulate briefly, if an offender is seen as a victim of forces beyond his control, then he obviously cannot help what he does and will likely do again. To prevent such acts from recurring (prediction), it is necessary to treat, or rather to compel, treatment, because "only we know what's best." Accordingly, definite sentences make little sense, since the time required for "cure" (or "rehabilitation") cannot be ascertained in advance (hence, indeterminacy). Thus, a crucial link is forged between time served and treatment, which creates in turn the additional link between coercion and cure.[45] And the ultimate price to be paid, which I consider fundamental to the concept of humanness, is *equity*.

Unlike the earlier retributive model of corrections, where the principle of equity was realized through a definite sentence structure of equal punishment for comparable offenses, the notion of equity has no meaning in the philosophy of rehabilitation. Treatment is not intended as punishment, so comparisons are invalid. That is to say, in making decisions which affect others, the treating of *each* person decided about as a *unique* individual means simply that there can arise no question of equity, since equity implies some basis for comparison. Thus, if one accepts the proposition that deprivation of liberty alone constitutes punishment,[46] then the price of imprisonment under the former system of retribution was simply deprivation of liberty. However, under the more recent system of rehabilitation, the price of

---

[44] Rothman, "Behavioral Modification . . ."     [45] Morris, *op. cit.*
[46] Paul Lerman, "Beyond Gault: Injustice and the Child," in Paul Lerman, ed., *Delinquency and Social Policy* (New York: Praeger Publishers, 1970), pp. 236–50.

imprisonment has become deprivation of liberty *plus* equity. Consequently, as a matter of public policy, if equity is seen as a precondition of humanness, we must decide what type of system is morally preferable.

Assuming a higher social value might be placed on retribution *with* equity than on retribution without, what might be done to realize a greater measure of humanness in our prisons and correctional system? First, on a more conceptual level, if indeed the product of imprisonment is punishment, irrespective of the rhetoric used to describe correctional intents, then the terms we use to define the purpose of incarceration should honestly reflect this impact on offenders. Wilkins has noted, for example, that *more* punitive (and dehumanizing) practices can be, and appear to have been, employed in the name of treatment than might otherwise obtain "if we were more honest and discussed punishment in clear and open terms." [47]

Second, if more equitable practices tend to be associated with the perception of man as a responsible being, and dignity, as Henry Miller observes, "inheres" in the concept,[48] then a greater measure of responsibility should be accorded to criminal offenders. Third, as the foregoing implies, the link should be broken between time served in prison and involvement in rehabilitation programs. As Norval Morris notes, "The total institution has such massive impact on its charges, its authority is so annihilative of free choice, that it is essential for us to protect, so far as we can for his sake and for ours, the prisoner's freedom *not* to be [involved] in any treatment program" (emphasis added).[49] In a word, participation in treatment programs should be made *voluntary*—an "unfettered opportunity," free of sanctions, deprived of no privileges and release in no way deferred, to decide on par-

[47] Leslie T. Wilkins, "Directions for Corrections," in *Proceedings of the American Philosophical Society,* June, 1974, p. 246.
[48] Henry Miller, "Value Dilemmas in Social Casework," *Social Work,* XIII, No. 1 (1968), 30.
[49] Morris, *op. cit.,* p. 20.

ticipation.[50] Coercion, then, beyond deprivation of liberty, must be eliminated from corrections.

Meanwhile, from a policy perspective, it seems to me that if the link between time served and treatment involvement is to be broken, which in turn implies an end to the coercive effects of indeterminacy, some form of fixed sentences should be reinstituted, which would also serve to confine the excesses of administrative discretion. Furthermore, in light of the earlier suggestion that offender involvement in treatment be made voluntary, a return to a definite sentence structure does *not* imply the elimination of rehabilitative programs for the correctional process; rather, such programs should be given a "facilitative" role within the context of punishments otherwise justified (or deserved).[51] In effect, a distinction must be drawn between the purposes of incarceration as punishment and the opportunities for training and assistance provided offenders *within* those purposes. Together, these conceptual and policy considerations suggest that power under the criminal law should be taken only in relation to, and be limited by, a past act as opposed to the future probability of criminality. Through such measures there would, in my view, be less hypocrisy, less coercion, and perhaps a greater degree of humanness.

[50] *Ibid.*, p. 19.    [51] *Ibid.*, pp. 26–27.

# Goals for Health Care
# in Other Nations

## MARION O. ROBINSON

A WORLD PERSPECTIVE on health care was lifted up
at the evening session on the Wednesday of Forum week by
way of presentations from distinguished leaders from five
countries. The meeting, sponsored by NCSW, with the help
of the Asia Foundation and the U.S. Committee of the International Council on Social Welfare, was presided over by Jay
L. Roney, Director, community planning staff, Social Security Administration.

In his remarks as moderator, Bertram S. Brown, M.D.,
Director, National Institute of Mental Health, reminded the
audience that the health and welfare of one nation are related to those of other nations "through the flow of people,
microorganisms, tourists, and refugees," as well as through
the flow of ideas, concepts, and values. He described briefly
work now being done by a small group of people at the international level on long-term perspectives concerning the
world health program, in which industrialized and developing countries—both of which were represented among the
evening speakers—present vastly different historical, political, social, and economic factors influencing health situations.

To take just the economic factor, which determines health
planning, nations with planned economy, those with a predominantly market economy, those rich in natural resources,
those poor in natural resources, together present an overwhelming diverse picture. He added that "one billion people
. . . live in countries with minimal social and economic structure and no natural resources," a fact which has become an

important issue in the international scene. Crosscutting these factors are current phenomena such as changes in family life, the women's movement, the struggle against racism, all affecting to some degree most of the nations of the world. It was Dr. Brown's opinion that "politics and political decisions and values will remain the critical determinants of health and human services," and he suggested that "health gives us a universal ethical and moral stand on which to urge our political authorities to act helpfully to all humanity."

From the local to the international level, concepts and questions presently concern those responsible for health development. One is the question of separate, parallel responsibilities for different authorities and disciplines required by complex health programs *versus* an increased sharing of responsibility among authorities and disciplines. Dr. Brown characterized this group of guest speakers as "a pilot experiment in bringing together people of different disciplines to share their special perspective."

Dr. M. Tajul Hossain of Bangladesh led off the evening's presentations. He was introduced by Dr. Brown as Secretary of the Ministry of Health, Population Control, and Family Planning for the Government of the People's Republic of Bangladesh; trained in Calcutta, New York, and in the United Kingdom; "a cardiac surgeon who could be making a fortune but instead is serving his people as a national leader."

Dr. Hossain sketched an interesting natural background of his country before describing the health delivery system. A hot, humid country, this Southeast Asian nation has six seasons, including a mild two-month winter and a prominent summer and monsoon. Only 5 percent of the land is forested; from 15 percent to 30 percent of the flat land surface remains under water, with seasonal variation. The Gangetic Delta, one of the most fertile lands on earth, has luxuriant growth of plant and animal life, most of which is "uneconomic and injurious to human society. . . . posing constant threat to human health and longevity." Population density is

1,400 per square mile in a land of 55,000 square miles. The population, now 75 million, is expected to double by the year 2000. Natural calamities such as floods, cyclones, crop failures, famine, and epidemics occur almost every year.

A predominantly poor-quality rice diet has influenced the metabolism and thinking process so that the people live by metaphysical and fatalistic attitudes. Social morality has been based on worship of hypothetical truth, goodness, and beauty, so that "the spirit of faith replaced the spirit of inquiry, [and] the society is more religious than scientific, more spiritual, superstitious, and atavistic then inquisitive. Primitive modes of agriculture have meant that cultivators have for ages been satisfied with two crops of rice in spite of limited lands and animals and growing families.

Liberation in 1971 found the country depleted of resources and values, and in crisis. The new Constitution defines the fundamental rights of citizens; the leadership aims "to establish a real welfare state"; the people "are determined to establish their rights."

Administratively, the country and its 64,000 villages, are being reorganized into 60 districts and 422 Thanas (counties), with the over-all aim to decentralize power.

Dr. Hossain characterized the manpower of his country as "uncared-for, underemployed, undereducated, suffering from undernutrition and ill-health." Basic health problems are overpopulation, undernutrition, and infection. The inherited health care system was curative-based, urban-based, and extremely limited as to medical and nursing personnel, hospital beds, medicines, and equipment. Public health measures had received little attention.

A five-year plan, drawn in 1972, outlined a health and population planning program. Under this, manpower—medical, paramedical, nursing, and auxiliary—is being educated, trained, organized, and utilized. Emphasis is on preventive measures; the aim, to promote good health rather than treat ill-health. A primary effort is toward education on fertility control, nutritional values of food, health care, and the history of communicable disease; sanitation, and hygienic measures.

The new plan prescribed integration of previously existing programs into one, manned by 12,000 multipurpose health workers, known as family welfare workers. Under this system, set up in 1974 following six months' training of the workers, the citizens of every locality will eventually be related to their own decentralized health institutions (Thana Health Complexes) through personal contact with workers who keep records on each family of health and family planning. Each Complex will have responsibility for 40,000 families (175,000 persons); each worker is assigned 800 to 1,000 families. Work on the Health Complexes has begun in 248 of the 422 Thanas. One small hospital for each Thana is written into the plan. Each of the 60 districts now has a modernized hospital of 50 to 100 beds.

At present, medical education in the country is carried by eight undergraduate colleges, one postgraduate school of medicine offering 26 specialties, one paramedical and one public health institute. About 7,000 doctors are now in practice; the aim is to increase their number to 30,000 in the next 25 years. Dr. Hossain emphasized that medical students are discouraged from going abroad for higher diplomas; rather, they are sent to specialized centers for training.

Particular effort has been made to step up nursing education and training, as there were only 700 nurses for 12,000 hospital beds. Now, 1,200 nursing students are admitted annually to schools of nursing under a crash program, and one postgraduate school of nursing is being established. A course for medical assistants is also being introduced to create a new type of substitute for qualified medical doctors.

Assistance is needed in obtaining educational apparatus, equipment and the printing of medical literature. Drugs and raw materials still have to be imported "out of meager foreign exchange earning."

Most diseases now prevalent are preventable by immunization, proper nutrition, and applying what is known about elimination of communicable diseases. Intestinal parasites from polluted drinking water produced a variety of major problem diseases. Malaria, though not eliminated, is under control. A vigorous campaign against smallpox is being waged. Tuberculosis is still a major problem, and skin infections are frequent.

Of the noncommunicable diseases now found in high incidence in other parts of the world—cancer, cardiovascular diseases, metabolic disorders—none has become a killer or even a major problem. Alcoholism and drug addiction, varicose veins, hiatal hernia, all are far less common than in the Western world.

The greatest problems, he said, are infant mortality, maternal morbidity, and multiple pregnancy. Regarding the last, he said the five-year plan stated, "No civilized method of contraception will be unacceptable to Bangladesh for sheer ecological viability of the nation."

Assistance from international organizations and friendly countries is forthcoming, concluded Dr. Hossain, but it is inadequate and sporadic. What is needed is "more generous, concerted, and comprehensive assistance programs." What is also needed is help to the unfortunate millions of his countrymen so that they may realize that "health is indeed a social and political right which they should strive for and achieve."

Dr. Satar Seraj, President of the Family Health Services Department of Afghanistan's Ministry of Public Health, was next introduced by Moderator Brown, who reminded the audience that Dr. Seraj's country was one of great diversity surrounded by the Soviet Union, China, and Iran. The speaker, he said, had been trained in his own country, at the London School of Hygiene and Tropical Medicine, and at the University of Paris. He added that this was Dr. Seraj's first visit to the United States mainland.

The Afghan Health Program, based on government policies broadcast in a comprehensive address to the nation by the national leader, has the objective of providing "health activities to get the people cured, so as to upgrade living standards and elevate the quality and quantity of training, while strengthening medical services and the national economy," said Dr. Seraj at the outset of his address. The program designed by the Ministry of Public Health aims to have doctors, specialists, and public health personnel trained theoretically and practically, and proposes that eventually Afghan personnel take complete charge of all responsibility for health activities. To achieve this, the country must rely on grants and assistance—financial, educational, training, and advisory—from friendly countries. He added that only projects and contracts compatible with the Afghan Health Program may be carried out.

Dr. Seraj outlined plans for development of both curative and preventive programs under the direction of the Ministry. In the curative program, the need for training for medical and laboratory personnel is most urgent. Now in process is the elevation of a few central hospitals and a number of those in the provinces to training center level. These centers will be responsible for determination of curriculum, following approval of the Health Minister; setting definitive training periods for various specialties, as well as for theoretical and practical work periods; and for final testing and certification.

Training instructors will be drawn from academic specialists in the medical colleges of the country and from among guest doctors serving in the curative programs in Ministry hospitals. Each specialist will work with one or two young Afghan physicians who, after training, will be assigned to provincial hospitals, thereby releasing less experienced physicians for their turn at the training center.

Development of a network of labs to facilitate the curative program begins with inauguration of central labs for diagnosis and development of work in X ray, electrocardiography, and histology. Here lab technicians will be brought in turn for training and, as with the physicians, returned to duty in the provinces.

As soon as it is financially possible, all specialized hospitals

in the capital city, both those now existing and those planned, will be turned into training centers so that Kabul will
become a center for diagnosis and treatment of all curable
diseases. Some of these institutions, for example, the Midwi-
fery Nursing School, will depend for training on foreign specialists.

Training in administration is also needed. Dr. Seraj
stressed the fact that guest doctors will not be accepted for
short periods of time and that the administration of hospitals, projects, traveling clinics, and distribution of food,
equipment, and supplies will all be carried by Afghans.

Foreign specialists and personnel will work only in the capacity of
instructors or advisors and will be assigned only to hospitals and
training centers. . . . [They] will be accepted at Afghan medical institutions only when they are trained in a specialty in one of the
medical fields so that they can provide useful services for the people. . . . no foreigner can indulge in practicing medicine of any
type outside his/her working location."

Preventive services are insufficient in rural areas, said Dr.
Seraj, and in some remote areas are entirely lacking. Therefore, an extremely important objective of the program is the
extension of these services into all parts of the country at a
village level.

Priorities in the preventive program are: a national campaign against communicable diseases, such as cholera, diph-
theria, malaria, smallpox, and so forth; lowering the incidence of infant and maternal mortality; and raising
nutrition levels. The preventive program is to be carried out
through one basic health center in each district (*woleswali*)
plus three or four subcenters. The aim is to have one such
center for each 5,000 persons. Personnel for each basic
center consist of a doctor, nurse, midwife, technician phar-
macist, dentist, sanitorian, and a few vaccinators, all of whom
would be Afghans. This team will have responsibility for
food distribution, the malaria eradication program, smallpox
vaccinations, and the detection of, and vaccination against,
tuberculosis. The campaign against other communicable dis-

eases will be "applied as such epidemic diseases break out."

To cope with malnutrition, research labs are studying the nature and extent of food lacks and food use, the results to be used by basic health centers.

Because of widespread illiteracy, Dr. Seraj said the educational program is being carried out through films, radio talks, and other audio-visual aids.

An immediate objective in the public health program is provision of healthy drinking water, with extension into fifteen provinces as the first step. A sewage disposal program, especially in the cities, is envisioned.

A school of public health to overcome the lack of trained personnel in the various specialties is planned, including the scientific training of personnel in making surveys and gathering statistical data; and vocational schools are to be set up by the Ministry to train technicians, sanitorians, pharmacists, and the like. Foreign personnel will be needed as advisers and instructors in this effort.

Dr. Brown next presented Dr. Junshiro Ohmura of Japan. A physician, Dr. Ohmura is Executive Director of the Kosei-dan in Tokyo, the organization which manages the pension fund for the private sector of industry, business, and health care, and a consultant to the Ministry of Health and Welfare. At present he is also a delegate to the World Health Organization.

Dr. Ohmura began with a description of significant changes in Japan's vital statistics since the end of the Second World War. The high prewar birth rate dropped rapidly in the first ten postwar years, even as the postwar baby boom was accelerating in the United States. About the time a decline in the rate set in for the United States, Japan's birth rate began to rise and in 1972 stood at 19.3 per 1,000 population as compared with 15.6 in the United States.

The rapid postwar decrease in birth rate was due to induced abortion, Dr. Ohmura explained; for a time, there were almost as many abortions as births. Since 1930 when this phenomenon reached its peak, with more widespread use of conception controls, the picture reversed. Contraceptive methods commonly employed are condoms and periodic abstinence. The IUD was put on the Japanese market in 1974. So far, oral pills are used only for endrocrine therapy.

Dr. Ohmura stated that the death rate in Japan is now the lowest in the world: 6.5 per 1,000 population (1972). Even when corrected for the lower proportion of the aged in the population, as compared with Western countries, only Sweden and the Netherlands have lower death rates. The life span for the Japanese male is 70.7 years; for the female, 76 years (1973 figures).

Since the 1940s, when infectious diseases such as tuberculosis, pneumonia, enteritis, and so on were the main causes of death, the degenerative diseases have risen to the top of the list. The five leading causes of death now are: cerebral vascular diseases, malignant neoplasms, cardiac diseases, fatal accidents, and senility. Due to the difference in diet habits between Japan and the United States, death from cerebral apoplexy is more frequent than death from cardiac diseases in Japan, while the reverse is true in the United States. However, Dr. Ohmura noted that increased use of Western diet habits in Japan has been accompanied by a sharp increase in death from cardiac disorders.

The death rate from gastric cancer in Japan is the highest in the world. For males, the next highest death rate from the malignancies results from lung and liver cancer; for females, these are uterine, liver, and breast cancers. Gastric cancer in both sexes and uterine cancer in women is on the decrease; cancer of the respiratory organs and pancreatic cancer is on the increase.

Since 1947 infant mortality in Japan has fallen from 76.7 per 1,000 live births to 11.7 (1972), the lowest in the world. The decrease in birthrate and death rate has rapidly changed the population structure, so that those in the productive years constitute a higher proportion of the total than the minor age group. An interesting development since the end of the war led Dr. Ohmura to remark that the image of the "tiny Japanese" may soon be disappearing: average body measurements of eleven-year-old boys show that height has increased by ten centimeters, body weight by seven kilograms, and chest circumference by four centimeters.

The high level of good health achieved in Japan in thirty years, the speaker felt, was due to the elevation of the nation's standard of living, the turning of the Japanese people from grain-centered diets to more protein-enriched ones, improvement of the environment, and the success of public health activities "pushed forward with U.S. aid in the postwar days." Among the last named is the tuberculosis control program (which disease topped the list of causes of death in 1947), which has introduced the galaxy of preventive and curative measures such as X rays, use of drugs, and chemotherapy.

Dr. Ohmura then described at length the system of medical insurance and public medical aid and current problems in each. The equivalent of $11 billion was paid for medical care in Japan in 1972—68.8 percent by sickness insurance, 13.6 percent by public medical aid, and 17.6 percent in charges paid by patients. (He pointed out that the comparable figure for patient payments in the United States in 1973 was 36.4 percent.) He estimated that medical care expenses in Japan amount to 4 percent of the gross national product.

All Japanese, except for needy families receiving assistance under the Daily Life Security Law, have compulsory coverage by the sickness insurance system. Under this, any insured person may consult with any participating doctor upon payment of the equivalent of seventy cents American at the time of the first consultation, and may be admitted to a hospital at a charge of twenty cents American per day for the first month.

Dependents of those covered by the employees' health insurance as well as those covered by national health insurance must pay 30 percent of their medical care expenses up to the equivalent of $100 a month, except for aged persons, infants, the mentally and physically handicapped, and those suffer-

ing from designated "intractable" diseases, all of whom receive free treatment.

The system of sickness insurance was established in 1927
for the benefit of industrial workers. White-collar workers
became eligible for coverage in 1940. In 1938 a system was
put in force for care of farmers, fishermen, and other self-
employed persons, following the depression when acute infectious diseases were prevalent and the poor physical condition of young men called up by the military was noteworthy.
In 1948, coverage became universal. Administered at the
community level, the program has been subsidized from the
national treasury in increasing proportion which has now
reached 50 percent of the total cost. The system now includes health insurance, seamen's insurance, daily workers'
insurance, four categories of mutual aid associations, national health insurance, and workmen's accident compensation.

Among present problems of the insurance system, the
most crucial is the financial dilemma. Shared payments of
employer and employee in small businesses paying lower
wages have required more subsidy of benefits from government. Medical care expenses between 1955 and 1970 increased nearly elevenfold, although Dr. Ohmura feels this is
due more to increasing demand than to increase of price.
Studies show that the average patient consults his doctor
eighteen times per illness (partly because drug dispensing is
often included in medical practice); and the frequency of
doctors' examinations among persons over seventy years of
age, who receive free medical care, is three times that of the
average demand.

Japanese patients take more medicine than do patients of
other countries, Dr. Ohmura explained. Drug dispensing may
be done by doctors, who can supply medicines free or for a
fraction of the cost at a pharmacy. Thus by 1970 the cost of
medicines represented 43.7 percent of the total of medical
care expenditures. Dr. Ohmura went on to say that overdosing
has become a matter of serious consideration to doctors in

Japan. For a time, a decrease in use was brought about by requiring patients to pay a portion of the cost but this was abolished because of opposition both from patients and doctors.

Medical care fees are paid according to a fixed tariff determined by the health insurance. Insurance fees are received by hospitals which in turn pay doctors on a fee-for-service basis. Dr. Ohmura feels the system serves to stimulate quantitative expansion rather than qualitative improvement.

In spite of these problems, costs have risen less rapidly than other consumer prices. For example, first-rate hospitals charge $17 a day, including the doctor's fee. Laboratory and other diagnostic fees may increase the cost to $30 a day.

The medical care delivery system is a problem in Japan, said the speaker. Seventy percent of the 8,188 hospitals are under private management. Public hospitals, under the auspices of universities, Red Cross, cooperatives, and social insurance funds, are maldistributed for regional coverage. The National Cancer Center, established in 1961, works through 160 local centers for examination and treatment of cancer in the early stages.

Resources for inpatient care included, in 1973, 103.5 hospital beds and 24.0 medical clinic beds per 10,000 population. The average length of patients' stay in hospitals is thirty-three days, as compared with seven days in the United States. In recent years this problem has been approached by efforts toward a more even distribution of the delivery system, including the preventive program, to ensure easily available services for local communities.

As of 1973, there were 125,302 doctors and 40,293 dentists in Japan; about half of them work as independent practitioners. Since the income of the latter is two or three times that of doctors who work in hospitals, there is a shortage of doctors, particularly in public services. About 2,000 doctors work in 829 public health centers. Twenty-two newly established medical colleges and medical departments in universities bring the total of these institutions to 68, which graduate about 3,200 doctors annually. The speaker predicted that by 1980 there would be 150 doctors for each 10,000 of the population.

A countermeasure against doctorless districts in remote areas is the founding of medical colleges by local governments where students on scholarship are required to work in designated areas for six years after graduation.

A happy development in Japan, said Dr. Ohmura, is that the government is said to be changing economic policy from "economic growth first" to "welfare first." However, he concluded: "Health is the right of people, but it is not to be given, but to be pursued. Government measures will not bear good fruit unless each individual consciously takes care of his own health."

Sēnora Lucila Leal de Araujo, Director of the Department of International Affairs, Mexican Social Security Institute, was then introduced to the audience by Dr. Brown. She chose as her topic "Basic Aspects in the Selection of Achievable Health Goals of Mexico," opening her discussion with the statement that in Mexico, as in other countries, consciousness of the need for health services developed rapidly as the concept of health as the absence of illness grew into the modern understanding of health as a state of complete well-being. At present, she went on to say, health needs are included in the "total constellation of our national objectives and the corresponding distribution of the public budget."

There is recognition in Mexico, said the speaker, that health objectives must be integrated with all the relevant aspects of the socioeconomic policies undertaken by the country for its over-all development. Thus they must be pursued simultaneously with such objectives as environmental control and preservation, prevention, nutrition, housing, clean water, sewerage, and education.

The current state of health of the population in Mexico, Sēnora de Araujo reported, varies considerably in relation to such factors as location, whether rural or urban; age groups;

and levels of income, education, and cultural background. Such heterogeneity implies, she said, that some of the existing health problems may be similar to those of the most developed countries, with their urbanization and rapid industrial growth. Yet at the same time, she added, Mexico faces some of the problems prevailing in the less advanced countries, and there is the need to devote a considerable part of available resources to programs designed to close the gap between rural and urban sectors.

Although there has been a general improvement in health standards in Mexico in the last decade, the incidence of contagious diseases and mortality rates among the rural population are still high, and life expectancy in general has not reached the desired level. She felt the main causal factors to be insufficient and inadequately distributed health services, particularly the number of hospital beds and of medical and paramedical personnel in relation to the population. To this should be added the fact that clean water, sewerage nutrition, housing, and education "are usually lacking or insufficient where they are most urgently required." In common with other countries in a similar stage of development, Mexico has a high population growth rate and suffers from an inflationary spiral affecting wages and cost of living as well as the cost of health services.

In the recent past, the Government of Mexico has placed major emphasis on planning and coordination of the institutions directly or indirectly working in the field of public health, and these efforts led, in 1973, to establishment of the National Health Plan, which sets out the basic health goals and the ways and means to achieve them. The over-all goal of the Plan is to raise the health standards of the entire Mexican population by sustained efforts to reduce the incidence of the lack of health while trying to eliminate causes of illness and to develop complementary social services.

The speaker expressed an underlying motivation in these words:

The population of Mexico is a predominantly young one. Almost half of it is under fifteen years of age. We consider they are the future of Mexico and to them especially, the National Health Plan hopes to grant the assurance that they will be protected against disease and sickness and will be more able to face the challenges of life on solidly based expectations.

Public and private agencies have established together the following long-range objectives:

1. To supply medical services for 30 million Mexican people by 1983

2. To increase life expectancy to sixty-eight years

3. To plan for more even distribution of physicians throughout the country

4. To achieve an index of one physician for each 900 people, and one dentist for each 5,000 people

5. To create a voluntary social service for community development

6. To establish a federal system of hospitals.

In line with its conviction that improvement of health services must go hand in hand with broad social development, the Government has drawn into planning the agencies devoted to environmental improvement, hydraulic resources, agriculture, and banking. The last named is to facilitate supplies of credit for low-cost housing, agricultural production, and increase of consumer goods at subsidized prices.

Policies have been "oriented with a sense of social justice," declared Sēnora de Araujo, "so that the population with fewer resources, especially in the rural areas, will be the one that receives the major benefits."

Pollution control is of major concern. The Agency of Environmental Control is giving priority to the control of pollution of water, food, and air caused by physical, chemical, and biological agents, based on extensive research. Particular effort is being made to improve the quality of food so that it will meet not only national standards but also those of the Food and Agricultural Organization of the United Nations.

The speaker concluded by reading to the audience the

thirty-four points contained in Mexico's National Health Plan approved by the Congress in 1973.

The final speaker on this international program was Dr. Krasarn Chartikavanij, Rector, Mahidol University of Medicine and Public Health, Bangkok, Thailand. In presenting the speaker to the audience, Dr. Brown explained that the university was a health sciences training center for doctors, nurses, and other health personnel. The moderator said also that Dr. Chartikavanij received his medical training in the United States.

The speaker began by giving facts about Thailand to orient his audience to the health picture he would give. Located in the Indochina Peninsula, Thailand is bordered on the east by Cambodia, Laos, South Vietnam, and North Vietnam; on the west, by Burma; on the north, by a narrow strip of land belonging to Laos which separates Thailand from the People's Republic of China; and on the south by a common border with Malaysia. The island of Singapore lies at the tip of the peninsula. Within an area of 200,000 square miles—about one and a half times the size of California—lives the Thai population of 40 million; about 6 million live in urban areas—more than half of them in the capital city, Bangkok. All but 5 percent of the population are Buddhist, the small remainder being Moslem and Christian. The average family size is 5.5 members. Eighty-five percent of the people have passed the compulsory four years of schooling. Almost 80 percent of the population live in rural areas; the main products of the country are agricultural, rice and maize being the main exports.

Successive governments of Thailand have had a policy of providing health care, but until recently good care has been given in the large cities, adequate care in the smaller cities, and the vast rural population has had access only to the simplest health measures, such as traditional herb medicines. The country has 200 first-class health centers, each available to about 50,000 people. The centers are staffed by public health nurses and other health workers. The maldistribution of doctors is illustrated by the fact that in Bangkok there is one doctor to 1,000 people, but in the rural areas there is one doctor for 22,000 people. Unevenness of distribution applies also to nurses, hospital beds, and allocation of the national budget.

The reluctance of health personnel to serve in the rural areas, while understandable because of primitive conditions, lack of good roads and means of communication, poor pay, and little or no equipment, has prompted medical schools to change from a hospital-based, Western type of curriculum to a work-study plan. Students are required to spend increasing amounts of time in community health and field work, public health students work for six weeks in the villages, and every medical graduate must serve the country for three years after graduation in any post of any area required by the national health service. The speaker added that many doctors elect to remain in practice in the area where they were first posted. New medical schools are being established in various regions of the country for training doctors in that region.

Like some other less developed countries, Thailand experienced a brain drain when half the medical graduates left the country for further study in Western countries, and perhaps half of these returned to practice in their native land. A radical change is now taking place: many fewer are leaving, partly because it has become more difficult to obtain good appointments in the United States, but partly because young graduates now seem to feel more social responsibility and tend to believe "that the graduate training available in their own country is more suitable for the work they will be required to perform in their future careers."

To improve the health delivery system, the Ministry of Health has merged the Department of Hospitals, which is concerned with treatment, with the Department of Health, which supervises the preventive aspect of health service. Now under consideration is the possible creation of another level of health worker who would be given limited powers for treatment under supervision, as another measure to improve health delivery. The problems involved, such as determining the level of training for this new kind of health worker and deciding whether or not they should be prepared to give in-service training to the public health nurses already posted in the 200 health centers, are being worked out. Another innovation for Thailand resulted from exchange visits between Thai doctors and those in the People's Republic of China: a system of "barefoot doctors" (semivoluntary health workers). Dr. Chartikavanij said that the Ministry of Health was planning to produce large numbers of these, and "it remains to be seen whether this transplant from one culture into another can be successfully integrated into our health system."

The present coalition government of Thailand has declared the policy of providing health care for all the people and has taken the step of offering free treatment to every person earning less than the equivalent of $50 a month, which income bracket would include 30 million people. Problems of funds, personnel, and accounting remain to be solved.

Until 1960 the high rate of population increase in Thailand was not viewed with alarm as there was sufficient food for all and enough remaining for export, and large families were greatly valued. However, a 1958 study by the World Bank Economic Commission showed that the rate of population increase was adversely affecting the country's economic expansion, and steps were taken to introduce a family-planning program. The IUD and the pill were well-accepted by urban dwellers but not by those in rural areas, who are slower to accept the need for change and continue to desire large families to work the land. Additional health workers have been recruited to work in the family-planning program, and plans are being made to incorporate population education into the school curriculum of the younger generation.

Following these five presentations, the speakers were guests at a reception.

# The Canadian Health Insurance Program

## MALCOLM G. TAYLOR

LIKE A NUMBER OF COUNTRIES, Canada has a federal
system of government with a central government and provincial governments. The present importance of this constitu-
tional arrangement lies in the fact that most matters relating
to health fall within the jurisdiction of the provinces, including the licensing of the health professions.

On the other hand, the federal government is able to intervene in this, as in other fields, by use of its spending powers.
It can offer large grants to the provinces to achieve federal
objectives within areas of provincial jurisdiction by establishing the conditions under which the grants will be
made.

Because all citizens contribute to the federal treasury from
which these funds are paid, no province has been able to
withstand the political pressure to make available to its citizens the largesse dispensed by the federal government. This
is a well-known phenomenon. The lure of the conditional
grant-in-aid is universally irresistible. It is this device that
provided the springboard for the launching of the Canadian
health insurance system.

Although the earliest recorded health insurance contract
in Canada was drawn up and notarized 320 years ago on the
Island of Montreal, the evolution of our public system spans
almost exactly fifty years. And, paradoxically, two of the most
important forces powering the ideological thrust for a pro-

MALCOLM G. TAYLOR is Professor of Public Policy, Faculty of Administrative Studies,
York University, Toronto, Canada.

gram to save lives were the experiences of two world wars.

The first war produced shocking statistics on the amount of preventable and reparable conditions among our young citizens that went unattended. It also introduced thousands of Canadians to national health insurance in Britain and, of course, provided them with the experience of the military medical services. A direct result was that in 1919 it was veterans elected to the legislature of British Columbia who forced the government to appoint the first royal commission on health insurance in Canada.

The Second World War reinforced those earlier experiences, but it did something more. Coming on top of the haunting memories of the deprivations of the depression, mobilization created a nation-wide commitment to the idea that out of the war must come not only defeat of totalitarianism but clear evidence that the democratic process could produce a better and more secure world in what Vice-President Henry Wallace had called "the century of the common man." Franklin D. Roosevelt's Four Freedoms and Churchill's and Roosevelt's Atlantic Charter captured the imagination, inspired the hopes, and gave promise of fulfillment of the aspirations of hundreds of millions.

The Canadian government took these aspirations seriously, and planning for health insurance began in January, 1940. As the war neared its end, other major programs were designed, and all of these were presented to the long-heralded Federal-Provincial Conference on Post-War Reconstruction, convened on August 6, 1945.

In opening the Conference, the Prime Minister said:

The enemies we shall have to overcome will be on our own Canadian soil. They will make their presence known in the guise of sickness, unemployment and want. It is to plan for a unified campaign in Canada against these enemies of progress and human well-being that we have come together at this time. This may well be the most important Canadian Conference since Confederation.

Among the federal proposals was an offer to pay 60 percent of the estimated costs of a comprehensive program of medical, hospital, dental, diagnostic, pharmaceutical, and nursing benefits. Unfortunately, however, the offer was part of a much larger package, and when other elements of the package were unacceptable, the Conference collapsed. It was not the only postwar dream to be shattered, either in Canada or elsewhere.

But it is one of the great virtues of a federal system that in a field of provincial jurisdiction the parts do not have to wait for the whole. Even before the Conference had foundered, the province of Saskatchewan had passed the necessary legislation authorizing the establishment of one of the major benefits—hospital insurance—to begin on January 1, 1947. Other provinces followed and by 1950 four of them had governmental programs. In 1955, the largest province, Ontario, decided to press the federal government to honor its 1945 promise, which it did by passing legislation in 1957. Fifteen years after the war, one of the benefits was available to all Canadians.

With that completed, the scenario began a rerun.

Now that Saskatchewan was receiving half the cost of its hospital insurance plan from the federal subsidy, the government decided to use these new revenues to pioneer again by introducing medical care insurance. Despite the opposition of the medical profession, which withdrew all but emergency services for twenty-three days, the program began on July 1, 1962. Other provinces introduced similar programs, and a federally subsidized national program was launched on July 1, 1968. By 1970 all Canadians were insured—a quarter century after that initial period of great expectations. When one considers the problems of administering programs of such magnitude and complexity, there may have been some inner wisdom in the body politic that resulted in the more cautious approach.

The impacts of the two programs were enormous. Gone were the financially crippling costs of hospital and medical bills; gone, too, was the array of devices that protected insurance funds but not patients: waiting periods, deductibles, experience rating, cancellable policies, higher premiums for the aged. To every Canadian—rich and poor, urban and rural, old and young, heads of families and their dependents— there is now available a comprehensive system of medical and hospital benefits. Also, on the positive side are a vastly improved network of hospital facilities and services, an expanded supply of health personnel, increased incomes for health workers, and the near disappearance of hospital deficits, with the net result that Canada probably enjoys as high a standard of medical and hospital services as any other nation.

In the wake of this transfer of the financing of medical and hospital services from the market economy to the political economy came new problems: assuring the right facilities in the right place, including resisting demands by local communities for more facilities than they needed; tough negotiations between the federal and provincial governments; equally tough negotiations with the providers of services; and, of course, in a period of rising inflation, concern over rising costs. But benefits are always accompanied by costs, and such problems are inevitably a part of the costs.

The two programs provide a full range of hospital services at the standard ward level and an equally wide range of services of physicians and surgeons at home or office or in hospital. These are standard benefits required by the federal legislation, and some provinces offer additional benefits. Hospitals are generally paid according to what is called a "global budget" system, and most physicians are paid by the fee-for-service method.

It is with respect to financing, however, that the diversity characteristic of federal systems is manifested. Prior to the introduction of the government programs about half the population had some degree of protection against hospital bills, and slightly over one third had some protection against medical bills under voluntary prepayment plans and commercial insurance. All of these were financed by premiums, frequently subsidized by employers. What the voluntary system had created was a ready-made tax source for govern-

ments. In the beginning, therefore, eight of the ten provinces used premiums as their primary source of revenue.
The other two used revenues from retail sales taxes. Gradually, other sources, such as the income tax, were used. One
by one, provincial governments have abandoned the use of
premiums until, at the present time, only one province uses
premiums for hospital insurance and only three use premiums for medical care insurance. In those provinces using
premiums, low-income earners and everyone over sixty-five
are exempt from payment. In seven provinces, medical and
hospital services are available, therefore, not on condition of
having paid an insurance premium, but simply on the basis
of being a bona fide resident. In those provinces, therefore,
it is no longer an *insurance* system. Entitlement to necessary
health services is a right.

One final aspect of revenue sources that remains for consideration is the Canadian experience with patient payments
or coinsurance. Despite the fact that the federal legislation
provides a disincentive to use patient charges, we do have a
few examples:

1. Alberta's original program required the patient to pay
$2.00 a day. It maintained this charge under the national
plan but abolished it in 1972.

2. British Columbia introduced coinsurance in 1952, with
rates ranging from $2.00 per day to $3.50, depending on facilities of the hospital, for a maximum of ten days per family
per year. This was extremely cumbersome to administer, and
in 1954 it was reduced to $1.00 per day where it now re-
mains, although no one can give a rational explanation for
the charge.

3. In Saskatchewan, following the 1964 defeat of the New
Democratic Party which had introduced medical care insurance in 1962, the new Liberal government introduced coinsurance payments on April 1, 1968, of $1.50 for office visits,
$2.00 for home and emergency (outpatient) visits, and $2.50
for the first ten days in hospital and $1.50 per day thereafter.

These charges remained in force until August 1, 1971,

when the New Democratic Party defeated the Liberal government, with the coinsurance payments being one of the major political issues of the election campaign.

The definitive study of this experience has been made by R. G. Beck. He concludes:

The effect of copayment in 1968 was a seven per cent reduction in overall utilization and reductions up to 24 per cent as family size and age of head of family were considered, with an average reduction of 18 per cent for the poor, these being as defined by the Economic Council of Canada.[1]

Taken together with other data, the conclusion must be drawn as Professor Evans of the University of British Columbia observes:

If cost escalation is not driven by patient behaviour then it cannot be controlled by measures which target the patient. Copayment (deductibles, co-insurance, ceilings, exclusions) will not limit the response of health care costs to insurance because they are directed at the wrong decision maker. National health insurance increased costs, but not apparently, through its impact on patient behaviour.[2]

4. There is one other type of patient payment—this one the result of extra billing by physicians. In general, there is no extra billing by participating physicians for insured general practice and referred specialist practice. However, in some provinces extra billing is permitted under certain circumstances where the patient has been informed and agreed in advance. What we call "opted out" doctors may extra bill, but their number is not great.

THE COSTS

Obviously, programs as comprehensive as these are expensive. The final figures are not yet released for fiscal 1973–74, but preliminary estimates indicate that costs were slightly over $3 billion for hospital care and $1.7 billion for medical

[1] R. G. Beck, "Demand for Physicians' Services in Saskatchewan" (unpublished Ph.D. thesis, University of Alberta, 1971).
[2] Robert Evans, "The Impact of National Health Insurance" (Mimeo; 1974).

care. As a result of costs of this magnitude, expenditures on health services in Canada in 1974 represented 7.3 percent of our gross national product (GNP) compared with 7.7 percent of the GNP in the United States.

PROBLEMS

As in many social security programs, part of the problem lies in the fact that more was expected of the programs than they were designed to achieve. In addition, there are problems of inequity in the distribution of personnel, particularly in the rural areas, and in providing access to primary care. There are also problems, shared with other countries, of how to substitute lower cost resources through the wider use of paramedical personnel, and of providing nursing homes for long-term patients who do not require the facilities of the active-treatment general hospital.

But these are not problems arising from the programs; they would have been confronted without a program, and in its absence there would have been fewer means to resolve them. As many critics of the British National Health Service suggest, part of the problem may lie in the fact that the new programs did not change the existing system or nonsystem enough.

LESSONS FROM THE CANADIAN EXPERIENCE

With this cursory examination of the Canadian programs, what have we learned? Some of the conclusions or lessons are as follows:

1. Comparing Canada with the United States, it seems reasonable to say that the costs of health services under the political economy have not risen much, if any, faster than they would have done under the market economy.

2. Canada has paid an unduly high and unnecessary cost because of the sequence in which it introduced the programs. By introducing first the most expensive element—hospital care—it was probably inevitable that we would overbuild acute-care hospital facilities. The incentives to do so were ex-

acerbated by the fact that despite the federal offer to include outpatient diagnostic services, the six largest provinces did not introduce this benefit in the first ten years because of opposition of the medical profession to such services being restricted to hospitals. This failure enhanced the demand for unnecessary inpatient admissions.

An equally serious defect is the fact that nursing homes and home-care programs are not shared-cost services, and this also created unnecessary demand for more expensive types of service.

It has always seemed to me that had we introduced medical services first, with financial incentives to establish group practice clinics or health maintenance organizations, and grants for the necessary clinic facilities, we would now be operating a superior service at less cost. But it requires more than vision in the real world. Governments respond to democratically determined imperatives, and it was hospital bills that were mortgaging people's lives and it was hospitals and not doctors that were in deficit, and so we acted as we did. But we could, and should, have been wiser.

3. The premiums method of collecting revenue is a more regressive form of taxation than any of the others, but even in the three provinces where it is used, the fact of federal and provincial subsidy results in the over-all system being slightly progressive in its tax incidence.

4. The 50 percent sharing by the federal government and the formulas it uses have an important distribution effect favorable to the lower-income provinces. For example, in the poorest province the number of physicians increased by 30 percent in four years.

5. The Canadian experience demonstrates that the division of a society into two classes of insurable and noninsurable citizens violates any principle of equal human rights and is a concept to be abjured. We have also abolished the concept of the charity patient, and with it the understanding that it was only the poor who served as the teaching material for the education of society's most prestigious profession.

6. We have achieved enormous reductions in administration costs, in two ways. First, the cost of administration of the programs is about 5 percent. Therefore, ninety-five cents out of every health dollar goes to health care. Secondly, there have been major reductions in the staffs of accounting departments in individual hospitals.

These are among the lessons. But over and above these, it seems to me that we have made a contribution to rational policy-making by laying to rest a number of myths that once held great sway. Among these are the following:

1. The myth that the delivery of health services must be extruded through the ideological molds of the insurance mechanism: we have almost virtually abandoned all the nonsense of waiting periods, deductibles, copayments, loss ratios, actuarial calculations. And yet the system works successfully.

2. The myth that payment of premiums is necessary in order to ensure patient responsibility: there are no discernible differences in patient demand under any revenue system.

3. The myth that copayments are necessary to ensure patient responsibility: they deter primarily the poor, and do not distinguish between deterring frivolous demand and genuine need.

4. The myth that the payment of a fee by the patient enhances the doctor-patient relationship: the president of a provincial medical association, one in a partnership of four obstetricians, told me that his three partners billed the Commission, while he billed the patient. As soon as he ceased to be president, he said, he would also bill the Commission. "None of us wishes to talk about money in the doctor-patient relationship."

5. The myth that a government-operated program is Socialism: that myth has no meaning in Canada; health insurance is supported by all political parties.

6. The myth that a government program would drive doctors out of the country: the brain drain of Canadian doctors to the United States has declined, and we have been forced

recently to put up barriers to those physicians who wish to immigrate to Canada.

7. The myth that a government program would reduce quality of care: increasing staff hours per patient day in hospital by 26 percent is one countermeasure. As a lay person, I am not qualified to be assertive here, but there are enough signs to satisfy me that the quality of care is, in fact, higher. An increase in the ratio of physicians to population from 1:860 in 1961 to 1:600 in 1974 and a doubling of the number of accredited hospitals must surely have improved over-all quality.

One could go on, but it is obvious that much of the conventional wisdom was wrong and that most of the predicted evils have not occurred. So, in creating a health service we also have destroyed a formerly powerful mythology. No Canadian would claim that the system is perfect, but it is a major advance on what we had.

In an evaluation of the Canadian system there are two outcomes that, however subtle and difficult to measure, must be accorded full weight. The first is that not only have we removed the economic barrier to higher quality care, but, in doing so, we have gone a long way in achieving one of Roosevelt's Four Freedoms—freedom from fear. We have abolished the fear of crippling health bills that can strike at any time but typically smite most of us when we retire on reduced incomes. The psychological effect has been extraordinary. Far from eroding moral fiber or sapping individual initiative, as the doomsayers predicted, our people have responded as if a great burden has been lifted from them, freeing their minds and spirits for positive purposes.

The second is that we have reinforced the confidence of Canadians in the democratic process. We have reaffirmed that citizens of a free society can, despite obstacles, opposition, and delays, collectively fulfill those individual aspirations that challenge a society to higher goals. In Canada, universally available, publicly financed health care has been joined to universal public education as one of the twin pillars on which a democratic society rests, ensuring that every one is assisted in striving toward the Greek ideal of a sound mind in a sound body.

We take pride in the fact that, acting together, through our elected parliaments, we have expanded every person's freedom, shielded every person's risk, reduced every person's fear, enhanced every person's confidence, and brightened every person's future.

Perhaps the paradox in the whole picture is that so few Canadians seem fully aware of the phenomenal change that occurred. We all now take it for granted, but its transcendent beauty is there for all to see.

# Problems and Prospects for a National Health Program

## PATRICK J. LUCEY

COUNTLESS SPEAKERS will address gatherings during the Bicentennial, reflecting upon the past two centuries of this nation, heralding the social and technological accomplishments of the Republic. Indeed, there is much to be proud of, much to praise. But just as this time is to be accepted as a time of hyperbole and redundant superlatives, let it also be accepted as a time for thoughtful reflection and harsh self-analysis. Let our 200th year be a time to see not only what is good about our nation and our people but also what is not so good—and then do something about it.

For here we are in our Bicentennial, and what do we find?

We find a nation whose fabric is strained, whose people are doubting their institutions, their leaders, perhaps even themselves. Sadly, dangerously, behind the frivolity and festivity of this Bicentennial there is a weakened spirit, a questionable resolve. Is it all worth it? Does it all matter? Does anything matter?

How far can we say this nation of promise and opportunity has come in 200 years when we find the conditions of life such as they are today—conditions conducive to endurance rather than excellence, complacency rather than concern, selfishness rather than service? They are conditions of life fostered by, and found in, both the private and public sectors. Culpability? There is enough blame for all of us.

The facts of life, the facts of living—of dying—speak for themselves:

PATRICK J. LUCEY is Governor of Wisconsin.

The United States is a world leader in the production of agricultural products, yet an estimated 20 million Americans suffer from malnutrition. More than 5,000 die each year because of inadequate diets.

In 1974, nearly 60,000 American infants died before they reached their first birthday. If we applied Sweden's infant mortality rate to the United States, 22,000 of those children would be alive today.

Public health practices vary in quality and coverage. In Texarkana, a community which is divided by a state line, 606 cases of measles were reported in Texas children (20 cases per 1,000 children), but only 27 cases in Arkansas children (one case per 1,000 children). Immunization in Texas has been left entirely to physicians in private practice; Arkansas has a public immunization program.

In Wisconsin, in a recent year, almost 100 women died from cervical cancer—deaths that could have been prevented by well-known methods of medical diagnosis and treatment.

If you are an expectant mother who is black, or Spanish-speaking, or a member of some other minority group, it is three times more likely you will die in childbirth than if you were a white mother. And if an American Indian in Wisconsin gets the flu, his chances of dying are twice as great as those of his white counterpart.

If you are poor, that also makes a difference in the care you may or may not get. Chicago, for example, has eight hospitals and five medical schools, but poor inner-city residents must seek their care at Cook County Hospital, where the wait may be many hours long.

These random statistics and examples represent, of course, only the surface. Each of us knows personally examples of how we have failed to meet the health needs of our citizens.

But on top of these examples, these instances of inadequacy, we also have the question of health care costs— skyrocketing costs, costs that often make adequate health care unaffordable even for some with moderate incomes. The average American now works a month each year just to pay doctors, hospitals, and health insurance companies. By 1980, we will be working two months annually for health benefits.

And so, nearly 200 years after our nation's birth, we find that, for too many, we have failed to deliver that first and most basic right of individuals, the right to life.

What could be a more basic concern of a society than the health of its people? America's answer in the last two centuries appears to be: "Almost anything."

Americans, as citizens and as a society, have given health a very low priority. Individually, most of us feel little personal responsibility for maintaining our own health; collectively, our efforts to assure that adequate health care is available to all who need it have been woefully inadequate.

Over the past ten years, specific frustration has developed about spotty accessibility, uncontrolled costs, and the questionable quality of health care services. Some 500,000 people live in counties where there is no practicing physician and no health care facility. In Lafayette County, Wisconsin, the physician-patient ratio is 1 to 4,400. That is less than the ratio in several Central American countries that receive financial assistance from the United States for their health programs. But even when rural areas claim a physician, he or she may be located at the county seat, miles from remote areas and reachable only over dirt and sometimes impassable roads. The distance may not be so great, but the barriers are, in some of our big cities. In Baltimore there are only 100 general practitioners for 550,000 slum dwellers, and all but 10 of them are at least sixty years old.

Those with access to medical help, however, have discovered that in these inflationary times health care costs have led the way in increases. Since the end of cost controls on April 30, 1974, hospital daily charges have increased 80 percent faster than the cost of living, and physicians' fees have gone up 50 percent faster.

Finally, one is prompted to ask: when we learn that an estimated 30 percent to 40 percent of some operations such as hysterectomies and appendectomies are thought to be unnecessary; when we learn we have a nation of drug-dependent people who spend $12 billion a year on prescription drugs; when we learn that the nutrition-poor diets of our children are promoted by a dearth of counteradvice to the $169 million-a-year advertising campaigns for sweets and soft drinks—what are we paying for?

But despite the pressure for change by the victims of a poorly functioning health care system, change has not occurred. And sadly, this is true because those who have taken an oath to protect our well-being have exploited their status, their wealth, and their special training to insist that the *status quo* continue.

The American Medical Association (AMA) and other obstructionists have perpetrated the free-market myth as the basis of their argument. This fable holds that quality health services can only be delivered in a free market where each consumer exercises his choice in terms of the type and level of health care which suits his taste. But when was the last time you heard of a health care consumer having the time or ability or opportunity to "shop around"? In fact, it is the provider—the physician, the hospital, the health professional—that decides what is needed and at what price.

And each time citizens or reformers question the *status quo,* particularly the *status quo* as it affects its pocketbook, organized medicine charges interference: interference in the free market, interference with the American way of life.

It happened when elected leaders sought to bring better health care through Medicaid and Medicare.

It happened when consumer advocates and elected leaders sought to end costly duplication and require some degree of rationality in facility construction and equipment purchases through certificate of need.

And it happened again when progressive leaders began an effort to develop a national health insurance program designed to aid each and every American citizen.

It is ironic, therefore, that the doctors who fought Medicare, the doctors who fight certificate-of-need requirements, and the doctors who are fighting national health insurance are using their powerful lobby to seek government help when their malpractice insurance costs increase. These doctors, who have told the people's advocates to keep hands off their profession in the past, are now blackmailing and even striking—demanding that government intervene on their behalf. What would their response be if we told them to shop around for malpractice insurance, it's the free-market way?

The professional outbursts we see and read about today are simply signs, however, of the level of political sophistication the medical profession has acquired in recent years. The AMA and its philosophical allies have bobbed, weaved, strategically retreated, and boldly attacked in their fight against the people's health care interests.

This political flexibility on the part of the AMA is nicely illustrated in its position on national health insurance. After strenuously opposing any national health insurance plan, the AMA finally offered its own version of what health insurance ought to be. Called "Medicredit," the proposal was quickly recognized for what it was: a transparent attempt to provide generously for the well-being of their own members. Medicredit would have brought no change in the organization of the health care system, and it featured the socially questionable device of tax credits for the purchase of private health insurance on a voluntary basis.

As pressure for reform has mounted in recent months, the AMA shifted position once again. Its latest ploy is to endorse compulsory private insurance for *selected* population groups. The AMA seems to be saying that we ought to be concerned about the health of some of the people all of the time and all of the people some of the time—but not all of the people all of the time.

But it is not merely the AMA that stands in the way of meaningful reform. In a recent issue of *Newsweek,* economist

Milton Friedman took after the Health Security bill much as a guided missile takes after its programmed target.[1] Friedman insults organized labor by asking it to oppose national health insurance because it will assist "simply average citizens" and remove from the bargaining table the question of medical care. He asks the rest of us to stand against this urgently needed reform by claiming that national insurance will generally reduce the quality of medical care, hurt the poor, increase medical costs, promote waste and duplication, and encourage doctors to leave the country. He does not argue that national health insurance will spread disease, destroy the family, and topple our system of government. But these items may have been deleted from his list by a cautious editor.

In truth, the problems Mr. Friedman identifies are with us now and must be laid squarely on the doorstep of the American medical establishment.

Mr. Friedman argues that costs will escalate if the Health Security bill is enacted and cites our experience under Medicare and Medicaid as proof. But it was the doctors who defeated attempts to make cost controls a feature of that program.

Mr. Friedman worries about the duplication of health care facilities. But, again, who stands foremost in opposition to certificate-of-need legislation?

Mr. Friedman postures about his concern for quality medical services. But does he honestly believe we can continue to provide one kind of care for those with wealth and status and not care at all about what happens to everyone else?

Well, despite the scare tactics of the AMA and Mr. Friedman, I believe effective national health insurance must and will be enacted by this Congress. It will not be easy and it will not come without commitments from people who, like social workers, must regard this achievement as the most important, and appropriate, reform of the Bicentennial year.

[1] Milton Friedman, "Leonard Woodcock's Free Lunch," *Newsweek*, April 21, 1975, p. 84.

But this will be true only if the reform we enact offers complete health care to every citizen.

It must be as concerned with malnutrition as with malignancy.

It must deal with health education as well as with emergency care.

It must offer complete health care to every American citizen without regard to race, social status, or income level.

And it must be financed through a combination of social insurance and taxation based upon ability to pay.

Important, too, is the long-term impact of such a program. National health insurance should do more than simply collect and distribute health care dollars. It should be designed and implemented to effect change and reform. It should be used to cut duplication and inefficiency in some areas and to establish decent care where there is presently little or none available.

Finally, an acceptable national health care program must be publicly accountable. It must be accountable not only at its inception, but in its implementation. Past experience has shown accountability to be an elusive goal and one that is easily avoided through token gestures or cosmetic trappings. This should *not* happen with national health insurance.

Public financing does not necessarily guarantee public accountability. Public discussion, and even consumer involvement in some decision-making, does not necessarily guarantee public accountability. And abandoning the present health care profit structure will not, in and of itself, guarantee public accountability.

The key to accountability is consumer involvement and consumer control. It must be involvement and control not in one isolated part of the system, but in health care decisions at all levels. The National Health Security bill attempts to provide that type of involvement in each health care decision. Through a consumer majority on national and local policy and administrative councils, the proposed National Health Security bill could go further than any other proposal in meeting the requirement for program accountability. In short, the bill not only contains incentives for consumer involvement, but also guarantees consumer majority representation on the bodies responsible for health care decisions in every area of importance.

In addition, every other health care improvement and reform I have outlined is similarly dealt with or can be dealt with in the National Health Security bill. It is, therefore, no surprise that the bill offered by Senator Edward Kennedy and Congressman James C. Corman is opposed so strenuously by the AMA and its allies like Milton Friedman.

It is no surprise, either, that the opponents of better and more equitable health care are attempting to use the nation's current economic condition as an excuse for inaction. Certainly, the Congress must be aware of the fiscal obligations it incurs and the cost of its actions. Economy in government should be a constant goal. But Congress must also be aware that this time of economic distress has allowed this nation to see for itself that fate and a layoff slip can, overnight, bring a health care nightmare to countless thousands of unemployed. It is a reality that cannot be allowed to continue.

Indeed, an innovative Congress could even use this opportunity—through a meaningful national health insurance act—to infuse a degree of productivity into our health care system. It could not only give this nation's citizens a better health care end product, but our nation's economy a leaner, more efficient economic entity.

And so, I challenge each of you to return home and look carefully at health care in your own community, your own state.

Return home and become an advocate for an equitable health service system for all Americans. Only through involvement by well-informed, highly motivated individuals can we hope to offset the well-heeled supporters of the *status quo*.

Return home and challenge your leaders to lead, to con-

front the doubt and cynicism of today with a quality of per-
formance worthy of trust, worthy of confidence.

Return home to prove that, through a commitment of the
people, this nation can act on behalf of the people. It can act
at last and once and for all to secure, in our Bicentennial
year, that first, important right our Founding Fathers
guaranteed for *all* the people: the right to *good* health, the
right to *life itself.*

# Institutes on Health and Health Care Delivery

## PATRICK McCUAN

THE INSTITUTES on Health and Health Care Delivery were envisaged as a means of developing in greater depth the theme of the 1975 Annual Forum: *Health as a Right: the Human and Political Dimensions*. They were designed with the expectation that by convening task forces composed of individuals with a wide diversity of program and policy experience to explore major issues in the health care field, major public policy statements would be produced which could be used by individuals, representatives of private organizations, service providers, and government agencies within the human services field as a basis for the development of national, state, and local public social policy. The task forces met several times prior to the Institutes to conceptualize their framework and to agree on principles for their reports. The task force preliminary reports which were presented at the five Institutes held in conjunction with the 1975 Annual Forum represented a melding of a wide range of viewpoints and experience. Subsequently, the task forces revised and expanded their preliminary statements into final reports, reflected in this article, to include points which emerged from the discussions in the Institutes and further refinements in their thinking.

The task forces launched their discussions from this basic premise: Although as a nation we are committed to seeing that all citizens have equal access to high-quality health care,

PATRICK McCUAN is a Special Projects Consultant to the National Conference on Social Welfare and served as project director of the five task forces.

our current system, or nonsystem, is fraught with inequities and maldistribution of services. However, major changes are imminent in the U.S. health care system. National health insurance is in the offing, and while some of the draft legislation proposes a comprehensive medical care plan, few recognize the central role "social" components should play in any national program. Also, the increasing scarcity of resources will force a reallocation of health resources, and decisions regarding these reallocations should be determined by generally accepted goals and policies.

INSTITUTE 1: SOCIAL COMPONENTS OF PHYSICAL AND
MENTAL HEALTH SERVICES

The purpose of this Institute was to place boundaries around the social component in physical and mental health services. The task force developed initial conceptual specifications covering the various aspects of the issue. This conceptual framework includes support services in the health system, style of life, financing, and administrative issues at various levels of government.

In its report [1] the task force refers to the social component as those aspects of a comprehensive health care approach which are nonmedical in nature, but essential in the acute phases of care and in the restoration and maintenance of health and well-being in the community setting. These are, in the main, social services outside the range of expertise of physicians but provided within a comprehensive care system and/or in cooperation with other institutional service systems.

INSTITUTE 2: HUMAN FACTORS IN LONG-TERM HEALTH CARE

This task force moved from the basic premise that the social welfare community has broad responsibilities for placing dependent, disabled, or elderly individuals into long-term health care arrangements and for payment of these services. The social welfare community also has much to contribute to

[1] *Social Components of Physical and Mental Health Services: Final Report of the Institute Task Force* (Columbus, Ohio: National Conference on Social Welfare, 1975).

the enhancement of the quality of life for individuals receiving such care. A significant body of research findings has emerged which tend to identify and confirm the importance of psychosocial components in the effective provision of health care. However, these ideas and approaches have not become a part of day-to-day planning for, or the provision of, or the assessment and evaluation of, long-term health care. Nor are they incorporated in the basic education of health care professionals.

The task force report [2] brought together several themes on which there was wide consensus into a set of principles of long-term health care, including recommendations for future action. The task force developed specifications for a definition of long-term social/health care which included the following elements:

1. Individuals in all age groups with chronic physical and mental handicaps and disabilities, including mental retardation and mental illness

2. Institutional and noninstitutional services

3. Emphasis on promotion of health as well as on prevention, rehabilitation, restoration, and maintenance

4. Focus on the individual's social, physical, and mental capacities and needs and on promotion of optimum functioning rather than just on illness and disability

5. Recognition of individual, familial, community, regional, and cultural differences in individual expectations, life-style requirements, and anticipated outcomes

6. Affirmation of needs of the individual as the nucleus for health care planning and provision of services rather than the services that are offered by specific institutions or programs

7. Continuity of provisions, services, and benefits rather than care or coverage related to separated or loosely coordinated episodes.

[2] *Human Factors in Long-Term Institutional Care: Final Report of the Institute Task Force* (Columbus, Ohio: National Conference on Social Welfare, 1975).

INSTITUTE 3: SOCIAL COMPONENTS OF HEALTH
MAINTENANCE ORGANIZATIONS (HMOs)

The task force suggested two basic choices on how the social component could be organized within the context of the medical care delivery system of an HMO: either the social component would be integrated within the medical way of organizing services or else the social component would be separately organized and linkages established between the medical system and the social system.

Another aspect which drew considerable attention was what social services should be mandated by the HMO Act as basic benefits to be provided by all qualified HMOs. How the basic primary care provider team functions within the rubric of the organization of the social component, including the advantages and disadvantages of patient care teams, was examined. A central underlying issue is how the social component should be financed. The task force concluded that although the HMO Act of 1973 is quite modest so far as mandated medical and social services are concerned, the fact that a higher level of benefits is required by the act than is usually provided by traditional insurance programs will encourage the inclusion of social components in HMO service delivery.

The extent to which social components are cost-effective within the context of medical services was also discussed.

The task force examined the extent and levels of government and consumer involvement in establishing regulations of cost, quality, and access to social services. They concluded that the current HMOs are far from ideal in regard to the fit between the services people say they want and what providers say they need. Specific detailed examples of innovative programs in operation are described in the final report.[3]

---

[3] *Social Components of Health Maintenance Organizations: Final Report of the Institute Task Force* (Columbus, Ohio: National Conference on Social Welfare, 1975).

INSTITUTE 4: THE IMPACT OF NATIONAL HEALTH INSURANCE
ON SERVICES TO THE MENTALLY ILL AND MENTALLY DISABLED

In this report,[4] the task force defined an appropriate role for
national health insurance in financing the care of the repetitive or continuing mentally ill and disabled, a group which
consistently has been denied equitable consideration in virtually all legislative proposals. In addition, the task force introduced an approach to providing a spectrum of needed
social support services, linked programmatically with insured
health services, but financed through other public and private mechanisms.

The task force was concerned by the lack of adequate, professionally developed guidelines for defining mental conditions in terms of social factors and levels of functioning,
rather than exclusively through medically oriented diagnostic
classifications.

The review of the current patterns of providing and financing care of the repetitive or continuing mentally ill and
disabled revealed that in spite of advances in the mental
health field in the past decade, this population continues to
receive services through a maze of costly, poorly coordinated,
health and other human service programs. The task force
recommends that the framers of national health insurance
should focus on developing a benefit structure which stresses
less costly service alternatives and workable review methods
in order to provide coverage for pressing health needs in an
economically feasible manner.

To assure such coverage, the task force recommended a
program which encompasses a range of health, health-
related, and supportive services designed to meet reasonably
the needs of all persons with acute, short-term, repetitive, or
continuing disorders, both mental and physical. This integrated program offers opportunities for improved health

[4] *The Impact of National Health Insurance on Services to the Mentally Ill and Mentally
Disabled, Final Report of the Institute Task Force* (Columbus, Ohio: National Conference
on Social Welfare, 1975).

care, more effective use of resources, and after a period of adjustment and the development of criteria for accrediting and monitoring services, cost savings through reduced utilization of the more expensive types of care. The interface of this programmatic program would be mandated in national health insurance legislation; the health services would be financed by insurance, and the other human services would be financed substantially through general public revenues.

INSTITUTE 5: ROLES FOR SOCIAL WORK IN COMMUNITY
MENTAL HEALTH PROGRAMS

Because of the scope and urgency of the mental health needs in communities throughout the United States, because of the congruence of the goals of community mental health and the professional mission of social work, and because of the increasing numbers of social workers in leadership positions in mental health programs, the task force gave thoughtful consideration to how alternative manpower utilization might strengthen the effectiveness of community mental health programs (CMH) and how social workers can help bring about such improvement.

The work of this task force embraced two major perspectives. Given the present stage of development of CMH programs and the reactionary mood of contemporary social-political affairs, an imperative first step makes it mandatory that professional social work organizations and CMH organizations strongly reaffirm their commitment to the original goals of the CMHC act. Second, the task force after reviewing the historical development of social work and community mental health concluded that there is an imbalance in the way that social work manpower is being utilized in CMH programs in that too much of the current manpower is used in the clinical area; that the clinical area itself needs to be expanded to involve more effort with client-related systems of home, work, school, and cultural groups; and that not enough manpower is being used in the nonclinical area.

The task force pointed out that social work, because of its

historical mission and functions, is in a unique position to contribute to the support of those service functions and objectives which are least well implemented and staffed, namely, work with other social and community systems to reduce unnecessary and harmful stress and to develop the support which these systems can provide clients in their recovery or adjustment from mental illness. The report [5] concludes with a detailed set of recommendations for specific actions to be taken by the social work profession and the community mental health field.

Unfortunately, the development of public social policy carries the connotation of something academic, esoteric, slightly outside the real world. In fact, it is very much a part of the real world and must be seen as such by the human service field if substantive rather than "first-aid" solutions are to be achieved to ameliorate inequities in our present systems. Before public policy is formulated, legislation written, or service delivery programs designed there must be agreement on the principles of how present and/or emerging social problems should be tackled and how they could be solved.

Some of the major public policy issues regarding the social components of the health care system have been clarified, and potential solutions have been suggested in these task force reports. The task forces on health and health care delivery have enabled NCSW to take a major step toward its goal of providing the education and information necessary for the development of public social policy. Thus, these task forces have forged yet another link in NCSW's chain of services whereby its efforts toward achieving the capacity to make an impact on national, state, and local public social policy can be accomplished—this, it is to be hoped, is no longer a dream but an imminent reality.

[5] *Roles for Social Work in Community Mental Health Programs: Final Report of the Institute Task Force* (Columbus, Ohio: National Conference on Social Welfare, 1975).

# *Appendix A: Program*

### *GENERAL SESSIONS*

## THE PRESIDENTIAL ADDRESS

*Speaker:* Melvin A. Glasser, International Union, United Automobile,
Aerospace and Agricultural Implement Workers of America-UAW,
Detroit; President, NCSW

*Respondents:* James R. Dumpson, Human Resources Administration,
New York

Joseph Maldonado, HEW, San Francisco

Mrs. Evelyn L. Blanchard, Bureau of Indian Affairs, Albuquerque, N.
Mex.

Tsuguo Ikeda, Seattle Atlantic Street Center, Seattle

## THE ECONOMIC HEALTH OF THE NATION

*Speaker:* Gardner Ackley, University of Michigan, Ann Arbor

*Respondents:* Herman Stein, Center for Advanced Study in Behavioral
Sciences, Stanford, Calif.

Mario Obledo, Secretary of Health and Welfare, California, Sacramento

Presentation of NCSW Distinguished Service Award and 75- and 50-year
Membership Plaques

## FACING UP NOW TO HUNGER IN THE UNITED STATES

*Speaker:* The Honorable Mervyn M. Dymally, Lieutenant Governor of
California, Sacramento

## THE MOST URGENT AND ACHIEVABLE GOALS FOR HEALTH CARE IN THEIR COUNTRIES

*Moderator:* Bertram S. Brown, M.D., National Institute of Mental
Health, Rockville, Md.

*Speakers:* Dr. Satar Seraj, Ministry of Public Health, Kabul, Afghanistan

Dr. M. Tajul Hossain, Health Secretary, Bangladesh

The Honorable Junshiro Ohmura, M.D., Ministry of Health, Tokyo,
Japan

Lucila Leal de Araujo, Instituto Mexicano del Seguro Social, Mexico
City, Mexico

Krasarn Chartikavanij, Mahidol University of Medicine and Public
Health, Bangkok, Thailand

PROBLEMS AND PROSPECTS FOR A NATIONAL
HEALTH PROGRAM
  *Speaker:* The Honorable Patrick J. Lucey, Governor of Wisconsin, Madison
Introduction of NCSW President 1975–76

### SECTION I: ECONOMIC INDEPENDENCE

THE CHALLENGE OF INCOME MAINTENANCE
  *Panelists:* Mitchell I. Ginsberg, Columbia University, New York
  Michael Mahoney, HEW, Washington
  Leonard Lesser, Center for Community Change, Washington
  Tom Joe, Seneca Corporation, Washington
  Alvin L. Schorr, Community Service Society of New York, New York

FULL EMPLOYMENT WITHOUT INFLATION
  *Speaker:* The Honorable Augustus F. Hawkins, U.S. Representative to Congress from California's 29th District, Washington
  *Discussants:* Bertram M. Gross, City University of New York, New York
  Mary Dublin Keyserling, Washington
  Paul Bullock, University of California, Los Angeles

KEYS TO ECONOMIC INDEPENDENCE—
IMPROVING MANPOWER TRAINING
AND JOB PLACEMENT
  *Speakers:* Curtis Aller, San Francisco State University, San Francisco
  S. Martin Taylor, Michigan Employment Security Commission, Detroit
  *Discussant:* Eunice Elton, Mayor's Office of Manpower, San Francisco

NATIONAL HEALTH INSURANCE—AN IMPERATIVE NOW
  *Speaker:* Lester Breslow, University of California, Los Angeles
  *Discussants:* Einar Mohn, Committee for National Health Insurance, Burlingame, Calif.
  Melvin A. Glasser, International Union, United Automobile Workers of America, Detroit

PUBLIC SERVICE JOB GOALS
  *Speakers:* Charles C. Killingsworth, Michigan State University, East Lansing
  Bonnie B. Snedeker, Olympus Research Corporation, Washington
  *Discussant:* Albert Pinon, Santa Clara Valley Employment and Training Board, San Jose, Calif.

### SECTION II: PROBLEMS OF EFFECTIVE FUNCTIONING

ADVOCACY AND LONG-TERM CARE:
THE ROLE OF THE OMBUDSMAN
  *Speakers:* The Honorable Martin J. Schreiber, Lieutenant Governor and Ombudsman, Wisconsin, Madison
  Arlene Warner, Idaho Department of Special Services, Boise

THE CAMPUS AS AN UNDERDEVELOPED COMMUNITY:
NEW CONCEPTS FOR STUDENT EFFECTIVENESS
*Speakers:* Russell Anderson, University of California, Berkeley
Marc Pilisuk, University of California, Berkeley
*Discussants:* James Nagel, University of California, Berkeley
Kenneth Huang, University of California, Berkeley
Jeri Anne Alberti, University of California, Berkeley

COMMUNITY SERVICES IN THE INNER CITY
*Speakers:* Robert Langer, National Assembly, New York
Rev. Samuel M. Carter, Clair-Christian United Methodist Church,
Chicago
*Discussants:* James Stewart, Chicago Youth Centers, Chicago
Samuel Rice, Chicago Housing Authority, Chicago
Robert Williams, Neighborhood City Halls, Detroit

HEALTH REVENUE SHARING AND MIGRANT WORKERS:
THE FUTURE OF MIGRANT HEALTH CENTERS
*Speakers:* David Davila, Centro de Information sobre el Alcoholism,
Walla Walla, Wash.
Frank Banales, Community Mental Health Task Force, Santa Barbara,
Calif.
*Discussant:* Ramon Mazon, Clinica de Salubridad de Campesinos,
Brawley, Calif.

INTEGRATION OF HUMAN SERVICES AT THE LOCAL LEVEL
*Speaker:* Stephen W. Lenhardt, Human Service Commission, Allegheny Co., Pittsburgh
*Discussants:* Thomas P. Coyle, Jr., HEW, Washington
Marie Callender, Washington

INTEGRATION OF HUMAN SERVICES AT THE LOCAL LEVEL
—IMPLEMENTATION
*Panelists:* David E. Epperson, University of Pittsburgh, Pittsburgh
Irvin L. Foutz, John J. Kane Hospital, Pittsburgh

AN INTERDISCIPLINARY APPROACH TO CHILD ABUSE
*Speakers:* Cheryl Munce, Children's Hospital and Medical Center,
Oakland, Calif.
Judith Rosenberg, Children's Hospital and Medical Center, Oakland,
Calif.
Joann Cook, Children's Hospital and Medical Center, Oakland, Calif.

MOVING FURTHER TOWARD HUMANIZATION OF PRISONS
AND THE CORRECTIONAL SYSTEM
*Speakers:* George I. Diffenbaucher, U.S. Bureau of Prisons, Washington
Ecford S. Voit, Jr., National Institute of Mental Health, Rockville, Md.

A NATIONAL SERVICE AND ADVOCACY MODEL FOR THE
SEVERELY DISABLED: SEX AND DISABILITY
 *Speaker:* Edward Roberts, Center for Independent Living, Berkeley,
 Calif.
 *Discussant:* John Hessler, University of California, Berkeley

NEW DIMENSIONS IN LONG-TERM HEALTH SERVICES
FOR THE ELDERLY
 *Panelists:* Warren Ponsar, California State University, Long Beach
 Hadley D. Hall, San Francisco Home Health Service, San Francisco
 Carol Erickson, Arizona State Health Department, Phoenix
 *Reactor:* Oscar Kurren, University of Hawaii, Honolulu

NUTRITION AS IT RELATES TO THE PHYSICAL AND
MENTAL WELL-BEING OF THE INNER-CITY FAMILY
 *Speakers:* Lillian Tauber, Model Cities/CCUO, Chicago
 Paul Hemphill, Mayor's Office on Senior Citizens, Chicago
 Elva Merrick, Loyola University, Chicago

RATIONAL PLANNING FOR EFFECTIVE SERVICE
DELIVERY TO THE AGED
 *Speakers:* Arthur Farber, University of Washington, Seattle
 Robert D. Krisologo, University of Washington, Seattle
 *Discussants:* Kenneth Caweroy, Department of Human Resources,
 Seattle
 Elizabeth Garlicks, Senior Services and Centers, Seattle
 Theodore Stevens, Snohomish County Senior Services, Edmonds,
 Wash.

RECONSIDERATION OF ADVOCACY: CLIENT-
RELATED APPROACHES
 *Speakers:* Charles Grosser, Columbia University, New York
 Brenda McGowan, Children's Defense Fund, New York
 *Discussant:* Douglas Glasgow, Howard University, Washington

SEXUALITY AND MENTAL HEALTH:
NEW TRENDS IN TREATMENT
 *Speakers:* Jay Mann, M.D., University of California, San Francisco
 Dr. Ian Barlow, University of California, San Francisco
 Dr. Joseph Katsuranis, University of California, San Francisco
 *Discussant:* June C. Stambaugh, University of California, San Fran-
 cisco

SKID ROW AND THE PUBLIC INEBRIATE: SOME ISSUES
IN SERVICE DELIVERY
 *Speakers:* Robert O'Briant, M.D., Garden Hospital, San Francisco
 William Petersen, Social Setting Detoxification Center, San Francisco
 Friedner D. Wittman, Study of Alcoholism Treatment Facilities,
 Berkeley, Calif.

SOCIAL WORK IN HEALTH MAINTENANCE ORGANIZATIONS:
A NEW PROFESSIONAL ROLE?

*Speaker:* Doman Lum, California State University, Sacramento
*Discussant:* Kathleen Obier Lells, University of California, Los Angeles

## STATUS AND PERCEPTION OF ORGANIZATIONAL CLIMATE IN PRISON
*Speakers:* Harris Chaiklin, University of Maryland, Baltimore
Harold Lohn, Levindale Research Center, Baltimore
*Discussant:* Richard Korn, Center for the Study of Criminal Justice, Berkeley, Calif.

## TRANSITION FROM MENTAL HOSPITAL TO COMMUNITY: PROBLEMS OF DEINSTITUTIONALIZATION
*Panelists:* Steven T. Segal, University of California, Berkeley
Stephen M. Rose, State University of New York, Stony Brook
John Goldmeier, University of Maryland, Baltimore

## WORK WITH THE DYING
*Speakers:* Sister Mary Louise Nash, Carlow College, Pittsburgh
Elizabeth Clark, University of Pittsburgh, Pittsburgh

## YOUTH IN NEED OF SERVICES FOR THEIR MENTAL WELL-BEING—A NATIONAL IMPACT
*Panelists:* Lynette Harris, Consolidated Neighborhood Services, St. Louis
Elizabeth Smith, Washington University, St. Louis
Russell Hogrefe, Chicago Youth Centers, Chicago
Joseph Boyd, Illinois State Scholarship Commission, Deerfield, Ill.
Tsuguo Ikeda, Seattle Atlantic Street Center, Seattle
Marie Hamburg, Department of Human Resources/SRA, Washington
Mrs. Natalie Levy, Board for Fundamental Education, Indianapolis

### *SECTION III: SOCIAL ASPECTS OF HEALTH*

## CULTURAL FACTORS AFFECTING THE UTILIZATION OF HEALTH SERVICES: TWO PERSPECTIVES
*Speakers:* Henrik L. Blum, M.D., University of California, Berkeley
Patricia A. Brown, University of Illinois, Chicago

## DELIVERING SERVICES TO THE RURAL POOR
*Speakers:* Mrs. Mary G. Leonidakis, University of Kentucky, Lexington
Fekreya Aly, University of Kentucky, Lexington
Lane J. Veltkamp, University of Kentucky, Lexington

## DEVELOPING LINKAGES AMONG HUMAN-SERVICE AGENCIES ON BEHALF OF ABUSED CHILDREN
*Moderator:* Michael Joan Schwartz, San Francisco Child Abuse Council, San Francisco
*Panelists:* Steffani B.
Curt Owen, San Francisco
Sherrill Lakin, Children's Hospital, San Francisco
*Discussant:* Norman Herstein, Sunny Hills Children's center, San Anselmo, Calif.

DIFFERENTIAL UTILIZATION OF MANPOWER
IN HEALTH SETTINGS
   *Speakers:* Thomas Briggs, Syracuse University, Syracuse, N.Y.
   Martin Nacman, Strong Memorial Hospital, Rochester, N.Y.
   Horace Ivey, Upstate Medical Center, Syracuse, N.Y.
   Helen Rehr, Mt. Sinai Hospital, New York

THE EFFECTS OF CATASTROPHIC EVENTS ON
THE INDIVIDUAL FAMILY
   *Speakers:* Myrna Kruckeberg, University of Michigan Hospital, Ann
   Arbor
   Joan Hagerty, University of Michigan Hospital, Ann Arbor
   Ronald Rozanski, University of Michigan Hospital, Ann Arbor
   M. Phyllis Hill, University of Michigan Hospital, Ann Arbor
   *Discussant:* David Kaplan, Stanford University Medical Center, Stan-
   ford, Calif.

HEALTH SERVICES IN THE OCCUPATIONAL SETTING:
A FOCUS FOR REHABILITATION AND PREVENTION
   *Speakers:* Philip Polakoff, M.D., University of California, Berkeley
   Robert Fowler, University of California, Berkeley

MENTAL HEALTH CARE AT THE WORK PLACE:
NEW OPPORTUNITIES FOR SERVICE DELIVERY
   *Speakers:* Paul A. Kurzman, Hunter College, New York
   Mrs. Carvel U. Taylor, CNA Financial Corporation, Chicago

ORGANIZATION AND DELIVERY OF HEALTH CARE IN
EMERGENCY MEDICAL SERVICES
   *Speakers:* Sidney Smock, M.D., University of Michigan Hospital, Ann
   Arbor
   Steve Frankel, University of California, Berkeley
   Steve McDermott, Bay Area Emergency Medical Service Project, San
   Francisco
   *Discussant:* Roma Guy, San Francisco Department of Public Health,
   San Francisco

PROBLEMS OF ROLE DEFINITION IN THE
HEALTH CARE TEAM
   *Speaker:* Luther Christman, Rush University, Chicago
   *Discussant:* Neil Bracht, University of Washington, Seattle

SOCIAL SERVICE IN INSTITUTIONS SERVING
MULTIETHNIC POPULATIONS
   *Speaker:* Federico Soufflee, Chicano Training Center, Houston, Texas
   *Discussant:* Porfirio J. Miranda, University of California, Los Angeles

THE STRENGTH IN US: SELF-HELP GROUPS IN THE
MODERN WORLD. SESSION I: THEORETICAL ASPECTS
   *Speakers:* Eugene I. Bender, University of California, Los Angeles
   Alfred H. Katz, University of California, Los Angeles

THE STRENGTH IN US: SELF-HELP GROUPS IN THE
MODERN WORLD. SESSION II: SELF-HELP GROUPS
AND THE PROFESSIONAL COMMUNITY
> *Panel Representatives from:* Alcoholics Anonymous, Cancervive, Cherksey Stroke Program, Gray Panthers, Mended Hearts, Project Nova, Recovery, Inc.

UPGRADING OF PERSONS IN DEAD-END JOBS:
A WORK-STUDY MODEL FOR OBTAINING CREDENTIALS
> *Speakers:* Seymour Lesh, National Committee on Employment of Youth, New York
> Lee D. Filerman, National Committee on Employment of Youth, New York
> Rae Weissman, National Committee on Employment of Youth, New York
> Stephanie Presseler, National Committee on Employment of Youth, New York

VOLUNTEERS AND PARAPROFESSIONALS: CURRENT ROLE
ASPECTS IN HEALTH CARE
> *Speakers:* Mrs. Cynthiane Morgenweck, New York University Medical Center, New York
> Hilde M. Lehmann, Adult Protective Services, San Diego, Calif.
> Paula Lugannani, University of Michigan Medical Center, Ann Arbor
> *Discussant:* Sheldon Siegel, University of Michigan, Ann Arbor


### SECTION IV: LEISURE-TIME NEEDS

CHANGING PATTERNS OF UNITED WAY FUNDING
> *Speaker:* Robert Young, Bay Area United Fund, San Francisco

COMMUNITY ARTS: A PRESCRIPTION FOR SELF-PRIDE
> *Speaker:* Kenneth Snipes, Karamu House, Cleveland

COMMUNITY INVOLVEMENT IN THE CREATION OF
A NATIONAL RECREATION AREA
> *Speaker:* Harvey Swack, Cuyahoga Valley Federal Park, Peninsula, Ohio

A COMMUNITY VIEW OF THE EDUCATIONALLY DEPRIVED
DELINQUENT YOUTH
> *Speakers:* Mrs. Noreen Haygood, Case Western Reserve University, Cleveland
> Mrs. Marjorie Hall, East End Neighborhood House, Cleveland

CREATING A CLIMATE IN A LEISURE-TIME AGENCY
FOR SOCIAL ACTION
> *Speaker:* Belle Likover, Jewish Community Center of Cleveland

DELIVERY OF HEALTH SERVICES VIA COMMUNITY BASED
VOLUNTARY AGENCIES
*Speakers:* David Phoenix, University of North Carolina, Chapel Hill
Sandra Johnson, University of North Carolina, Chapel Hill
John Hatch, Durham, N.C.

DEVELOPMENTAL GROWTH THROUGH RECREATION
*Speaker:* Barbara Reynolds, Cleveland State University, Cleveland

GROUPING USERS OF SCENIC AREAS IN TERMS OF THEIR
PSYCHIC NEEDS—A MANAGEMENT APPROACH
*Speaker:* Arthur Bernstein, Department of Human Resources, Grants
Pass, Ore.

THE GROWING PROBLEM OF LEISURE-TIME:
PRESENT KNOWLEDGE FOR FUTURE PLANNING
*Speaker:* Jordan I. Kosberg, Florida State University, Tallahassee

THE LIFELONG LEARNING MOVEMENT:
EDUCATION AFTER 50
*Speaker:* Ruth Glick, Case Western Reserve University, Cleveland

NEW ROLES FOR THE OLDER ADULT VOLUNTEER
*Speaker:* Mary Sequin, University of Southern California, Los Angeles

SERVICING AND FUNDING NEW PROGRAMS FOR
ETHNIC MINORITY
*Speaker:* George Nishinaka, Special Service for Groups, Los Angeles

SUCCESSFUL PROGRAMMING WITH TEEN-AGE
STREET GANGS USING MINI-BIKES
*Speaker:* Alan Kumamoto, YMCA National Youth Project, Los
Angeles

VALUES CHILDREN DERIVE FROM GAMES
*Speaker:* Shraga Scrok, Case Western Reserve University, Cleveland

THE WEEKEND ADDICT
*Speaker:* Courtney Brown, New York State Division of Human Rights
and Hunter College, New York

*SECTION V: PROVISION AND MANAGEMENT OF
SOCIAL SERVICES*

AGENCY RESPONSIBILITIES IN MANAGERIAL
AND STAFF DEVELOPMENT
*Speaker:* Sharon L. Rickert, Greater Cleveland Neighborhood Centers
Association, Cleveland

EVALUATION OF HEALTH DELIVERY SYSTEMS:
SOME NEW PERSPECTIVES
*Panelists:* John L. McAdoo, University of Maryland, Baltimore
Harriette Pipes McAdoo, Howard University, Washington

Joseph G. Teresa, University of Michigan, Ann Arbor
Elizabeth Watkins, Case Western Reserve University, Cleveland

INSTITUTING MANAGEMENT BY OBJECTIVE AND PROGRAM
BUDGETING: PITFALLS AND SERVICES
*Speakers:* Robert L. Bond, Greater Cleveland Neighborhood Centers
Association, Cleveland
Sharon L. Rickert, Greater Cleveland Neighborhood Centers Association, Cleveland
Joseph T. Hairston, Greater Cleveland Neighborhood Centers Association, Cleveland
Victorina Peralta, Philadelphia Department of Public Welfare, Philadelphia

LEGAL SERVICES FOR THE ELDERLY
*Speakers:* Paul S. Nathanson, National Senior Citizen Law Center, Los
Angeles
Terry Donnelly, San Francisco

MANAGEMENT OF INTERDISCIPLINARY TEAMS IN
MENTAL HEALTH
*Speakers:* Carolyn M. Hiltner, Pittsburgh Child Guidance Center, Pittsburgh
Max G. Magnussen, Pittsburgh Child Guidance Center, Pittsburgh

A MODEL: RESEARCH AND DEMONSTRATION PROGRAM
IN DRUG ABUSE PREVENTION
*Speakers:* Sharon L. Rickert, Greater Cleveland Neighborhood Centers
Association, Cleveland
Edna F. Roth, Case Western Reserve University, Cleveland
Mary H. Gilmore, Geauga County 648 Board, Chardon, Ohio

THE NURSING HOME CRISIS
*Speaker:* Val J. Halamandaris, U.S. Senate Special Committee on
Aging, Washington
*Discussants:* Sidney Friedman, Jewish Home for the Aged, San Francisco
Dolores A. Davis, Federal City College, Washington

REVENUE SHARING: ISSUES AND DIRECTIONS FOR ACTION
*Speakers:* Robert S. Caulk, Human Care Services Program, San Diego,
Calif.
Ernest Jenkins, West Sears Roebuck YMCA, Chicago

SOCIAL SERVICES FOR THE UNEMPLOYED, 1930 AND 1975:
COMPARISONS AND CONTRASTS
*Speaker:* Milton D. Speizman, Bryn Mawr College, Bryn Mawr, Pa.
Jean Haring, Bryn Mawr College, Bryn Mawr, Pa.
Robert L. Woodson, National Urban League, New York

SECTION VI: SOCIETAL PROBLEMS

DEINSTITUTIONALIZATION: HOW FAR AND HOW FAST
HAVE WE COME?
*Speakers:* Stanley B. Thomas, Jr., HEW, Washington
Wyatt C. Jones, Brandeis University, Waltham, Mass.
Robert E. Trimble, National Council on Crime and Delinquency, San
Francisco

DENVER-SEATTLE INCOME-MAINTENANCE EXPERIMENTS
*Speaker:* Robert G. Spiegelman, Stanford Research Institute, Menlo
Park, Calif.

HAS AMERICA THE MATERIAL AND POLITICAL RESOURCES
TO FULFILL ALL EXPECTATIONS?
*Speakers:* Robert Harris, Urban Institute, Washington
Irwin Garfinkel, University of Wisconsin, Madison

IMPERATIVES OF HEALTH CARE AND FINANCING
*Speaker:* Howard Ennes, Equitable Life Assurance Society of the U.S.,
New York
*Reactor:* Mrs. Beatrice Phillips, Beth Israel Hospital, Boston

MINORITIES TODAY
*Speakers:* Yolanda Sanchez, City University of New York, New York
Harry L. Kitano, University of California, Los Angeles

TITLE XX—ITS SIGNIFICANCE FOR THE DELIVERY OF
SOCIAL SERVICES
*Speaker:* James S. Dwight, Jr., HEW, Washington
*Discussants:* Herschel Saucier, Georgia Department of Human Re-
sources, Atlanta
Evan E. Jones, Jr., Utah Department of Social Services, Salt Lake City

AUTHORS' FORUM

ADMINISTRATION: MANAGEMENT METHODOLOGIES
*Speakers:* Kenneth R. Wedel, University of Kansas, Lawrence
Leonard Rutman and Brian Segal (coauthors), Carleton University,
Ottawa, Canada
Thomas Owen Carlton, Virginia Commonwealth University, Rich-
mond
Gerald Fisher, University of Wisconsin, Madison, and Lowell E.
Wright, Madison, Wis. (coauthors)
Judy Bablitch and Richard Master, Rock County Department of Social
Services, Janesville, Wis., and Gerald Fisher, Rock County Department
of Social Services, University of Wisconsin, Madison (coauthors)
Joe R. Hoffer, Ohio Department of Public Welfare, Columbus

ADMINISTRATION: STRUCTURE AND PROCESS
*Speakers:* John P. Myers, University of Kentucky, Lexington
Nancy Hooyman, University of Minnesota, Duluth
Barry R. Gordon, Florida International University, Miami, and Philip

Hines,, West Virginia College of Graduate Studies, Charleston (coauthors)
AGING
*Speakers:* Jeffrey R. Solomon, Miami Jewish Home and Hospital for the Aged, Miami
Abraham Monk, State University of New York, Buffalo, N.Y., and Frank B. Endres, Research and Planning Council of Greater Buffalo, Buffalo, N.Y. (coauthors)
Eloise Rathbone-McCuan, Levindale Hebrew Geriatric Center and Hospital, Baltimore
Elizabeth Huttman, California State University, Hayward
ALCOHOLISM
*Speakers:* Fidelia A. Masi, and Bradley Googins, Boston College, Chestnut Hill, Mass. (coauthors)
Mrs. Muriel McGuigan, Los Angeles County Department of Social Services, Pasadena, Calif.
Phyllis R. Miller, University of Maryland, Baltimore
COURTS AND CORRECTIONS
*Speakers:* Kenneth Viegas, University of Oregon, Eugene
Joe Hudson, Minnesota Department of Corrections, St. Paul, and Burt Galaway, University of Minnesota, Duluth (coauthors)
Mark Pogrebin, Florida State University, Tallahassee
EDUCATION FOR SOCIAL WORK
*Speakers:* Michael S. Kolevzon, Virginia Commonwealth University, Richmond
Wayne D. Duehn and Nazneen S. Mayadas, University of Texas, Arlington (coauthors)
Joyce A. Brengarth, University of Pittsburgh, Pittsburgh
Cordell H. Thomas, the ROAD, Inc., Philadelphia
FAMILY
*Speakers:* Burt Galaway, University of Minnesota, Duluth
Philip Coltoff, Children's Aid Society, New York
Jane H. Pfouts, University of North Carolina, Chapel Hill
John S. Wodarski, University of Tennessee, Knoxville
Enola K. Proctor, Washington University, St. Louis
HEALTH
*Speakers:* Dolores I. Rodriguez, Women's Hospital, Los Angeles
Shirley Weber, Rutgers University–Camden College of Arts and Sciences, Camden, N.J.
J. M. Kapoor, Indiana University–Purdue University, Indianapolis
HEALTH AND MANPOWER
*Speakers:* Mary B. Hans and Richard J. Doran (coauthors), Veterans Administration Hospital, Albany, N.Y.
Linda Vanek, Washtenaw County Community Mental Health Center, Ann Arbor, Mich., and Thomas J. Powell, University of Michigan, Ann Arbor (coauthors)

MENTAL HEALTH
*Speakers:* Robert M. Casse, Jr., Barry M. Daste, and Darlyne Nemeth (coauthors), Louisiana State University, Baton Rouge
Felice Perlmutter, Temple University, Philadelphia
Stuart A. Kirk, University of Kentucky, Lexington

SOCIAL WORK EDUCATION: SENSITIZING
TO NEW CONSTITUENCIES
*Speakers:* George Hoshino, University of Minnesota, Minneapolis
Judith Lacerte, University of Kentucky, Lexington
Joseph Giordano, American Jewish Committee, New York, and Sidney Pinsky, Long Island Jewish–Hillside-Medical Center and Columbia University, New York (coauthors)

SOCIAL WORK PRACTICE: PROFESSIONAL CONCERNS
*Speakers:* Paul Abels, Case-Western Reserve University, Cleveland, and Sonia Abels, Cleveland State University, Cleveland (coauthors)
Nazneen S. Mayadas and Wayne D. Duehn, University of Texas, Arlington (coauthors)
Samuel A. Richmond and Sonia Abels, Cleveland State University, Cleveland, and Paul Abels, Case-Western Reserve University, Cleveland (coauthors)
Daniel I. Rubenstein, West Virginia College of Graduate Studies, Charleston

## *ASSOCIATE GROUPS*

### ALLIANCE OF INFORMATION AND REFERRAL SERVICES

COST ANALYSIS OF INFORMATION AND REFERRAL SERVICE
*Speakers:* Jerry Banks, C. L. Hohenstein and Associates, Atlanta, Ga.
Gershone Cooper, Cooper and Company, Stamford, Conn.
*Reactor:* Marjorie Carpenter, Community Information and Referral Service, Minneapolis

INFORMATION AND REFERRAL ROUNDTABLE: LINKING
COMMUNITY CONSUMERS AND SERVICES—
CLASSIFICATION OR CHAOS?
*Speaker:* Frances Gilbert, Information Center of Hampton Roads, Norfolk, Va.
*Reactors:* Thomas Deahl, Microfilm Systems, MICRODOC, Philadelphia
Rae Brooks, Office of the Mayor, New York

INFORMATION AND REFERRAL ROUNDTABLE:
SERVING THE ELDERLY
*Speakers:* Evelyn Fraser, United Community Services of Metropolitan Detroit
Kathleen Heard, Southeastern Arizona Governments' Organization, Bisbee
*Reactor:* Margaret Presser, Community Council, Phoenix, Ariz.

PROVIDING INFORMATION AND REFERRAL SERVICES
IN THE RURAL AREAS
*Speakers:* Stephen Webster, University of Tennessee, Knoxville
Nola Hughes, Wyoming Information and Referral Service, Cheyenne

ROLE OF THE PUBLIC AND PRIVATE SECTORS IN THE
DELIVERY OF INFORMATION AND REFERRAL SERVICES
*Panelists:* Don Wortman, HEW, Washington
Thomas Parrott, Social Security Administration, Baltimore
Elinor Walker, U.S. Public Health Service, Rockville, Md.
Morris Cohen, HEW, Washington
James Burr, HEW, Washington
*Panelists:* Lois Hardt, M.D., National Easter Seal Society, Chicago
Corazon Esteva Doyle, Community Council, Phoenix, Ariz.
Robert Wedgeworth, American Public Library Association, Chicago
Hamp Coley, United Way of America, Alexandria, Va.

AMERICAN ASSOCIATION OF WORKERS FOR CHILDREN

DEVELOPING MANPOWER FOR TWENTY-FOUR-HOUR-A-DAY
PROGRAMS SERVING CHILDREN AND THEIR FAMILIES
*Panelists:* Stevanne Auerbach-Fink, Parents and Child Care Resources,
San Francisco
F. Herbert Barnes, Lakeside School, Spring Valley, N.Y.
Brian F. Cahill, California Association of Children's Residential Centers, Sacramento
Paul D'Agostino, Florida Mental Health Institute, Tampa
Norman Herstein, Sunny Hills, San Anselmo, Calif.
Ralph Kelly, St. Agnes Convent, Sparkill, N.Y.
Edward Leong, Salvation Army, Honolulu
Norman V. Lourie, Department of Public Welfare, Commonwealth of
Pennsylvania, Harrisburg
Delmar J. Pascoe, M.D., Child Mental Health Specialist Training Project, Santa Barbara, Calif.
Norbert Rieger, M.D., Child Mental Health Specialist Training Project, Santa Barbara, Calif.

AMERICAN FOUNDATION FOR THE BLIND

VISUAL IMPAIRMENT: A CONDITION OF AGING
*Speakers:* Mrs. Milton Schiffman, National Council on Aging, San
Francisco
Benjamin Wolf, National Council on Aging, San Francisco
Irene M. Burnside, R.N., University of Southern California Gerontology Center, University Park, Calif.

AMERICAN JEWISH COMMITTEE

THE NEW ETHNICITY AND THE NEW PLURALISM:
PERSPECTIVES ON BUILDING COALITIONS
FOR HUMAN SERVICES

*Panelists:* Irving M. Levine, American Jewish Committee, New York
Michael Novak, Rockefeller Foundation, New York
Percy Steele, Urban League–Bay Area, San Francisco
Mary Anna Colwell, Laras Foundation, Corte Madera, Calif.
Lillian Rubin, Wright Institute, El Cerrito, Calif.
Douglas Glasgow, Howard University, Washington
Harry L. Kitano, University of California, Los Angeles
Manuel Miranda, University of California, Los Angeles

AMERICAN NATIONAL RED CROSS

DO VOLUNTEERS HAVE A FUTURE IN HEALTH SERVICES?
*Speaker:* Mrs. Theodore O. Wedel, American National Red Cross, Washington
*Discussants:* Mrs. Harriett Naylor, HEW, Washington
Mrs. Jill Ruckelshaus, National Center for Voluntary Action, Washington
Peter Miller, Veterans Administration, Washington
Gen. John F. McMahon, Volunteers of America, New York

AMERICAN PUBLIC WELFARE ASSOCIATION

EVALUATING SOCIAL SERVICES:
IMPLICATIONS OF TITLE XX
*Panelists:* George P. Hoshino, University of Minnesota, Minneapolis
Robert T. Clifford, Atlantic County Welfare Board, Atlantic City, N.J.
Al Kohls, Hennepin County Welfare Department, Minneapolis

ASIAN AMERICAN SOCIAL WORKERS

ASIAN AMERICANS: A CASE OF BENIGHTED NEGLECT AND
THE BILINGUAL-BICULTURAL SERVICE DELIVERY
IMPLICATIONS TO THE NATIVE AMERICANS AND
SPANISH-SPEAKING AMERICANS
*Speaker:* Tom Owan, Social Security Administration, Baltimore
*Reactors:* Phyllis J. Cross, Bureau of Indian Affairs, Washington
Edward Rivera, California State Department of Health and Welfare, Sacramento
Lambert Choy, Donaldina Cameron House, San Francisco

HEALTH AND SOCIAL SERVICES: THE DILEMMA FACING
THE NEW IMMIGRANTS
*Panelists:* Grace Pena Blaszkowski, San Diego County Human Relations Agency, Bonita, Calif.
Po S. Wong, Chinese Newcomers' Service Center, San Francisco
*Reactors:* Tom Kim, Bay Area Coalition of Koreans, San Francisco
Lily Lee Chen, Los Angeles County Department of Social Services, Elmonte, Calif.

ASSOCIATION OF AMERICAN INDIAN SOCIAL WORKERS

BROKEN TREATY OF BATTLE MOUNTAIN. FILM:
BATTLE MOUNTAIN: WESTERN SHOSHONE

*Speakers:* Joan Bordman, Western Staff of National Committee on Indian Work, Newark, Calif.
E. Dan Edwards, University of Utah, Salt Lake City

INDIAN HEALTH CARE AND PROGRAMS
*Speaker:* Loren Sekayumptewa, University of Utah, Salt Lake City

ASSOCIATION OF VOLUNTEER BUREAUS

GRANT EVALUATION: WHO WANTS WHAT?
*Panelists:* Ken Phillips, United Way of America, Palo Alto, Calif.
Bill Somerville, San Mateo Foundation, Burlingame, Calif.
Robert Woodruff, HEW, San Francisco
Kenneth Schremp, California Office of Criminal Justice Planning, Sacramento

MANAGEMENT BY OBJECTIVES
*Speaker:* Philip Cavan, California Department of Health, Berkeley

MANAGEMENT PARALLELS EVALUATION
*Speaker:* Philip Cavan, California Department of Health, Berkeley

COUNCIL ON SOCIAL WORK EDUCATION

EDUCATING SOCIAL WORKERS FOR THE HEALTH
PROFESSIONS
*Speakers:* Marie Simmons, University of California Medical Center,
San Francisco
Phyllis Rochelle, San Francisco State University, San Francisco

HISTORICAL PERSPECTIVES ON SOCIAL WORK PRACTICE:
POTENTIAL USE OF HISTORICAL MATERIALS IN FILES
OF SOCIAL AGENCIES AND ORGANIZATIONS
*Cochairmen:* Gary A. Lloyd, University of Houston, Houston, Texas
Imogene S. Young, University of Illinois, Chicago

PREPARING SOCIAL WORK PRACTITIONERS TO WORK
WITH OLDER ADULTS: AN EDUCATIONAL DESIGN
*Speaker:* Margaret E. Hartford, University of Southern California, Los
Angeles
*Discussant:* Mary O'Day, University of California, Berkeley

FAMILY SERVICE ASSOCIATION OF AMERICA

AIDES TO THE ELDERLY
*Panelists:* Mrs. Martha Newmark, Jewish Family Service of Los
Angeles
Mrs. Sharel Krimsky, Jewish Family Service of Los Angeles
Mrs. Sandra Seskind, Jewish Family Service of Los Angeles

ADVOCACY FOR SPANISH-SPEAKING FAMILIES
*Panelists:* J. Donald Cameron, Family Service Agency of San Mateo
County, Burlingame, Calif.
Carol Goodman, Family Service Agency of San Mateo County, Burlingame, Calif.

Paul Baca, Family Service Agency of San Mateo County, Burlingame, Calif.

Esther Talavera, Family Service Agency of San Mateo County, Burlingame, Calif.

Angie Corder, Family Service Agency of San Mateo County, Burlingame, Calif.

INTERNATIONAL UNION, UNITED AUTOMOBILE, AEROSPACE
AND AGRICULTURAL IMPLEMENT WORKERS OF AMERICA, UAW

## IN DARK AND DANGER—THE FIGHT FOR
## COAL MINERS' HEALTH
(Walter P. Reuther Memorial Lecture)
   *Speaker:* Arnold Miller, United Mine Workers of America, Washington

MENNINGER FOUNDATION

## CHILDREN AND THEIR FAMILIES: DO SETTINGS REALLY
## SUPPORT AUTONOMY AND GROWTH?
   *Speakers:* Sara P. Hill, Menninger Foundation, Topeka, Kans.
   Donald Holcomb, Menninger Foundation, Topeka, Kans.
   Arthur Mandelbaum, Menninger Foundation, Topeka, Kans.

## IMPLEMENTATION OF PATIENTS' TREATMENT RIGHTS IN A
## PRIVATE PSYCHIATRIC HOSPITAL
(C. F. Menninger Memorial Hospital)
   *Speakers:* Marcella Baird, Menninger Foundation, Topeka, Kans.
   Virginia Heisey, C. F. Menninger Memorial Hospital, Topeka, Kans.
   Mabel Remmers, Menninger Foundation, Topeka, Kans.
   Loretta Class, Menninger Foundation, Topeka, Kans.
   Anthony Tangari, Menninger Foundation, Topeka, Kans.

## WHAT ARE THE RIGHTS OF STAFF?
   *Speaker:* Arthur Herman, Menninger Foundation, Topeka, Kans.

NATIONAL ASSOCIATION OF BLACK SOCIAL WORKERS

## NABSW—GOALS AND DIRECTIONS IN HUMAN
## DEVELOPMENT AND SERVICES
   *Speaker:* Jay Chunn, National Association of Black Social Workers and
   Howard University, Washington
   *Discussants:* State and local representatives from NABSW

NATIONAL ASSOCIATION OF SOCIAL WORKERS

## BARRIERS TO HEALTH SERVICES DEVELOPMENT
## AND DELIVERY IN RURAL AREAS FROM THE
## PERSPECTIVE OF NATIVE AMERICANS, MIGRANTS,
## AND MOUNTAIN PEOPLE
   *Speakers:* Paul Campbell, University of Tennessee, Knoxville
   Manuel E. Aguirre, California State University, Fresno
   Wilma Morgan, Indian Hospital, Redlake, Minn.

CHILD ABUSE: THE SOCIAL WORK RESPONSIBILITY
    *Panelists:* Elsa Tenbrook, Extended Family Center, San Francisco
    Peggy Hall, Extended Family Center, San Francisco
    Ann Harris Cohn, Berkeley Planning Associates, Berkeley, Calif.

THE DELIVERY OF HEALTH AND MENTAL HEALTH
SERVICES TO ETHNIC MINORITY POPULATIONS:
BREAKING THE BARRIERS
    *Panelists:* Julian Rivera, Adelphi University, Garden City, N.Y.
    William I. Gore, Milwaukee County Mental Health Center, North Division, Milwaukee, Wis.
    Jim Miyano, Greater Los Angeles Community Action Agency, Los Angeles

THE EXPANDING PARAMETERS OF SOCIAL WORK PRACTICE
IN HOSPITAL SETTINGS
    *Speakers:* Gerald Beallor, Montefiore Hospital and Medical Center, Bronx, N.Y.
    Marie Y. Simmons, University of California Medical Center, San Francisco
    Marguerite V. Hodge, Lung Association of Los Angeles County, Los Angeles

HELPING VS. INFLUENCING: SOME POLITICAL ELEMENTS
OF ORGANIZATIONAL CHANGE
    *Speaker:* George A. Brager, Columbia University, New York City

INFORMATION UTILIZATION AND THE
PROTECTION OF PRIVACY IN HEALTH
AND MENTAL HEALTH SERVICES
    *Speakers:* John P. Fanning, HEW, Rockville, Md.
    Gareth Hill, Berkeley, Calif.
    Rinna B. Flohr, Department of Public Health, City and County of San Francisco

LICENSING AND ETHNIC MINORITIES
    *Panelists:* Rafael Aguirre, El Paso State Center for Human Development, El Paso, Texas
    Amy Mass, Asian American Social Workers, Whittier, Calif.
    Janet Burton, Federal City College, Washington

NEW DIMENSIONS IN FEMINIST COUNSELING
    *Speakers:* Patricia Gallagher, San Anselmo, Calif.
    Ruth Pancoast, Washington
    Lynda Martin Weston, Feminist Counseling Collective, Washington
    *Discussants:* Alma Arnold, University of Washington YWCA, Seattle
    Francisca Flores, Chicano Service Action Center, Los Angeles

NEW MODES OF CLINICAL PRACTICE
    *Speakers:* Jordan I. Zarren, Growth Therapy Associates, Syracuse, N.Y.
    Vermeice D. Thompson, Berkeley, Calif.
    Ruth Hill, Berkeley, Calif.

RESEARCH UTILIZATION AND HEALTH CARE PROGRAM
*Speakers:* Grant Loavenbruck, Community Council of Greater New York, New York
Dr. Thomas E. Backer, Edward Glaser and Associates, Los Angeles
Jack Rothman, University of Michigan, Ann Arbor

THE ROCKY ROAD TO VENDORSHIP
*Speakers:* Nancy A. Humphreys, California State Polytechnic University, Pomona
Estelle R. Gabriel, Chicago

SOCIAL COMPONENTS IN LONG-TERM CARE PROGRAMS
FOR THE AGED
*Speakers:* Hugh J. Sloan, HEW, San Francisco
Ruth E. Weber, University of Georgia, Athens

STRATEGIES FOR IMPACTING DELIVERY OF HEALTH
SERVICES AT LOCAL, STATE, AND NATIONAL LEVELS
*Speakers:* Hobart Burch, National Assembly of National Voluntary Health and Social Welfare Organizations, New York
H. Frederick Brown, University of Chicago, Chicago
Greta Glugoski, San Francisco State University, San Francisco

TRENDS AFFECTING THE USE OF SOCIAL WORKERS
IN HEALTH SETTINGS
*Panelists:* Evelyn McNamara, Society for Hospital Social Work Directors, Chicago
Claire R. Lustman, Veterans Administration, Washington
Mrs. Corinne Wolfe, University of the Highland, Las Vegas, N. Mex.

WAR IS NOT HEALTHY FOR CHILDREN AND OTHER
LIVING THINGS: THE DOMESTIC/DEFENSE CONTROVERSY
*Speaker:* Edward L. King, Coalition for National Priorities and Military Policy, Washington.

WHITNEY M. YOUNG, JR., MEMORIAL LECTURE
*Introduction:* Henry A. Talbert, National Urban League, Los Angeles
*Speaker:* Aileen C. Hernandez, Hernandez Associates, San Francisco
Presentation of Social Worker of the Year and Public Citizen of the Year Awards

NATIONAL ASSOCIATION FOR STATEWIDE
HEALTH AND WELFARE

TITLE XX—BOON OR BOONDOGGLE?
*Speakers:* A. Rowland Todd, Wisconsin Council on Human Concerns, Madison
Murray B. Meld, Connecticut Social Welfare Conference, Hartford
Charles Hall, HEW, San Francisco
Robert Langer, National Assembly of National Voluntary Health and Social Welfare Organizations, New York
Charles P. Devereux, California Department of Health, Sacramento

*Respondent:* James Wimberly, Texas United Community Services, Austin, Texas

### NATIONAL COUNCIL ON THE AGING

## HOW THE PUBLIC SEES THE AGING: HOW THE AGING SEE THEMSELVES
*Speaker:* Jack Ossofsky, National Council on the Aging, Washington

## THE MEDIA AND SOCIAL PERCEPTION OF OLDER PERSONS
*Speaker:* Louis Hausman, National Council on the Aging, Washington

### NATIONAL COUNCIL IN ALCOHOLISM

## FAMILY THERAPY: KEY FOR PREVENTION OF ALCOHOLISM
*Speaker:* Lorraine Hinkle, Rutgers University, New Brunswick, N.J.

## STRATEGIES FOR PREVENTION OF ALCOHOLISM
*Speakers:* Juanita Palmer, National Council on Alcoholism, New York
Katherine Pike, National Council on Alcoholism, San Marino, Calif.

### NATIONAL COUNCIL FOR HOMEMAKER-HOME HEALTH AIDE SERVICES

## HOME CARE AS A RIGHT FOR THE AGING: THE IMPLICATIONS FOR HOMEMAKER-HOME HEALTH AIDE AND SUPPLEMENTARY SERVICES
*Speaker:* Harriet Miller, National Retired Teachers Association/American Association of Retired Persons, Washington
*Discussants:* Hadley D. Hall, San Francisco Home Health Service, San Francisco
Esther C. Gilbertson, R.N., HEW, San Francisco

## HOME CARE AS A RIGHT FOR CHILDREN WITH SPECIAL DISABILITIES: THE IMPLICATIONS FOR HOMEMAKER-HOME HEALTH AIDE SERVICES
*Panelists:* Patricia W. Soyka, National Council for Homemaker-Home Health Aide Services, New York
Mrs. Vera M. Burke, Jewish Family Services, New York
Delmar J. Pascoe, M.D., San Francisco General Hospital, San Francisco

### NATIONAL FEDERATION OF SETTLEMENTS AND NEIGHBORHOOD CENTERS

## SETTLEMENT ADVOCACY AND IMPLEMENTATION OF NEIGHBORHOOD HEALTH SERVICES
*Speakers:* Lynette Harris, Consolidated Neighborhood Services, St. Louis
*Panelists:* Eugene Coleman, Canon Kip Community House, San Francisco
Richard Park, Golden Gate Neighborhood Centers Association, San Francisco

Peter Gibb, Telegraph Hill Neighborhood Association, San Francisco
James Soler, Union Settlement, New York
Charles Goodrich, M.D., Mt. Sinai School of Medicine and Union Settlement, New York
Edith Mas, Union Settlement, New York
Ralph Flores, El Barrio Young Peoples Health Clinic, New York

NATIONAL HEALTH COUNCIL

## WHITHER GOEST CHARITY AND VOLUNTARY ACTION: WILL THEY SURVIVE? IN WHAT FORM? AT WHOSE EXPENSE?

*Moderator:* Pauline Miles, National Health Council, New York
*Speaker:* Leonard L. Silverstein, Commission on Private Philanthropy and Public Needs, Washington
*Reactors:* Alvin L. Schorr, Community Service Society of New York, New York
Jayne Shover, National Easter Seal Society for Crippled Children and Adults, Chicago

PLANNED PARENTHOOD—WORLD POPULATION

## THE MEDICAL AND LEGAL RIGHTS OF TEENS AND MINORS TO SEXUALITY SERVICES

*Speakers:* Gene Vadies, Planned Parenthood–World Population, New York
Lelia Hall, Planned Parenthood–World Population, New York
Nancy Fischer, HEW, Chicago

SCHOOL OF SOCIAL WORK, CALIFORNIA
STATE UNIVERSITY, SACRAMENTO

## VIETNAMESE REFUGEES AND ORPHANS

*Speakers:* Benjamin F. Finley, Afro-American Family Community Services, Chicago
David Nesmith, American Friends Service Committee, Philadelphia
Joseph H. Reid, Child Welfare League of America, New York
Carol Johnson, California State University, Sacramento

TRABAJADORES DE LA RAZA

## MOBILIZATION FOR HEALTH IN THE SPANISH COMMUNITY—TWO APPROACHES

*Panelists:* Rudolfo Sanchez, National Coalition of Spanish-speaking Mental Health Organizations, Los Angeles
Carmen Isales de Weil, Department of Instruction, San Juan, Puerto Rico

## SELECTIVE HEALTH CARE LEGISLATION— IMPLICATIONS FOR THE SPANISH-SPEAKING COMMUNITY

*Panelists:* Pereta Rodriguez Balian, Health Resources Administration, Rockville, Md.

Leticia Diaz, HIBHC, Rockville, Md.
Floyd Martinez, M.D., Colorado Division of Mental Health, Denver

VETERANS ADMINISTRATION SOCIAL WORK SERVICE

HEALTH CARE IN THE VA FOR THE SEVENTIES
*Speaker:* Carleton Evans, M.D., Veterans Administration, Washington
*Panelists:* Gerald Charles, M.D., Veterans Hospital, San Francisco
Harold Sox, M.D., Veterans Hospital, Palo Alto, Calif.
*Discussant:* Warren Stimpert, Veterans Administration, Washington

## INSTITUTES

HUMAN FACTORS IN LONG-TERM HEALTH CARE
Partially supported by the Division of Long-Term Care, National Center
for Health Sciences Research

Task Force
*Chairman:* Ruth Knee, Arlington, Va.
*Members:* Elaine Brody, Philadelphia Geriatric Center, Philadelphia;
Betty Reichert, Model Allied Community Services, San Diego, Calif.;
Kurt Reichert, San Diego State University, San Diego, Calif.; Brahna
Trager, Special Committee on Aging, San Geronimo, Calif.

THE IMPACT OF NATIONAL HEALTH INSURANCE ON
SERVICES TO THE MENTALLY ILL AND
MENTALLY DISABLED
Supported by the National Institute of Mental Health

Task Force
*Chairman:* Dale Farabee, M.D., Farabee and Associates, Lexington, Ky.
*Members:* William Bechill, University of Maryland, Baltimore; Carlton
L. Engquist, Veterans Administration, Washington; Henry A. Foley,
Colorado Office of Social Services, Denver; William Goldman, M.D.,
Massachusetts Commissioner of Mental Health, Boston; John A.
Hackley, Hillhaven Foundation, Tacoma, Wash.; Ina J. Javellas, Conference of Social Workers in State and Territorial Mental Health
Programs, Oklahoma City; Ruth Knee, Arlington, Va.; Faustina Knoll,
Community Health and Social Services, Detroit; Dorothy P. Rice,
Social Security Administration, Washington
*Staff Consultant:* Alice H. McCarty, Domestic Council Committee on
the Right of Privacy, Washington.
*NIMH Project Director:* James Stockdill, National Institute of Mental
Health, Rockville, Md.

ROLES FOR SOCIAL WORK IN COMMUNITY
MENTAL HEALTH PROGRAMS
Supported by the National Institute of Mental Health

Task Force
*Chairman:* John B. Turner, University of North Carolina, Chapel Hill
*Members:* Jack Bartleson, National Institute of Mental Health, Seattle;
J. Wilbert Edgerton, North Carolina Division of Mental Health Ser-

vices, Fayetteville, N.C.; Ernesto Gomez, Our Lady of the Lake College, San Antonio, Texas; Marshall Jung, Hahnemann Medical College and Hospital, Philadelphia; Abraham Lurie, Long Island Jewish-Hillside Medical Center, New Hyde Park, N.Y.; James W. Osberg, M.D., North Carolina Department of Human Resources, Raleigh, N.C.; Howard J. Parad, University of Southern California, Los Angeles; Hazel G. Price, University of Louisville, Louisville, Ky.; Eugene Rivera, Nord Mental Health Center, Lorain, Ohio; Gilbert Sanchez, Mental Health Services, Tucson, Ariz.; Martin Schwartz, Virginia Department of Mental Health and Mental Retardation, and Virginia Commonwealth School of Social Work, Richmond; Carl Scott, Council on Social Work Education, New York; Cecil G. Sheps, M.D., University of North Carolina, Chapel Hill, N.C.

*NIMH Advisory Committee:* Ford H. Kuramoto, National Institute of Mental Health, Rockville, Md.; Juan Ramos, National Institute of Mental Health, Rockville, Md.; Milton Wittman, National Institute of Mental Health, Rockville, Md.

## SOCIAL COMPONENTS OF HEALTH MAINTENANCE ORGANIZATIONS
Sponsored by NCSW

Task Force
   *Chairman:* Anthony R. Kovner, United Automobile Workers of America, Detroit
   *Members:* Mildred Arrill, HEW, Washington; Robert Harrington, M.D., Permanente Medical Group, San Jose, Calif.; J. Paul Racine, Metro Health Plant, Detroit; Helen Smith, M.D., University of Pennsylvania, Philadelphia

## SOCIAL COMPONENTS OF PHYSICAL AND MENTAL HEALTH SERVICES
Supported by the National Institute of Mental Health through the Minneapolis Medical Research Foundation

Task Force
   *Chairman:* Robert Morris, Brandeis University, Waltham, Mass.
   *Members:* Delwin M. Anderson, Arlington, Va.; Philip D. Bonnet, M.D., Johns Hopkins University, Baltimore; Sylvia Clarke, *Social Work in Health Care;* Melvin A. Glasser, United Automobile Workers of America, Detroit; Thomas Kiresuk, Minneapolis Medical Research Foundation, Minneapolis; Sol Levine, Boston University, Boston; Thomas Plaut, National Institute of Mental Health, Rockville, Md. Maurice Russell, New York University Medical Center, New York; Robert Straus, University of Kentucky, Lexington
   *Staff Consultant:* Harris Chaiklin, University of Maryland, Baltimore

### NATIONAL CONFERENCE ON SOCIAL WELFARE

## ALTERNATIVE SYSTEMS OF DELIVERING HEALTH CARE: DO THEY MAKE A DIFFERENCE? THE CALIFORNIA EXPERIENCE

*Speakers:* C. Donald Hankins, Occidental Life Insurance Company, Los Angeles

Jack Light, California Medical Association, San Francisco

Boyd Thompson, American Association of Foundations for Medical Care, Stockton, Calif.

Arthur Weissman, Kaiser Foundation Health Plan, Oakland, Calif.

EFFECT OF COPAYMENT ON MEDICAID SERVICES: AN EVALUATION OF THE EIGHTEEN-MONTH CALIFORNIA EXPERIMENT

*Speaker:* Milton I. Roemer, M.D., University of California, Los Angeles

*Discussant:* Jean Hoodwin, HEW, San Francisco

THE INTERRELATIONSHIP BETWEEN SOCIAL WELFARE AND HEALTH ACTIVITIES: A DISCUSSION OF RECENT FEDERAL INITIATIVES

*Speaker:* William A. Morrill, HEW, Washington

PREPAID HEALTH PLANS FOR PROFIT: THE CALIFORNIA EXPERIENCE

*Speakers:* Alfred W. Childs, M.D., University of California, Berkeley

Joanne B. Stern, University of California, Berkeley

Steven Passin, California Department of Health, Sacramento

*Discussants:* Margaret Greenfield, University of California, Berkeley

William Mandel, M.D., University of California, San Francisco

THE REDUCTION OF PATIENT CENSUS IN CALIFORNIA MENTAL HOSPITALS: WHAT'S HAPPENING TO THE PATIENTS AND TO THE HOSPITALS?

*Speakers:* Arthur Bolton, Arthur Bolton Associates, Sacramento, Calif.

J. Frank James, M.D., Fresno County Department of Health, Fresno, Calif.

Robert Rubenstein, M.D., Mt. Zion Hospital, San Francisco

### NCSW AUDIO-VISUAL COMMITTEE

A PLAYS FOR LIVING PRODUCTION: THE INNER TIGER

One-act play by Virginia Coigney about child abuse, depicting the problems of reporting the incident, and the treatment of the child as well as the parents. Staged by the Plays for Living Company in San Francisco.

USE OF VIDEO-TAPE MATERIALS AND EQUIPMENT: WORKSHOP

*Discussion leader:* Russ Lowe, Chinese for Affirmative Action Committee, San Francisco.

### U.S. COMMITTEE, ICSW

A LOOK AT THE CANADIAN'S NATIONAL HEALTH INSURANCE EXPERIENCE: IMPLICATIONS FOR U.S. POLICY

*Speaker:* Malcolm G. Taylor, York University, Toronto, Canada

*Discussant:* Richard Splane, University of British Columbia, Vancouver, Canada

**A LOOK AT THE MEXICAN SOCIAL SECURITY EXPERIENCE: IMPLICATIONS FOR U.S. POLICY**

*Speaker:* Lucila Leal de Araujo, Instituto Mexicano de Seguro Social, Mexico City, Mexico

# Appendix B:
# Organization of the
# Conference for 1975

## OFFICERS

*President:* Melvin A. Glasser, Detroit
*First Vice-president:* Shelton B. Granger, Philadelphia
*Second Vice-president:* Jay L. Roney, Baltimore
*Third Vice-president:* Steven A. Minter, Cleveland
*Secretary:* Edward W. Francel, Louisville, Ky.
*Treasurer:* Emerson C. Wollam, Columbus, Ohio
*Past President:* Phillip M. Hauser, Chicago
*President-elect:* Norman V. Lourie, Harrisburg, Pa.
*Executive Director:* Margaret E. Berry, New York and Columbus, Ohio

### NATIONAL BOARD
(*includes officers listed above*)

*Term expires 1975:* Mrs. Leonard H. Bernheim, New York; William C. Fitch, Washington; Arnold Gurin, Waltham, Mass.; Joseph A. Hall, Cincinnati; George D. Nickel, Arcadia, Calif.; Daniel Thursz, Baltimore

*Term expires 1976:* Mrs. Arlin Adams, Philadelphia; Mrs. Ellouise De-Groat, Window Rock, Ariz.; Mrs. Nellie Gustafson, Indianapolis; Tsuguo Ikeda, Seattle; Jose Pepe Lucero, San Antonio, Calif.; Elizabeth Davis Pittman, Omaha, Neb.; James H. Sills, Jr., Wilmington, Del.

*Term expires 1977:* P. R. Balgopal, Houston, Texas; Kenneth L. Brown, Boston; Clarence Coleman, New York; Sam S. Grais, Minneapolis; Dorothy Hollingsworth, Seattle; Mrs. Virginia M. Smyth, Atlanta, Ga.; Wilbert Tom, San Francisco.

*Representative from NCSW Committee on Public Relations:* Donald F. Bates, New York

*Representative from National Association for Statewide Health and Welfare:* Robert S. Burgess, Providence, R.I.

*Chairman, U.S. Committee of ICSW:* Norman V. Lourie, Harrisburg, Pa.
*Chairman, Combined Associate Groups:* C. Milton Jackson, Washington
*Legal Consultant:* Rudolph Janata, Columbus, Ohio

## COMMITTEE ON NOMINATIONS

*Chairman:* Thomas J. Powell, Ann Arbor, Mich.
*Vice-chairman:* J. Julian Rivera, Brooklyn, N.Y.

*Term expires 1975:* Saul Bernstein, Dennis, Mass.; Mrs. Freona C. Moore, Topeka, Kans.; Thomas J. Powell, Ann Arbor, Mich.; J. Julian Rivera, New York; Mrs. Elaine Rothenberg, Richmond, Va.; Mrs. Fay H. Williams, Indianapolis

*Term expires 1976:* Duane Beck, Atlanta, Ga.; Helen Daniels, Indianapolis; Sister Mary Immaculate, San Antonio, Texas; Richard E. Streeter, Cleveland; Mrs. Helen Johnstone Weisbrod, Salem, Ore.; Leontine R. Young, Newark, N.J.

*Term expires 1977:* Mrs. Pereta R. Balian, New York; Harold Hagan, Washington; Mrs. Michael Harris, New York; Joseph I. Hungate, Jr., Columbia, S.C.; Mrs. Gerald Kirshbaum, Stamford, Conn.; Rosa C. Marin, Rio Piedras, Puerto Rico; Eleanor Wasson, Los Angeles

### COMMITTEE ON PUBLIC RELATIONS

*Chairman:* Donald F. Bates, New York
*Vice-chairman:* Mrs. Adele Braude, New York
*Term expires 1975:* Joan Buck, New York; Ronald Kozusko, New York; Mrs. Betty Leslie Lund, Norwalk, Conn.; Mrs. Elly Robbins, New York
*Term expires 1976:* Herbert S. Fowler, Washington; Carlton E. Spitzer, Washington; John R. Stampfli, Rochester, N.Y.; John D. Williams, New York
*Term expires 1977:* Mrs. Elma Phillipson Cole, New York; Frank Driscoll, New York; Richard Earl, New York; Robin Elliott, New York; Mrs. Farida Ghani, New York; Guichard Parris, New York; William Perry, Roslyn, Va.; Daniel J. Ransohoff, Cincinnati; William C. Tracy, New York

### TELLERS COMMITTEE

*Chairman:* Merriss Cornell, Columbus, Ohio

### EDITORIAL COMMITTEE

*Chairman:* Magdalena Miranda, Bethesda, Md.
*Members:* Salvador Alvarez, San Jose, Calif.; James Leiby, Berkeley, Calif.; Marion Robinson, New York; Carl Scott, New York

### U.S. COMMITTEE OF ICSW

*Chairman:* Norman V. Lourie, Harrisburg, Pa.
*Vice-chairman:* Morton I. Teicher, Chapel Hill, N.C.
*Secretary:* Martha Branscombe, Chapel Hill, N.C.
*Treasurer:* Nelson Jackson, Pelham, N.Y.
*Representatives of National Organizations:* American Council of Voluntary Agencies for Foreign Service, Theron Van Scoter, New York; American Public Welfare Association, Edward T. Weaver, Washington; Council of International Programs for Youth Leaders and Social Workers, Henry B. Ollendorff, Cleveland; Council on Social Work Education, James R. Dumpson, New York; Jack Svahn, HEW, Washington; National Assembly for National Voluntary Health and Social Welfare Organizations, Mrs. Alexander B. Ripley, Los Angeles; National Association of Social Workers, Benjamin P. Finley, Jr., Chicago.

*Members-at-large:*

*Term expires 1975:* Mrs. Margery Carpenter, Washington; Dr. Maureen Didier, Albany, N.Y.; Douglas Glasgow, Washington; Margaret Hickey, Tucson, Ariz.; Joe R. Hoffer, Columbus, Ohio; Hector Sanchez, Washington; John B. Turner, Chapel Hill, N.C.

*Term expires 1976:* Charles Chakerian, Richmond, Va.; Eugenie Cowan, New York; Phyllis M. Harewood, Brooklyn, N.Y.; Bernard E. Nash, Washington; Terushi Tomita, Johnson City, Tenn.; John B. Twiname, Washington; Mrs. Corinne H. Wolfe, Las Vegas, New Mex.

*Term expires 1977:* Mrs. Fannie Allen, Boston; Mrs. Evelyn Blanchard, Albuquerque, N. Mex.; Mrs. Caroline Komunonwire, Brooklyn, N.Y.; Schuyler M. Meyer, Jr., New York; Patrick Okura, Rockville, Md.; J. Julian Rivera, Brooklyn, N.Y.; Jerry A. Shroder, New York

*Liaison:* NCSW Program Committee, Mrs. Margery Carpenter, Washington; NCSW, Shelton B. Granger, Philadelphia

*Subcommittee Chairmen:* Nominating Committee, Bernard J. Coughlin, Spokane, Wash.; U.S. Exhibit, John S. Glaser, Alexandria, Va.; Future Role and Resource Development: Bernard Shiffman, New York; Cooperative International Projects: Mitchell I. Ginsberg, New York; Interamerican Conference: Mary Catherine Jennings, Washington

*Members of Committee of Representatives,* ICSW, Norman V. Lourie, Harrisburg, Pa.

*Officers of ICSW (residing in U.S.)* Dorothy Lally, Washington, Vice-president; Charles I. Schottland, Waltham, Mass., immediate past president; Secretary General, ICSW: Mrs. Kate Katzki, New York

## COMMITTEE ON PROGRAM
## FOR THE 102ND ANNUAL FORUM

*NCSW President and Chairman:* Melvin A. Glasser, Detroit

*Past President:* Philip M. Hauser, Chicago

*President-elect:* Norman V. Lourie, Harrisburg, Pa.

*Members-at-large:* Ronald Boltz, Syracuse, N.Y.; Sol Gorelick, Brooklyn, N.Y.; Matilde Goyco, New York; Marshall Jung, Drexel Hill, Pa.; Kathy Leff, Baldwin, N.Y.; Gloria Lopez McKnight, Detroit; Florence Rice, New York; Paul Ruiz-Solomon, Roslyn Heights, N.Y.

*Representatives of National Social Welfare Organizations:* American Public Welfare Association, Phyllis Simmons, New York; Council on Social Work Education, Nancy Coleman, New York; National Assembly of National Voluntary Health and Social Welfare Organizations, Robert Langer, New York; National Association of Social Workers, James Craigen, Washington; National Association of Statewide Health and Welfare, Susan Beard, Charleston, W. Va.; National Health Council, Mrs. Pauline Miles, New York

*Liaison Members:* HEW, Stuart Altman, Washington; NCSW Audio-Visual Committee, Mrs. Claire Pittman, Washington; NCSW Combined Associate Groups Committee, C. Milton Jackson, Washington and Eloise Waite, Washington; NCSW Public Relations Committee, Mrs. Elly Robbins, New York; U.S. Committee of the International Council on Social Welfare, Mrs. Margery Carpenter, Washington

NCSW SECTIONS

SECTION I. ECONOMIC INDEPENDENCE
*Chairman:* Mrs. Mary Dublin Keyserling, Washington
*Vice-chairman:* William B. Neeman, Ann Arbor, Mich.
*Members:* Mitchell I. Ginsberg, New York; Sar A. Levitan, Washington;
Gilbert Y. Steiner, Washington; S. Martin Taylor, Detroit

SECTION II. PROBLEMS OF EFFECTIVE FUNCTIONING
*Chairman:* Milton Wittman, Rockville, Md.
*Vice-chairman:* Barbara K. Shore, Pittsburgh
*Members:* Martin Adler, Pittsburgh; Robert Z. Apte, Berkeley, Calif.;
Joyce Brengarth, Pittsburgh; Dr. Juan Buono, Washington; Milton Curry,
Chicago; Irvin Foutz, Pittsburgh; Patricia Gilroy, Washington; William
Hall, Pittsburgh; Hector Sanchez, Chevy Chase, Md.; Hugh Sloane, San
Francisco; Ruth Succop, Pittsburgh; Margaret M. Wynee, Pittsburgh
*Ex officio:* Augustin Gonzalez, New York; Alfred Katz, Los Angeles

SECTION III. SOCIAL ASPECTS OF HEALTH
*Chairman:* Jules Schrager, Ann Arbor, Mich.
*Vice-chairman:* Stephen Loebs, Columbus, Ohio
*Members:* Neil Bailey-El, Chicago; Jean Dockhorn, Baltimore; Tony Kov-
ner, Detroit; Paula Lugannani, Ann Arbor, Mich.; James Lyon, East Lans-
ing, Mich.; Mabel Meites, Lansing, Mich.; Seymour Mirelowitz, Chicago;
Elisio Navarro, Ann Arbor, Mich.; Jean Robinson, Ann Arbor, Mich.; Jean
Wright, Ann Arbor, Mich.

SECTION IV. LEISURE-TIME NEEDS
*Chairman:* Robert L. Bond, Cleveland
*Vice-chairman:* Arthur Bernstein, Grants Pass, Oreg.
*Members:* Paul Abels, Cleveland; Letha Arrants, Chicago; Josephine Bas-
kerville, Chicago; Herman Eigen, Cleveland Heights, Ohio; Joseph Garcia,
Cleveland; Marjorie Main, Cleveland; George Nishinaka, Los Angeles;
Shig Okada, Cleveland; Richard Park, San 'Francisco; Barbara Reynolds,
Cleveland; Audrey Simmons, Burlingame, Calif.; Kenneth Snipes, Cleve-
land; Mrs. Ellie Sutler, Cleveland, William Wolfe, Cleveland

SECTION V. PROVISION AND MANAGEMENT
OF SOCIAL SERVICES
*Chairman:* Hobart C. Jackson, Philadelphia
*Vice-chairman:* Mrs. Mildred Murphy, Oklahoma City
*Members:* Fannie L. Allen, Boston; Alfred Armstead, St. Louis; Merle
Broberg, Bryn Mawr, Pa.; Dolores Davis, Washington; Caroline P. Dotson,
New Orleans; Mildred Freeney, Chicago; Hyacinth Graham, Philadelphia;
Lorraine Hathaway, Philadelphia; Benjamin J. Kendrick, Chicago; Valerie
L. Levy, New York; Victorina Peralta, Philadelphia; Sharon L. Rickert,
Cleveland

SECTION VI. SOCIETAL PROBLEMS
*Chairman:* Robert Morris, Waltham, Mass.
*Vice-chairman:* Jere L. Brennan (deceased)

*Members:* Edward Burke, Chestnut Hill, Mass.; G. Ramsey Liem, Chestnut Hill, Mass.; Joseph Meisels, Boston; Steven A. Minter, Cleveland; Julio Morales, Waltham, Mass.

## NCSW AUDIO-VISUAL COMMITTEE
*Chairman:* Mrs. Claire Pittman, Washington
*Vice-chairman:* Mary Flynn, Washington
*Honorary vice-chairmen:* Lt. Col. Belle Leach, New York; Herbert F. Lowe, New York
*Members:* Ann P. Booth, New York; John M. Couric, Washington; William Duke, Washington; Barbara Fenhagen, Washington; Ray E. Hiebert, College Park, Md.; Dr. Irmagene Holloway, Arlington, Va.; Dr. Warren Johnson, Washington; Morton Lebow, Rockville, Md.; Maurice McDonald, Washington; George Manno, Washington; Theresa Morrison, New York; Mario Pellegrini, Alexandria, Va.; Bill Perry, Arlington, Va.; Mrs. Elsa A. Porter, Washington; Bernard Posner, Washington; Carlton E. Spitzer, New York; Dr. Wil J. Tannenbaum, New York; Ruth Walter, Washington; Gwen Wong, Washington

## COMMITTEE ON COMBINED ASSOCIATE GROUPS

*Chairman:* C. Milton Jackson, National Retired Teachers Association/American Association of Retired Persons, Washington
*Vice-chairman:* Eloise Waite, American National Red Cross, Washington

## PROGRAM CHAIRMEN OF ASSOCIATE GROUPS

AFL–CIO Department of Community Services: John J. McManus
Alliance of Information and Referral Services: Corazon Esteva Doyle
American Association of Workers for Children: Mrs. Martha Innes
American Council for Nationalities Service: Sidney Talisman
American Foundation for the Blind: Dorothy Demby
American Friends Service Committee: Marjorie C. Seeley
American Home Economics Association: Muriel Yager
American Humane Association, Children's Division: Vincent De Francis
American Jewish Committee: Mrs. Ann G. Wolfe
American National Red Cross: John F. McGowan
American Public Welfare Association: Benjamin O. Hendrick
Army Community Service, Department of the Army: Lt. Col. D. T. Owen
Asian American Social Workers: Marshall Jung
Association for Voluntary Sterilization: Mrs. Evelyn Bryant
Association of American Indian Social Workers: Mrs. Marcia P. Steele
Association of Puerto Rican Social Service Workers: Aida Burnett
Association of Volunteer Bureaus: Mrs. Marjorie M. Bolton
Big Brothers of America: Francis X. Shevlin
Child Study Association of America/Wel-Met: Mrs. Rita Rabinowitz
Child Welfare League of America: Maxine Phillips
Council of Jewish Federations and Welfare Funds: Charles Zibbell
Council on Social Work Education: Nancy Coleman
Executive Council of the Episcopal Church: Woodrow W. Carter

Family Service Association of America: Emlicia Mizio
Florence Crittenton Association of America: Mrs. Helen Johnstone Weis-
brod
International Union, United Automobile, Aerospace and Agricultural Im-
plement Workers of America, UAW: Andrew W. L. Brown
The Menninger Foundation: Richard S. Benson
National Assembly of National Voluntary Health and Social Welfare Orga-
nizations: Robert Langer
National Association for Statewide Health and Welfare: Maurice P. Beck
National Association of Housing and Redevelopment Officials: Mrs.
Dorothy Gazzolo
National Association of Social Workers: Virginia S. Cooke
National Board, YWCA of the U.S.A.: Vivian Grove
National Center for Voluntary Action: Kerry Kenn Allen
National Committee on Employment of Youth: Jeffrey Newman
National Conference of Jewish Communal Service: Sophie B. Engel
National Council for Homemaker-Home Health Aide Services: Mrs. Mary
G. Walsh
National Council of Churches of Christ in the U.S.A.–Committee on Social
Welfare: Hulbert James
National Council of Jewish Women: Mrs. Helen Powers
National Council of Senior Citizens: Rudolph T. Danstedt
National Council on Alcoholism: Mrs. Juanita Palmer
National Council on the Aging: Mrs. Rebecca Eckstein
National Easter Seal Society for Crippled Children and Adults: Mrs.
Rhoda Gellman
National Federation of Settlements and Neighborhood Centers: Richard
Bargans
National Federation of Student Social Workers: Minerva Atuna
National Health Council: Mrs. Pauline Miles
National Jewish Welfare Board: Mitchell Jaff
National Legal Aid and Defender Association: James F. Flug
National Multiple Sclerosis Society
National Public Relations Council of Health and Welfare Services: Donald
F. Bates
National Retired Teachers Association/American Association of Retired
Persons: C. Milton Jackson
National Urban League: Jeweldean Londa
Planned Parenthood-World Population: Lelia V. Hall
The Salvation Army: Brig. Mary E. Verner
Save the Children Federation/Community Development Foundation: Mel-
vin E. Frarey
Trabajadores de La Raza: Joseph Suarez
Travelers Aid–International Social Service of America: Halema Haigney
United Cerebral Palsy Associations: Ernest Weinrich
United Church Board for Homeland Ministries, Division of Health and
Welfare: Chenoweth J. Watson
United HIAS Service: Muriel Bermar

United Methodist Church, Board of Global Ministries: Lula Garrett
United Presbyterian Church, Health, Education, and Social Justice: Antonio A. Medina
United Seamen's Service: Lillian Rabins
United Service Organization: Alan Kassin
United Way of America: Henry Weber
Veterans Administration, Central Office: Claire R. Lustman and Mrs. Natalie J. Cave
The Volunteers of America: Lt. Col. Belle Leach

# Index